YOU & YOUR
PET BIRD

YOU & YOUR
PET BIRD

DAVID ALDERTON

Photography by
CYRIL LAUBSCHER

NEW YORK: ALFRED A. KNOPF
1994

A DORLING KINDERSLEY BOOK

Project Editor Susan Thompson
Art Editor Nigel Partridge
Assistant Editors Marcus Hardy, Helen Townsend
Production Manager Meryl Silbert

**BARRABAND
PARAKEET
COCK**

Reproduced by GRB Grafica
Fotoreproduztion, Verona Italy
Printed and bound by Wing King Tong, Hong Kong
Published July 1, 1992
Second Printing, March 1994

Library of Congress Cataloging-in-Publication Data
Alderton, David. 1956 –
You & your pet bird / David Alderton. – 1st ed.
p. cm.
"A Dorling Kindersley book" –
"A Borzoi book" –
ISBN 0-679-74061-9 : $15.00
1. Cage Birds.   I. Title. II. Title: You and your pet bird.
GV995.D66 1992
796.342′ 2 – dc20
91–58565 CIP

THIS IS A BORZOI BOOK, PUBLISHED
BY ALFRED A. KNOPF, INC.

CONTENTS

CHATTERING LORY HEN

CHAPTER ONE

INTRODUCTION

BLACK-HOODED RED SISKIN *(above) This rare South American finch was used in a breeding program during the 1920s to create the ancestors of today's Red Factor Canaries.*

LONDON FANCY CANARIES *(left) This breed became extinct during the early years of the present century. It was especially popular among canary fanciers in the London area during the Victorian era.*

KEEPING BIRDS

Bird-keeping is an interest with many different facets. You may, for example, simply want to keep a single bird in a cage in your home as a companion, or you might decide to set up an aviary in your garden. This could be landscaped with plants to provide an attractive and secluded environment for a colorful selection of small finches or other species of bird.

A BRIEF OVERVIEW

All the birds covered in this book are fairly easy to look after, and thrive in indoor or outdoor surroundings. For some birds, it may be necessary to provide additional heating and lighting during the colder months of the year. This obviously depends to some extent on where you live, as well as the species concerned. Most parrots are hardy once they are acclimatized to living outdoors, but the small finches may have to be brought inside for the winter in temperate areas, if no source of electricity is available in their quarters. Larger softbills can usually stay in an outdoor aviary throughout the year, and some species, such as various laughing thrushes, often live at quite high altitudes in the wild, where temperatures regularly fall below freezing. Even so, many softbills may benefit from additional warmth during the colder months, and giving them extra lighting will allow them to have a longer feeding period. This applies to many recently imported birds, though some, once acclimatized to living outdoors in temperate areas, may subsequently also be able to overwinter without heating or lighting.

EXHIBITING BIRDS

Among domesticated species, where different color forms are well known, there are standards established to permit the exhibition and judging of such birds. The standard itself is a picture in words, which provides a description of the ideal visual appearance of a variety. In this way judges can compare the features of one individual with those of another. Points are available for all the individual features of a bird, with some features scoring more points than others.

TALENTED TALKER The African Gray Parrot has been cherished as a pet for centuries, and is now also being widely bred in aviaries.

Most Numerous Bird *Experts estimate that the Red-billed Weaver, an African finch, may have a population of up to 10,000 million.*

Canaries and Budgerigars rank among the most popular of all the exhibition birds, although the Zebra Finch along with the Bengalese or Society Finch, are usually also well represented at bird shows.

The exhibition aspect of bird-keeping provides owners with a good opportunity to meet people with similar interests, and to form new friendships. There are both local shows and larger regional or national events staged in most countries where bird-keeping clubs and societies are established. Specialist bird-keeping magazines usually advertize forthcoming events.

Bird Origins

Many finches originate from Africa and Asia, where they are regarded as crop-eating pests. Existing nonselective methods of control, such as poisoning waterholes or attacking roosting sites with napalm, kill the birds, and also kill many other species, as well as damaging the environment. Exportation of certain birds is permitted, and provides some financial recompense for the damage the birds cause, but the numbers of birds involved are tiny compared with the overall populations, so the birds continue to be slaughtered.

The keeping and breeding of birds that are not fully domesticated is known as "aviculture," and people interested in this field are described as "aviculturists." In contrast, bird-keepers who concentrate on domesticated species, breeding them primarily for their coloration or for exhibition purposes, are referred to as "fanciers." The term "fancy" originated in the Victorian period, and describes the selective breeding of both plants and livestock, which was extremely fashionable at that time.

Traditionally, the canary has been closely associated with mining areas, and breeds such as the Yorkshire Fancy have evolved

here. The close bond between miners and canaries stems from the use of these birds to detect poisonous gases underground in the pit shafts, since a lack of oxygen will eventually cause canaries to pass out. Their cages were equipped with their own oxygen supply, so that the miners could revive their invaluable birds later.

FINANCIAL OUTLAY

Prices of birds vary considerably. Finches are relatively cheap, while parrots, especially if they are hand-raised, are more costly, and this price is a direct reflection of the care and attention needed to rear their chicks.

In return for your investment of a hand-raised parrot, however, you should receive a lifelong companion. Most larger species have a potential lifespan equivalent to our own. The many dangers they face in the wild mean that few birds attain their natural lifespan, but pet parrots are documented as living for up to a century. Even smaller species such as the Cockatiel can live well

VICTORIAN FANCIERS Judges debate the merits of a Scotch Fancy Canary, a popular bird of the period.

LIFE SAVER Canaries are still often associated with mining, and the use of them in mines produced many breeds.

into their twenties, and breed successfully for much of their lifetime. There is a record of a male parrotlet that successfully produced chicks up to the age of 18. Budgerigars often have a shorter life than other psittacines, with the average lifespan being about seven years. However, some Buderigars can live into their twenties. The oldest known example was 29 years old when she died in London in 1977.

IMPORTING BIRDS

Strict regulations apply to the movement of birds internationally. Under the Convention on International Trade in Endangered Species (CITES), a licensing system operates for the movement of parrots and many other birds. A period of quarantine is mandatory in most countries.

The care of imported birds after release from quarantine is initially demanding, but the vast majority settle well. A nationwide survey carried out in 1990 in Britain revealed that the mortality of birds imported during the previous year was just 7 percent, while finches in the wild sustain an annual mortality of well over 80 percent.

The lively nature of parrots, their attractive coloration, and their willingness to breed in aviaries have ensured that this particular group of birds is very popular with bird-keepers. They are kept not just as companions but also, very importantly, for the purpose of breeding.

In the islands of the Caribbean there are several endemic Amazon parrots. Although they are protected by conservation laws, they still face a constant threat from hurricanes. With their tiny population of less than 100 individuals in some cases, their reproductive potential needs to be maximized. Techniques that have been

pioneered for the breeding of common species can now be applied successfully to species that are facing an uncertain future in the wild. Taking all the eggs from a nest after the hen has finished laying will stimulate her to lay again. The first clutch of eggs can then be incubated artificially and the chicks hand-reared, while the hen can be left to hatch her second clutch naturally. Under normal circumstances, many parrots, especially the bigger species, are preoccupied with chicks and lay only once a year or even less frequently.

There is a growing realization among conservationists that aviculture can make a real contribution to the preservation of endangered species, and techniques for releasing birds into the wild are likely to become more sophisticated in the future. The principal concern of environmentalists, then, must be whether or not there will be sufficient habitats into which birds such as this can be one day successfully reintroduced.

ENDANGERED SPECIES The future of parrots from the Caribbean, such as the rare St. Vincent Amazon, can be assured by captive breeding programs.

ORIGINS OF BIRD-KEEPING

Bird-keeping as a hobby dates back more than 4000 years, and appears to have arisen quite distinctly from keeping birds as a source of food. Special cages of different designs have been recorded in various early civilizations. Those in the area of the Nile valley were traditionally rectangular, while circular cages were favored by the people living close to the Indus river, farther to the east. In Egypt, early hieroglyphs have been found depicting all manner of birds, including doves, parrots, ibises, and ducks, which were kept as part of exotic menageries.

ANCIENT CONTACTS

Many birds that are popular pets today, such as the Greater Hill Mynah, have been kept in their homelands as companions for millennia. On feast days in India, mynahs were publicly displayed on floats, and pulled through the city streets by oxen. These birds later became known as "sacred grackles" in Ancient Greece, where bird-keeping was already flourishing more than 2000 years ago.

Dealers specialized in breeding and selling birds, with the most expensive being peacocks, which were highly valued for their plumage. Some of the more common types of goldfinch were popular song birds for the home. Children kept jackdaws as pets and let them live at liberty in their gardens. They trimmed the flight feathers of young birds and by the time these had regrown the jackdaws were so tame they did not attempt to fly away.

Tame birds feature prominently in early art and culture. The Greek playwright Aristophanes, writing in about 400 B.C.,

CANARY ORIGINS
A 17th century drawing.

frequently included references to birds such as goldfinches in his work. These early Greek links with birds survive today in the popular Alexandrine Parakeet, a species that bears the name of Alexander the Great. It is believed that the generals of his army took these and other psittaculid species with them when they returned home to Greece after the invasion of northern India in 327 B.C.

TALKING BIRDS
The ability of some birds to mimic the human voice was already known to the Ancient Greeks, although only corvids, such as crows and jackdaws, and starlings were kept for this purpose. Before Alexander the Great invaded India, parrots were virtually unknown outside their native lands. However, there is one earlier report by Ctesiphon, personal physician to King Artaxerxes and court naturalist, at the beginning of the fifth century B.C. He wrote of rare talking birds, referred to as

DOMESTICATED SONGSTER This painting of a goldfinch by Carel Sabritious (1624–1654) confirms pet birds' popularity in Europe several hundred years ago.

bittakos by the Indian merchants who described them to him. Once discovered by the Greeks, parrots became highly prized and were kept in cages made of the finest metals with elaborate inlays of ivory and other precious materials.

By Roman times, courses designed to teach parrots to mimic the human voice were well established. These birds were usually taught words of greeting, and their wealthy owners employed slaves whose specific task was to care for the parrots and to encourage them to talk. Pliny the Elder, writing in the first century A.D., gave special instructions for the training of parrots. He held that each bird needed to be housed on its own in a darkened room to help it to concentrate. Without any distractions, it would soon start to mimic

individual words, followed by distinct phrases. During the reign of the Emperor Tiberius (A.D. 14–37), a raven kept by a cobbler was able to recite the Emperor's name and that of his sons. When the bird was killed by a jealous neighbor, the cobbler's friends took it upon themselves to lynch the man responsible. Many people paid their respects at the bird's funeral. Ravens were also put on display at barbers' shops to attract and amuse customers. The bullfinch was a particularly popular songbird with the Romans. They trained it to sing specific tunes in a way that is similar to how Roller Canaries and other singing breeds are taught today.

INTO EUROPE

Less documentation exists on bird-keeping in Europe in the period after the Romans, but there are clear indications that it became widespread. Birds were popular pets at court, usually housed in the Queen's quarters. In the thirteenth century, exotic species reached Europe and these were very highly valued by Frederick II, the Holy Roman Emperor at the time.

In 1493, when Christopher Columbus returned triumphant from his voyage of discovery to the New World, he brought with him a pair of Cuban Amazon parrots (*Amazona leucocephala*) for his patroness, Queen Isabella of Spain. While in England in the sixteenth century, Henry VIII kept an African Gray Parrot at Hampton Court. This bird used to call to the boatmen on the River Thames and then mimic their demand to be paid for the journey.

By the fifteenth century, canaries were well known in Europe. Portuguese sailors are credited with originally bringing these attractive finches from the Canary Islands to Europe. Many of the portraits of fashionable ladies, which were painted at this time, also included a domesticated canary perched delicately on their fingers.

MODERN TRENDS

From the 1580s, farmers on the Canary Islands were encouraged to breed their native canaries for export. It is unclear when the first yellow canaries appeared, but they were bred selectively in parts of Austria before the end of the seventeenth century. When the Austrian mines were shut down in the eighteenth century, the miners moved with their birds to the Harz Mountain region of Germany. Canaries were sold from there all over Germany, and traveled to England from ports in the Low Countries. The birds were sold in specially designed wooden cages, which were recognized as a mark of quality.

In the eighteenth century, canaries were popular in coffee houses throughout Europe. Their song attracted customers and this, in turn, helped to stimulate a domestic demand for pet birds. Traveling troupes of canaries are also known to have been taken around Europe, to perform for customers in taverns.

Although canaries are best known for their singing abilities, they can also mimic the human voice. For these reasons, they attracted considerable attention from the general public and, by Victorian times, a strong specialist interest in canaries was discernible. The ancestors of many of today's type breeds came into existence at this time, although some of these, such as the London Fancy, have been lost.

New type breeds continue to be developed. The most radical achievement in canary breeding during this century has been the development of the red factor birds, which are the result of a quest for pure red canaries in the 1920s.

THE BUDGIE BOOM

The Budgerigar has a much shorter history of domestication than the canary. Its powers of mimicry were first described in the 1780s by Thomas Watling, a forger who had been deported to Australia. He had obtained a Budgerigar, which lived with him in Port Jackson. Watling's employer, Dr. James White, was amazed, on entering his assistant's home, to be greeted by the Budgerigar saying "How do you do, Dr. White?" Yet it was not until the naturalist John Gould returned to England in 1840 that the Budgerigar became well known outside its homeland. The pair of Budgies that Gould brought back was kept by his brother-in-law,

PARISIAN FRILLED CANARY One of the more bizarre birds bred today, this canary's feathers are pronouncedly curved, giving it an attractive ruff.

Charles Coxen, and soon bred. More Budgerigars soon reached Britain, and a huge trade in these birds developed, with as many as 50,000 Budgies imported annually by the end of the 1850s.

Almost inevitably, as domestication proceeded, new colors started to appear, with reports of light yellows in Belgium in 1872, and in Germany in 1875. An explosion of colors followed, each helping to maintain the public's interest in the birds.

SPECIALIZATION

Many of the birds that were made available for domestication during the early part of the twentieth century arrived in Europe by ship. Journeys could take months. With the advent of commercial air services after the

BUDGERIGARS *This plate, taken from Gould's book* The Birds of Australia, *published from 1851 to 1869, is one of the first ever depictions of Budgerigars.*

VICTORIAN PASSIONS *This spectacular nineteenth-century structure was designed to feature not only birds, but also fish and plants.*

Second World War, birds could be moved rapidly and safely around the world, and a number of hitherto unknown species became available to aviculturists. This has triggered a demand for specialist foods and equipment, and today it is quite easy to cater for species that once had a reputation for being delicate.

The trend now is for specialization, with people concentrating on particular groups of birds. In America, a number of societies have been established for breeders with specialist interests, such as Amazon parrots and macaws. This trend encourages members to acquire specific expertise, which one hopes will help them to establish their own captive-bred stock.

THE ANATOMY OF THE BIRD

F light is not unique to birds. In the past the pterosaurs, with wingspans of up to 12 meters (39 ft), dominated the skies before birds had evolved. Bats, a widespread group of mammals, share the flying skills of birds, although their bodies are very different. It is the presence of feathers that distinguishes birds from all other creatures that have conquered flight, and their success can be judged by the fact that more than 8000 species are recognized today.

THE BASIC BIRD

The evolutionary development of birds remained unknown until 1861, when a group of workers in a limestone quarry in Solnhofen, southern Germany, split open a block of stone, which revealed the fossilized remains of what appeared to be a primitive bird. There was unmistakable evidence of feathers attached to its upper limbs and forming a tail, as in the modern birds we know today. Other anatomical features served to confirm the relationship of this fossil to modern birds. A wishbone, resulting from the fusion of the collar bones, was apparent. This showed that the creature actually flew, rather than simply using its wings for gliding.

Christened *Archaeopteryx* (meaning "ancient wings"), this primitive bird was about the size of a large pigeon. In some respects, however, it showed similarities to bipedal dinosaurs, such as *Compsognathus,* a small carnivorous dinosaur of the time.

Yet *Archaeopteryx* itself was probably not the only ancestor of modern birds. There are a number of anatomical differences

between the two, which cannot be reconciled by those evolutionary changes that have been noted to date. It seems quite probable that there were other forms of primitive bird present at the same time as *Archaeopteryx*, and that these unknown ancestors provided the lineage through to today's many and varied species. Their fossilized remains may still await discovery.

ARCHAEOPTERYX *Dating back approximately 150 million years, this primitive bird fossil has various features in common with those found in today's birds.*

RECONSTRUCTION *Based on the available evidence, Archaeopteryx may have looked rather like this in life.*

sternum, that is a characteristic feature of modern birds. It is at this point on the skeleton that the muscles responsible for the power of flight are attached.

Through studying its anatomical features, scientists believe that *Archaeopteryx* was, in fact, an insectivorous predator. It could run on the ground as well as fly, and its claws may have helped it to climb around in the tree canopy so that it could catch insects there as well. Only six specimens of *Archaeopteryx* have been unearthed to date, all of which were found in northern Europe – although a single fossilized feather of unknown origin has been discovered in Spain. It seems likely that birds developed during the Jurassic Period, between 213 and 144 million years ago, and that it was their power of flight that helped them to become established as a distinctive animal group.

PRIMITIVE SURVIVOR *With claws on its wings and feet, this hoatzin chick clings onto a branch.*

Modern birds have all but lost any trace of the three claws that *Archaeopteryx* had on the front edge of each of its wings. However, this characteristic has survived in one avian species, the hoatzin *(Opisthocomus hoatzin)*, which lives in the jungles of Amazonia. When they hatch, hoatzins have two fully functional claws on the front edge of each wing, which help the young birds to move around in the tree tops. The development of its flight feathers is slower than in other birds, but when they are developed, the claws are shed. *Archaeopteryx* also had teeth, a characteristic that is not shared by any modern species of birds, although it is still evident in some modern species of reptile.

The long legs of *Archaeopteryx* suggest a basically terrestrial lifestyle, and there is no supporting fossil evidence to suggest the development of the breastbone, or of the

THE BIRD'S SKELETON

The survival of most birds depends on their flying ability. Excessive weight compromises this, so, not surprisingly, the skeleton of a bird is much lighter than that of a mammal. However, this is achieved at a cost, and the skull of a bird is thin and susceptible to fracturing. In aviculture, the most vulnerable groups are the Australian parakeets, which are the quickest in flight and may collide with the aviary framework, and quails, which tend to be nervous and may attempt to fly vertically from the ground with considerable force.

Further lightening of the bird's head has also been made possible by the absence of teeth, and the powerful muscular jaws associated with them. The other noticeable feature of a bird's skull is the size of the eye sockets. Vision is its most crucial sense, and the eyes are correspondingly large. The inner dark area, the pupil, is surrounded by the iris, which is highly colorful in some species.

STRUCTURAL STABILITY

The vertebral column is more variable in birds than in mammals. Fusion of some of the vertebrae, occasionally over the ribs and more commonly over the hindleg area, provides increased stability. This ensures that when the bird walks, rather than flies, the weight of its body is more evenly distributed along its length.

In theory, birds could encounter difficulties in both flying and walking because of the position of their center of gravity. They would be inclined to fall forward, but their dual means of locomotion is made possible by skeletal adjustments in the vicinity of the pelvis. Here, the hip joint is basically identical to that of mammals, with the acetabulum at the top of the femur fitting snugly into the pelvis, but there is a significant difference. The femur is directed forward, and is effectively held in position quite tightly against the body by muscles. This means that while the femur is far less mobile than in humans, for example, it helps to shift the focus of the hind limbs much closer to the bird's center of gravity.

Flexibility within the bird's leg stems from what is actually the knee joint, rather than higher up the limb. The equivalent of our ankle joint, where the tibia and metatarsus meet, extends down to the toes, terminating in claws.

FLIGHT MUSCLES

To provide effective thrust, the bones in the wing move together. The humeral area is the main site for muscular attachment. As the bird's wing beats downwards, special bones prevent its chest being crushed. The thrust of the wing articulates with the scapula on each side of the body. The coracoid and the wishbone provide reinforcement. The sternum attaches to the coracoid, and here the flight muscles have a broad area for attachment.

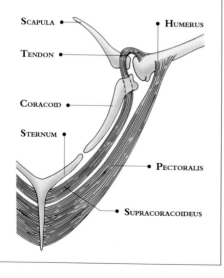

SCAPULA

TENDON

CORACOID

STERNUM

HUMERUS

PECTORALIS

SUPRACORACOIDEUS

Not surprisingly, the bird's forelimbs show the greatest diversity. Since these are used solely for locomotion, the high degree of digital specialization has disappeared. In fact, only the counterparts of the second, third, and fourth digits remain. This trend is already clearly visible in *Archaeopteryx* (see pages 16–17). The metacarpals are fused, providing a strong attachment point for the primary flight feathers. The skeletal structure of the wing is relatively constant, but the actual shape of the feathers can be quite variable, depending on the flying capabilities of the species concerned.

The chest cavity is reinforced by the unusual structure of the ribs. The ribs have projections, known as uncinate processes, which are directed backwards, overlapping each other. These help to provide support, especially in diving birds.

Since the wing profile is rigid, no extra, weighty muscles are needed to maintain its shape, and its efficiency is improved. In cross section, the wings are honeycombed. This lightens the load of the pectoral muscles during flight. These muscles, attached to the keel of the sternum, may account for half of the bird's body weight.

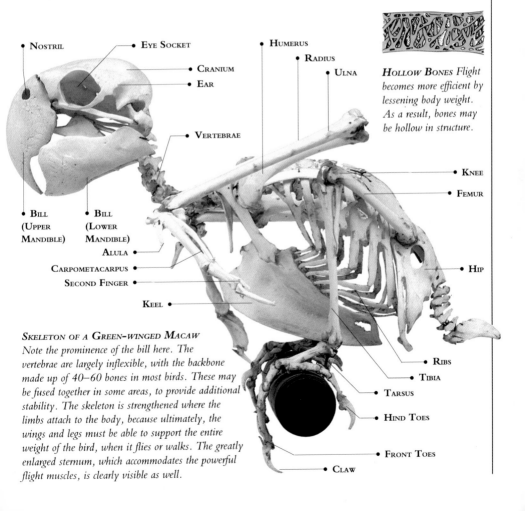

- NOSTRIL
- EYE SOCKET
- CRANIUM
- EAR
- VERTEBRAE
- HUMERUS
- RADIUS
- ULNA

HOLLOW BONES Flight becomes more efficient by lessening body weight. As a result, bones may be hollow in structure.

- KNEE
- FEMUR
- HIP
- BILL (UPPER MANDIBLE)
- BILL (LOWER MANDIBLE)
- ALULA
- CARPOMETACARPUS
- SECOND FINGER
- KEEL
- RIBS
- TIBIA
- TARSUS
- HIND TOES
- FRONT TOES
- CLAW

*SKELETON OF A GREEN-WINGED MACAW
Note the prominence of the bill here. The vertebrae are largely inflexible, with the backbone made up of 40–60 bones in most birds. These may be fused together in some areas, to provide additional stability. The skeleton is strengthened where the limbs attach to the body, because ultimately, the wings and legs must be able to support the entire weight of the bird, when it flies or walks. The greatly enlarged sternum, which accommodates the powerful flight muscles, is clearly visible as well.*

THE DIGESTIVE SYSTEM

Irrespective of the particular species of bird, the basic design of their digestive tract is similar. Seeds are usually cracked to extract the kernels, and other foods are also broken into smaller pieces using the bill, so they can be swallowed easily. Pigeons and doves differ from other seed-eaters, however, in that they do not dehusk the seed before swallowing it.

From the mouth, the food travels down the esophagus, or gullet, and then usually passes into the crop. This is essentially a storage organ, and if the bird has had little to eat recently, the food will quickly proceed further into the digestive tract. In certain birds, notably pigeons and doves, the lining of the crop undergoes a change early in the incubation period, which is triggered by the hormone prolactin. The crop begins to produce a white secretion, sometimes described as "crop milk," which is rich in proteins and fats. This nourishes the chicks for the first days after they hatch.

The crop is usually of no significance in the digestive process of a bird, with the single exception of the bizarre hoatzin, which feeds almost exclusively on plant matter and needs to consume vast quantities in order to meet its daily metabolic requirements. For them, the digestive process does actually begin in the crop.

After the food passes through the crop, it reaches the proventriculus, also known as the

LUNGS These are not very flexible in birds.

STOMACH Also known as the proventriculus.

KIDNEYS Located close to the backbone.

GIZZARD Usually has muscular walls.

INTESTINE/PANCREAS These are involved in the absorption of foodstuffs.

CROP Food is stored here, before it passes into the digestive tract.

HEART Birds have a very rapid heartbeat.

LIVER The liver is an important storage organ for some vitamins, such as vitamin A and D_3.

CLOACA The digestive, reproductive, and urinary tracts meet here.

DIGESTIVE TRACT OF PARROT Parrots usually feed in the early morning and prior to dusk, and it is at these times that they will fill their crop. When they have young birds to feed, however, they have a tendency to eat more frequently.

BILL SHAPES

The shape of the bill reflects the bird's feeding habits. Nectar-feeders, such as sunbirds, have narrow, pointed bills; finches, which consume large quantities of seed, have short, stout bills to help them crack the seeds and extract the kernels. Birds that eat insects and berries have a non-specific bill shape – moderately long and broad to turn over leaves, grab any insects, and pluck berries from branches. Parrots' bills are very powerful to cope with hard-cased seeds.

ST. HELENA WAXBILL

SENEGAL PARROT

VARIABLE SUNBIRD

glandular stomach. Here the food is mixed with mucus, hydrochloric acid, and pepsin – an enzyme responsible for breaking down proteins into other smaller groups of amino-acid residues.

The ventriculus itself is the muscular organ within the digestive tract, and it is here that seeds are ground down. The thickness of the surrounding muscle depends fully on the bird's diet. Parrots fed primarily on dry seed tend to have a thick-walled ventriculus, whereas nectar-feeding species, such as lories, usually have only a relatively thin-walled ventriculus.

Seed-eating birds usually also eat some grit, which lodges in the gizzard to take the place of teeth. The rough edges of the grit grind up the seeds and prevent the particles of food from coalescing and forming an obstruction.

Birds' intestines are less developed than those of mammals. The pancreas connects to the duodenal loop, as does the liver via the bile duct. Pancreatic juice plays an important role in the digestive process by producing enzymes, which help to break the food down into its components so that

they can then be absorbed into the bird's body. Lower down in the digestive tract, blind-ending tubes known as ceca may be present; these are most prominent in birds that feed on vegetation. In them are beneficial bacteria that break down the plant cellulose so that it can be digested. Parrots lack ceca altogether, and they are only rudimentary in various other species, including hummingbirds.

The rectum is the end of the digestive tract, and also leads into the cloaca, where the urinary and sexual openings are also found. The avian kidneys are located on either side of the vertebral column, close to the synsacrum. The urine that birds produce is largely in the form of uric acid, the white constituent of birds' droppings, rather than in the form of urea, as is the case with mammals. Birds do not possess a bladder (with the exception of the ostrich), and so the the uric acid passes directly, via the ureters, to the cloaca. In the cloaca, water is reabsorbed back into the bird's body, so that when the uric acid is finally excreted, it is normally in the form of a semi solid, whitish concentrate.

FLIGHT AND FEATHERS

The bird's wing is basically an airfoil. This means that as the wings cut through the air, the air is forced above and beneath them at different rates. The upper surface is raised compared with the hollow lower surface, so air rushes over the top of the wing at a faster rate, reducing the pressure. The rigid leading edge of the wing ensures that the air will always be divided in the same direction, and the pressure differential between the upper and lower surfaces provides lift.

The shape of the bird's wings has a direct effect on its flying abilities. Birds with relatively broad wings, such as vultures, are able to soar on warm air currents without having to expend much energy on flapping their wings. The air is thinner because of the heat, so there is more lift available from the warmth rising off the land. It is for this reason that migratory birds prefer to fly over land rather than over sea, where these warm currents, known as thermals, are absent.

THE FUNCTIONS OF FEATHERS

Long primary flight feathers, which maintain the bird in the air, are situated on the back edge of the wing. There are usually eleven in total, six fixed to the metacarpal part of the wing, and the remaining five extending to the wing tip, running along the phalanges. The number of primaries varies according to species.

There may be more variation in the number of secondary flight feathers, with perhaps only half a dozen in small passerines, while albatrosses, with their highly developed gliding skills, may have as many as forty. The secondary flight feathers are attached to the ulna, and closer to the body there are smaller tertiary flight

THE MOLTING SEASON

In the Budgerigar, for example, as with all parrots, the molt begins with the shedding of the fifth primary feather. Feathers on either side of this are shed in turn, and before the tenth primary has fully regrown the cycle could have started again. Molting usually takes place at least once during a year and frequently twice annually. A few species, such as various weavers and whydahs, molt at the start of the breeding period, undergoing a dramatic change in appearance. For most of the year, cocks resemble their relatively dull partners, but they are suddenly

HEAVY MOLT Amethyst Starling molting from juvenile to adult plumage.

transformed from their eclipse plumage by a prenuptial molt into strikingly colorful individuals. These species emphasize another function of plumage, which is its use for display purposes. In the majority of cases, molting will not interfere with the bird's flying ability. However, ducks, swans, and geese shed all of their flight feathers at the same time. This handicaps them for a month or more, often forcing them to migrate to a safer area where they will be less exposed to predators. Deprived of the power of flight, birds are largely defenseless against predators unless they can run or swim well. Temperature and light exposure can also affect molting, which can be significant in the case of pet birds.

ALULA Formed by short feathers resembling small quills, they are important for stability in flying birds, and assist swimming in some ducks. •

WING COVERTS These overlap to cover the
• remaining surface.

*THE BIRD'S PLUMAGE
Feathers are not only
important to birds for flight.
They also help to retain
body heat, and may be
used by some birds for
display purposes.*

PRIMARY FEATHERS These provide the major thrust when flying. The number of primaries varies slightly, and in finches for example, there are usually ten on each wing.

SECONDARY FEATHERS These attach to the part of the wing closest to the body, near the ulna. Shorter than primaries, they are also important in flight.

BODY PLUMAGE This comprises contour feathers that generally lie quite flat, outlining the shape of the body. Their tight structure helps to retain body warmth and repel rain. •

TAIL FEATHERS These are • very variable in shape. In the case of parakeets the tail feathers are long, whereas parrots are recognized by the short length and often square shape of their tail feathers. The same basic distinction serves to separate lories from lorikeets.

feathers in the skin adjoining the humerus. The remaining surface of the wing is covered with feathers known as coverts, which lie so that their broad edges are toward the rear of the wing, thus reducing air resistance during flight. The main thrust when a bird flaps its wings emanates from the primary flight feathers. These open as the wing moves upwards, allowing air between them. When there is a downward movement, these feathers lie flat on each other forcing the bird forward. The "bastard wing," or alula, at the tip of the leading edge of the wing, maintains air flow locally over the top of the wing, and reduces turbulence. As well as being required for flight, feathers are also important for insulation. The body temperature of birds tends to be significantly higher than that of

PARROT'S TAIL
FEATHER

RED LORY BODY FEATHERS

FEATHER FLAW Note the lines across the parrot's tail feather. These indicate a poor diet when the feather was developing. There is nothing that can be done at this stage, until such time as the plumage is shed. The bird itself is not handicapped in any way by this flaw.

mammals, averaging between 41–43.5°C (106–110°F). Small birds lose heat at a faster rate than large birds, and thus require more effective protection. The average covering of feathers totals about 6 percent of a bird's body weight, but in small titmice this figure is doubled, affording better protection against the elements.

MOLTING

In the vast majority of species, feathers develop in specific tracts over the bird's body – a process known as pterylosis. However, the number of feathers varies according to the season, and birds in temperate areas tend to have more feathers in winter than in summer. Molting is controlled by hormones that the endocrine system produces, which ensures that damaged or worn feathers can be shed and replaced regularly, so that the bird suffers the minimum of handicap.

During molting, a bird's energy requirements increase. Its food intake increases accordingly, and dietary

shortages during the molt may result in stunted feathering and abnormal changes in coloration. Ring-necked Parakeets, for example, may develop odd yellow feathers in among their otherwise green plumage. Provided that you correct the deficiency, however, the feathers will regrow normally at the next molt.

The blood supply to the plumage is only temporary, lasting throughout the growth period. After this, feathers are effectively dead, possessing neither innervation nor a blood supply. Any changes in feathering that occur at the time of the molt will remain until the plumage is replaced at the next molt. This is particularly important to bear in mind if you have birds such as canaries, which may need color-feeding (see page 157). Start using the coloring agent just before the molt occurs and continue throughout this period.

*REPLACEMENT PLUMAGE
The plumage is likely to become damaged and worn, and is usually replaced annually, during a molt. A food supplement for captive stock is recommended at this time of year.*

BUDGERIGAR
SECONDARY
FEATHERS

COCKATIEL PRIMARIES

THE RESPIRATORY SYSTEM

There are significant differences between the respiratory system of a bird and a mammal. A bird has two lungs, but these are comparatively rigid. A number of air sacs are also located within the bird's body. These sacs extend to some of the larger hollow bones, such as the humerus, and are described as being "pneumatic."

OXYGEN DEMAND

The exertions of flight demand a high oxygen intake. Although the lungs of birds are relatively small compared with those of mammals, they are more efficient, irrespective of altitude. Gaseous exchange is facilitated by tiny capillaries in the lungs, which ensure that oxygen is taken up by the red blood cells there, and that carbon dioxide is released. The air sacs themselves are not directly involved in this process, but they are vital to the efficiency of the system, acting rather like bellows. When the bird breathes in, air passes through to the posterior air sacs. Then, when it exhales, the air moves through the lungs, passing into the anterior air sacs and out of the bird's body.

These movements are controlled by two different sets of muscles. Unlike mammals, birds lack a diaphragm to establish a pressure differential between the chest and abdominal cavities. Instead, the intercostal muscles stimulate inhalation by broadening the bird's chest area, and the abdominal muscles then compress the chest, triggering exhalation. A slight modification is required during flight – the pectoral muscles move the sternum forward and then away from the vertebrae as they constrict and relax.

The major advantage of the respiratory system of birds is that it ensures a thorough change of air on exhalation. In mammals, a proportion of the existing air always remains in the lungs. The arrangement of the bird's blood vessels also ensures that the uptake of oxygen can be carried out with maximum efficiency. Blood returning to the lungs, with a low oxygen content, meets air that has already passed through the lungs. This still contains some oxygen, however, and this gas diffuses into the blood, triggering the release of carbon dioxide. As the blood moves closer to the lungs, it encounters progressively more oxygen, causing the blood to become progressively saturated with oxygen.

In addition to their role in respiration, the air sacs are also used for display purposes by some birds, such as frigate birds (*Fregata* species). The male's bright red gular pouches inflate with air during courtship, helping to attract a mate.

THE AVIAN RESPIRATORY SYSTEM This relies to a great extent on the nine air sacs, which assist air passage through the respiratory system.

TRACHEA (WINDPIPE)

LUNG This is close to the vertebral column.

ABDOMINAL AIR SAC

POSTERIOR THORACIC AIR SAC

ANTERIOR THORACIC AIR SAC

CHAPTER TWO

BIRD VARIETIES

KIKUYU ZOSTEROPS (above) These attractive little softbills can be kept and bred quite easily in groups.

ECLECTUS PARROT (left) While many parrots can be impossible to sex visually, there is a striking difference in this species, with hens being mainly reddish, and cock birds being predominantly green.

INTRODUCTION TO BIRD VARIETIES

Consider a number of points when choosing a bird. For a companion, start with a youngster that has recently left the nest, but feeds independently. An older individual will settle well into an aviary, but it is unlikely to develop the same rapport with its owner. Select suitable birds for your environment. Some large parrots, for example, are too noisy for outside aviaries in suburban gardens.

CHOOSING A BIRD

If your main concern is for a "talking" bird, you cannot do better than the African Gray Parrot or Greater Hill Mynah. Less costly than these species are Budgerigars and Cockatiels, both of which are talented mimics with cheerful temperaments. Cockatoos have very affectionate natures, and they whistle well, but their vocabulary is limited.

If you are choosing a bird for breeding purposes, then look for a young bird. Although it may take several years before it breeds successfully, it should be guaranteed a long reproductive life. If your interest is in establishing an exhibition stud, start with a clear idea of the ideal type for the bird concerned. Although the show standard is useful in this regard, the best thing to do is attend as many shows as possible. You will then see the types of bird that are winning and, equally important, observe why the others fail.

BUDGERIGARS These relatively inexpensive birds are bred in a wide range of colors, are talented mimics, and are not temperamental when mature. They have long been cherished as pets, and can be bred easily, in groups or as individual pairs. They are good birds for exhibiting.

GRAY-WINGED SKY BLUE BUDGERIGAR

FINCHES In general, finches are adaptable and often nest quickly once released from quarantine. They live well in groups, but rarely become tame. Additional heat and lighting may be needed in cold weather.

SPICE FINCH

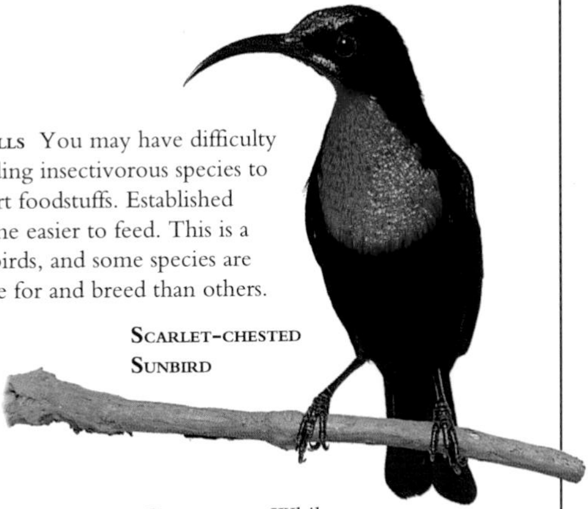

SOFTBILLS You may have difficulty persuading insectivorous species to take inert foodstuffs. Established birds will become easier to feed. This is a diverse group of birds, and some species are much easier to care for and breed than others.

SCARLET-CHESTED SUNBIRD

GOLDEN-MANTLED ROSELLA

PARROTS AND COCKATOOS While parrots are most often thought of as "talking birds," the larger species are most talented. Such birds are also likely to be very costly to purchase, and many species have loud, raucous calls. Smaller species are more suitable for aviary surroundings.

COCKATIELS AND PARAKEETS Cockatiels share many of the attributes of Budgerigars in terms of nature and mimicry. While some parakeets become tame, rosellas are one of a group of very popular Australian species that are kept and bred in aviary surroundings, rather than being housed in the home.

SENEGAL PARROT

CANARIES Cock birds can make superb songsters, and there is an exciting range of breeds and colors to choose from, if you are interested in breeding and exhibiting birds. Canaries are not destructive to woodwork, and can be housed alongside finches if required.

RED FACTOR CANARY

ZEBRA FINCH
Poephila guttata

The Zebra Finch is an ideal bird for the newcomer to bird-keeping, although it also attracts a strong following among experienced fanciers and exhibitors. The birds are easy to breed and raise since they make diligent parents. Zebra Finches are available in a crested form and a wide variety of color forms, which makes them popular with experienced bird-keepers. At shows, they are normally exhibited as pairs.

CHARACTERISTICS

LENGTH: *10cm (4in).*

AVERAGE LIFESPAN: *5 years.*

SEXING: *Hens of most varieties have no barring; their bills are also a paler red.*

BREEDING DETAILS: *Incubation lasts 13 days; fledging occurs 18 days later.*

YOUNG BIRDS: *Bills have brown markings; their tails are also shorter when they first leave the nest.*

MALE PLUMAGE The cock has a bright red bill and orange cheek patches.

FEMALE PLUMAGE The hen's body color is duller than that of the cock.

BREAST The cock has zebra-like barring on the breast.

FOOD & HOUSING Offer Zebra Finches a mix of millets and plain canary seed, augmented with softfoods and greenfood, such as seeding grasses and chickweed, especially during the breeding period. You can house a group of Zebra Finches in a small outdoor aviary, with a 1.8m- (6ft-) long flight. If you live in a temperate area, it is advisable to provide the birds with additional lighting and warmth during the winter. Alternatively, you can keep a pair indoors comfortably, in a breeding cage.

FAWN PENGUIN COCK

MUTATIONS
There are fawn, chestnut-flanked white, silver, and cream mutations of the Zebra Finch. You can easily breed them, and most are widely available.

BREEDING Given either a basket or a box, Zebra Finches are likely to nest in due course. They may have five or more chicks at a time; the young birds themselves are likely to breed from about nine months. Once the hen has laid eggs, withdraw nesting material and only provide greenfood that is finely chopped, otherwise she may bury the eggs.

GOULDIAN FINCH
Chloebia gouldiae

With its stunning coloration, and the three different head colors all found in the wild, the Gouldian Finch from Australia is one of the most popular with enthusiasts. However, it is one of the more expensive finches, and pairs are not always ready breeders. To increase your chances of breeding success, use Bengalese Finches as foster parents for the eggs and chicks, but always give Gouldian Finches an opportunity to rear their own offspring.

RED-HEADED COCK

PLUMAGE All three mutations are brightly colored. Cocks have vivid, purple breasts, yellow underparts, and green backs.

BILL Just prior to nesting, the tips of cocks' bills turn cherry-red.

YELLOW-HEADED COCK

MUTATIONS *The red-headed form is dominant to the black-headed; and the yellow-headed is a dilute form of the red-headed. Lilac- and white-breasted forms are bred in all head colors.*

FOOD & HOUSING Feed Gouldian Finches a quality foreign finch mix, combined with a little niger seed. Some breeders also like to add rock salt and powdered charcoal to the grit to aid the birds' digestion. Gouldian Finches are usually housed in indoor flights because they are quite sensitive to low temperatures. Watch for any signs of wheezing in this species because it could indicate that the birds are infected with air-sac mites.

BLACK-HEADED COCK

TAIL Short tails are characteristic of finches.

BREEDING Gouldian Finches can be bred in their flights, but it is best to use breeding cages if you want to breed mutations. They tend to nest during the winter in northern climates and therefore need extra protection. Wean chicks carefully to prevent them "going light." If there are any fatalities during weaning, seek advice from a vet as the cause may be infectious.

CHARACTERISTICS

LENGTH: 12.5cm (5in).
AVERAGE LIFESPAN: 7 years.
SEXING: Hens are paler than cocks.
BREEDING DETAILS: Incubation lasts 15 days; fledging occurs 21 days later.
YOUNG BIRDS: Plumage is predominantly greenish and much duller than that of adults.

JAVA SPARROW (RICE BIRD)
Padda oryzivora

As its name suggests, the Java Sparrow probably was confined originally to Java and nearby Bali, but it is now found over much of southeast Asia as well as further afield. The white Java Sparrow has a long history, possibly originating in China as many as 400 years ago. Several appealing color variants are well established, including a pure white form and a fawn form. Strangely enough, these color mutations tend to breed more readily than the normal form.

BREEDING For the best breeding results, keep Java Sparrows in groups, separate from other birds. Sometimes only dominant pairs attempt to breed, but providing a variety of nest-sites and plenty of nesting material should help to overcome this problem.

BILL The powerful bill enables the Java Sparrow to crack larger seeds than most finches. It may help to distinguish the sexes; a hen's bill is often paler.

PLUMAGE The plumage of these lively birds is invariably immaculate, making them a good choice for exhibiting.

FAWN MUTATION COCK

MUTATIONS
Pied Java Sparrows vary considerably; some are mainly colored, whereas others are primarily white. Crossing a white with a normal usually yields some pied offspring. The fawn mutation first appeared in a breeder's aviaries in Adelaide, Australia, during the late 1950s, and has since become very popular around the world. Crossing fawn pieds with whites yields fawn pieds.

CHARACTERISTICS
LENGTH: 14cm (6in).
AVERAGE LIFESPAN: 7 years.
SEXING: Scientific sexing required; cocks sing.
BREEDING DETAILS: Incubation lasts 14 days; fledging occurs 28 days later.
YOUNG BIRDS: Bills are dark; plumage is streaked on the breast.

FOOD & HOUSING Java Sparrows favor plain canary seed and millets, along with some paddy rice and greenfood. These birds can live in an outdoor aviary throughout the year, provided that they are both properly acclimatized and have snug, dry roosting quarters. Do not house them with waxbills, as they might bully the smaller birds. Watch for any signs of aggression in this group.

ORANGE-CHEEKED WAXBILL
Estrilda melpoda

These West African finches are among the smallest members of the waxbill clan, and are relatively easy to obtain. They are widely kept, probably because they are so easy to look after. However, they may prove rather shy, often hiding in a planted aviary when you are in the vicinity. Some become tamer with time. They usually prove compatible with other waxbills of similar size, rarely acting in an aggressive manner when kept in a community aviary. It is better to avoid boisterous companions, which may interfere with the birds' nesting activities.

CHARACTERISTICS

LENGTH: *10cm (4in).*
AVERAGE LIFESPAN: *4 years.*
SEXING: *Visually difficult; hens may be paler, with smaller orange cheek patches.*
BREEDING DETAILS: *Incubation lasts 12 days; fledging occurs 21 days later.*
YOUNG BIRDS: *Plumage is paler than in adults; the head is grayish brown.*

BILL The term "waxbill" refers to the bill coloration of this group of birds. It resembles the color of sealing wax.

CHEEKS The orange cheek plumage is characteristic of this species. It takes about six weeks to become apparent in chicks.

RUMP The red plumage on the rump of this cock bird is unique to the Orange-cheeked Waxbill.

TAIL The tail is important for communication between Orange-cheeked Waxbills. The cock bird flicks the tail back and forth when displaying to his mate.

FOOD & HOUSING Panicum millet and other small cereal seeds likely to be included in a foreign finch mix are readily accepted by Orange-cheeked Waxbills. They also eat a selection of greenfood and invertebrates. This species is happiest in a densely planted flight, especially as the birds prefer to nest close to the ground. As they are not completely hardy, you will need to bring them inside during cold weather. Release them into an outside flight in the spring, once all risk of frost has passed. For the best success in breeding, make sure that the birds are settled in their breeding quarters as soon as possible in the spring.

BREEDING
Provide nestboxes and avoid disturbing Orange-cheeked Waxbills unnecessarily during the breeding season, or they may react by abandoning the nest, even if they already have chicks. Given privacy, however, a pair may have two or even three clutches in a season. Supplying livefood of suitable size is essential when there are young chicks in the nest – a regular supply of whiteworm is ideal rearing food.

RED-CHEEKED CORDON BLEU
Uraeginthus bengalus

When first acquired, Red-cheeked Cordon Bleus tend to need careful management, but ultimately they settle well and nest readily in the right surroundings. Pairs will often breed very well in spacious, indoor quarters, so it is not essential to house them in an outdoor aviary. Plants here may help to encourage nesting.

FOOD & HOUSING Offer Red-cheeked Cordon Bleus a foreign finch seed mix, with plenty of soaked seed, fresh seedheads, and small livefood, such as whiteworms. When feeding, these birds normally eat on the ground, in contrast to the estrildid group of waxbills, which pick seeds directly from grassheads. Nectar, provided in a sealed drinker, helps to settle recently acquired birds. Coming from the warm and arid climate of southern Africa, they dislike the cold and damp. In warm weather you can keep them in a well planted, sheltered aviary. If it is cold, however, you must provide adequate heat and additional lighting.

BREEDING Red-cheeked Cordon Bleu pairs may be aggressive to other blue waxbills while breeding, so keep them separate. Other waxbills, however, are perfectly safe. They may build their own nest but, for breeding purposes, often favor nesting baskets. Livefood is essential for rearing chicks.

CHEEKS Cocks have red markings on both cheeks. On rare occasions, these cheek markings may be yellow.

MALE PLUMAGE Cocks are usually more brightly colored than their mates.

VARIETIES
Blue-capped Waxbills (Uraeginthus cyanocephala) *can be sexed easily, as hens have brown heads.*

BLUE-CAPPED WAXBILL COCK

CHARACTERISTICS
LENGTH: 12.5cm (5in).
AVERAGE LIFESPAN: 8 years.
SEXING: Hens of all species are paler than cocks.
BREEDING DETAILS: Incubation lasts 12 days; fledging occurs 21 days later.
YOUNG BIRDS: Lacking the red cheek patches of cock birds; resemble hens due to paler coloration; legs are darker at first.

RED-EARED WAXBILL
Estrilda troglodytes

For many years, the immaculate little Red-eared Waxbill from Northern Africa has been commonly available, but it has never proved particularly easy to breed. This is partly because it is not always easy to sex reliably – keeping a group together offers the best prospects of breeding success. Red-eared Waxbills can be housed with other waxbills, but it is not a good idea to keep them alongside bigger birds such as mannikins, who may well bully them.

BREEDING Red-eared Waxbills can have up to three broods during the summer, if you provide them with suitable nesting material, such as dried grass and moss. Cocks tend to display with nesting material in their bills, bobbing up and down in front of a potential mate. As with all waxbills, livefood is of great importance during the breeding period. Watch for hybridization in these birds if they are housed with other waxbills, since this makes it impossible to establish pure lines, and the resulting offspring are likely to be infertile.

EYES A red area of plumage surrounds the eyes.

TAIL The cock holds his tail vertically during the courtship display.

BILL The bill coloration resembles that of sealing wax.

BODY The lack of barring on the body distinguishes Red-eared Waxbills from other estrildids.

CLAWS To protect both the eggs and the chicks, trim the parents' claws before the start of the breeding season.

FOOD & HOUSING Offer Red-eared Waxbills a diet of foreign finch seed mix, chickweed, fresh grass seeds, and small invertebrates. They do not need to be housed in a large enclosure, but you should plant it well to encourage successful breeding. The birds can then forage for any invertebrates attracted to the vegetation. In an aviary, it is not unknown for them to breed on the ground, choosing to build their nest in a well-concealed locality. You should provide separate cold weather accommodation, although you can keep these birds in the shelter during bad weather if additional heating and lighting are available. Their plumage is normally immaculate, even when housed indoors, though a light spray of water helps it stay in top condition. Red-eared Waxbills are social by nature, and the fact that two individuals are observed preening each other does not necessarily indicate that they are a pair.

CHARACTERISTICS
LENGTH: 10cm (4in).
AVERAGE LIFESPAN: 5 years.
SEXING: Cocks' abdomens are usually a darker shade of pink than hens' abdomens.
BREEDING DETAILS: Incubation lasts 12 days; fledging occurs 21 days later.
YOUNG BIRDS: Bills are dark; eye-stripes are dark pink.

ST. HELENA WAXBILL (COMMON WAXBILL)
Estrilda astrild

For the beginner, St. Helena Waxbills provide a good introduction to this group of birds. They are one of the more adaptable members of the genus, making them quicker to acclimatize than some of their relatives. Nevertheless, they require adequate winter-time protection in temperate areas. Once established in their quarters, they are often quite ready to nest – they have been bred successfully in both cage and aviary surroundings. Since they are not aggressive birds, you can house them successfully in the company of related species.

MALE PLUMAGE Cocks have bright abdominal plumage, which makes identification easy. Since they are found over a wide area of southern Africa, the coloration of St. Helena Waxbills can show slight regional variations. •

BREEDING During the breeding season, provide suitable nesting material, such as dried grass and moss, or commercial nesting material, available in pet stores. Exposure to driving wind or rain can cause breeding pairs to desert their nests during warmer weather, but extra protection offered by an enclosed aviary prevents this, and also keeps cats from disturbing breeding birds, which may result in eggs or chicks being fatally chilled.

CHARACTERISTICS

LENGTH: 11.5cm (4½in).
AVERAGE LIFESPAN: 5 years.
SEXING: Cock birds have dark pink plumage on their abdomens.
BREEDING DETAILS: Incubation lasts 12 days; fledging occurs 21 days later.
YOUNG BIRDS: Bills are dark; red eye-stripes are smaller than those in adults.

EYES The eye-stripe is seen in both sexes.

FLANKS Similar in appearance to Red-eared Waxbills, the St. Helena Waxbill is more heavily barred on the flanks.

CLAWS If the claws are too long, the bird is at risk of becoming caught up in the netting in its quarters.

FOOD & HOUSING Offer St. Helena Waxbills staple foreign finch mixture, millet sprays, some greenfood, and livefood. In the wild, this species feeds on grassheads and relies on its claws to keep its balance on narrow perches. The long, spindly claws may cause the birds to become caught up in their enclosure, so you will need to trim them back occasionally. Trim the claws of the St. Helena Waxbill before the start of the breeding season to prevent eggs being punctured or young chicks being dragged from the nest. These waxbills thrive in an aviary planted with suitable grasses and small shrubs. The design of such an aviary should also offer extra protection against the elements, and so should be enclosed on all sides except the front. With this design, you will need to water the plants in the enclosure.

GOLDEN-BREASTED WAXBILL
Amandava subflava

Tiny and colorful, Golden-breasted Waxbills have long been avicultural favorites, and have been bred successfully to numerous generations by dedicated enthusiasts. They are not usually aggressive and can be housed with related species that are unlikely to molest them. The birds pictured below are the most usual form of the species, but you may see a slightly larger race, known as Clarke's Waxbill (*A. s. clarkei*), with less striking plumage.

> ### CHARACTERISTICS
> *LENGTH: 9cm (3½in).*
> *AVERAGE LIFESPAN: 8 years.*
> *SEXING: Hens are paler; they also lack the red eye-stripes, which are characteristic of cocks.*
> *BREEDING DETAILS: Incubation lasts 12 days; fledging occurs 21 days later.*
> *YOUNG BIRDS: Bills are dark; plumage is duller than in adults; they have no eye-stripes.*

FOOD & HOUSING Offer Golden-breasted Waxbills a foreign finch mix, with millet sprays, greenfood, and small livefood. Since they are so small, these waxbills should be kept in quarters with mesh that does not exceed 1.25cm (½in) square, otherwise they may escape. Although they can live quite happily in an outdoor aviary during the summer, in temperate parts of the world you should provide warm winter accommodation.

BREEDING When a pair looks ready to breed, provide nesting baskets. Waxbills will neglect their chicks if deprived of whiteworm or similar livefood when they are breeding, since they have a strong instinct for livefood at this stage. Even though they may accept softfood, which will provide variety and be sufficiently nutritious for their diet, it is not an adequate substitute since it will not satisfy the birds' strong desire for livefood.

EYES The red eye-stripe is a feature associated with cocks only.

UNDERPARTS The cock has much brighter golden underparts than the hen.

FLANKS Dark barring on the flanks is usual, but some of these finches show more pronounced areas of black plumage, a phenomenon known as induced melanism. This can prove transitory, with normal feathering reappearing at the next molt. However, it is possible that the black areas will spread further.

FEMALE PLUMAGE Hens can be recognized by their duller plumage. Since they are found over a wide area of Africa, south of the Sahara, local variations occur in coloration as well as size. Hens often remain close to their mates, and they may frequently preen each other. In terms of size, the Golden-Breasted Waxbill is the smallest of all the waxbills.

BENGALESE FINCH
Lonchura domestica

The origin of the Bengalese Finch is a mystery, because it does not occur in the wild. It is thought to be the result of selective crossbreeding, done centuries ago in China, with the Striated Mannikin (*Lonchura striata*) and other related species. Records show these birds occuring in Japan around the sixteenth century, and they were first seen in the West in 1860, when two pure white Bengalese Finches were acquired by the London Zoo. Later, in 1871, the first of the chocolate-colored Bengalese Finches reached Germany from the Orient; they were followed by fawn and more white forms. Today, these birds are kept all over the world, and rank among the most popular finches. They are highly valued as foster parents for Australian grassfinches, such as Gouldian Finches, who often are not reliable parents. Social birds, Bengalese are also known as Society Finches, particularly in North America.

PLUMAGE This bird's color is chestnut; self chocolate is the darkest of the Bengalese colors.

LEGS Rings of differing color, attached to the legs, can identify proven cocks and hens.

CHARACTERISTICS

LENGTH: 10cm (4in).
AVERAGE LIFESPAN: 5 years.
SEXING: Scientific sexing required; cocks sing.
BREEDING DETAILS: Incubation lasts 12 days; fledging occurs 21 days later.
YOUNG BIRDS: Plumage is duller and underparts are paler than in adults.

TAIL The cock fans his tail feathers as part of the breeding display.

MARKINGS Since it differs from bird to bird, the pattern of markings is impossible to predict.

FAWN AND WHITE COCK

MUTATIONS *The fawn and white Bengalese mutation often has white areas on its head, which vary in extent.*

BREEDING When a pair appears ready to mate, provide them with suitable nesting material, such as dried grass or moss, or commercial nesting material. Avoid housing Bengalese Finches alongside other mannikins, or they may interbreed.

FOOD & HOUSING Offer Bengalese Finches standard foreign finch seed mix plus some greenfood. They are reasonably hardy and social birds by nature, so they will live happily in an outdoor aviary in the company of waxbills and other smaller finches.

SILVERBILL
Lonchura malabarica

The two types of Silverbill, *Lonchura m. malabarica* and *L. m. cantans*, originate from India and Africa respectively. They are equally easy to look after and normally nest quite readily, either in cage or aviary surroundings. The more colorful Pearl-headed Silverbill *(Lonchura griseicapilla)* is easily recognized by its gray head and white speckling on the sides of the face and throat, and has pinkish brown underparts, while the *L. m. malabarica* has fawn underparts. It is difficult to distinguish between the sexes, but if you start off with five or six birds, there is every likelihood that you will have at least one pair. At the breeding season, cocks not only sing to attract a mate, but also dance, holding nesting material in the bill.

BREEDING When a pair appears ready to breed, provide a basket or box for nesting. You can rear chicks successfully without giving them small livefood; feed them daily on fresh egg food or softbill mix, both valuable sources of extra protein. Like many smaller finches, these are prolific, producing as many as eight eggs in a typical clutch. They may also nest two or three times in succession. Breeding results are likely to be best in an outside aviary.

CHARACTERISTICS
LENGTH: *10cm (4in).*
AVERAGE LIFESPAN: *5 years.*
SEXING: *Hens are often smaller, with redder tails; cocks sing in breeding period.*
BREEDING DETAILS: *Incubation lasts 12 days; fledging occurs 21 days later.*
YOUNG BIRDS: *Similar to adults.*

HEAD Dark markings on the head are a characteristic of the Silverbill, whose common name derives from the silver color found on its bill.

RUMP The Silverbill from India can be identified by its white rump; Silverbills from Africa have black rumps.

LEGS This bird's lightly scaled legs show that it is still young; older birds have more heavily scaled legs.

FOOD & HOUSING Silverbills thrive on a diet of small millets and the ingredients found in foreign finch mixtures. They will also take some greenfood, such as seeding grasses. You can house Silverbills alongside waxbills, as they are not aggressive. They can be kept in an outside aviary, but will require additional heating and lighting during cold weather. In temperate countries, keep them outside for one summer, before allowing them to winter outdoors.

SPICE FINCH (NUTMEG FINCH)
Lonchura punctulata

Spice Finches span a wide area of Asia, from India to mainland China. They also inhabit numerous islands, including the Philippines. The common name may have arisen because Spice Finches were first brought to Europe on ships returning with valuable spices from the Orient. Given their wide geographical spread, it is not surprising that a number of different forms exist, which vary somewhat in plumage and overall size. Social birds by nature, you can keep groups of these finches together. Start with a number of birds from one source to ensure that they are of the same race.

CHARACTERISTICS

LENGTH: *12.5cm (5in).*
AVERAGE LIFESPAN: *5 years.*
SEXING: *Scientific sexing required; cocks sing.*
BREEDING DETAILS: *Incubation lasts 12 days; fledging occurs 21 days later.*
YOUNG BIRDS: *Similar to adults, but are generally duller in appearance.*

FLANKS The degree of markings on the flanks varies according to the race concerned. This bird has barring along its flanks.

UPPER PARTS The depth of reddish brown coloration on the upper parts of the birds varies.

BILL The color of the bill ranges from dark gray to black in this species of finch.

MARKINGS Certain Spice Finches have more colorful breast markings than others.

FOOD & HOUSING A mixture of millets and canary seeds suits Spice Finches well. They also appreciate livefood and greenfood. Unlike most mannikins, they show a preference for livefood. Feed them this intermittently through the year, and offer plenty to pairs with chicks. Chickweed and meadow grass are favored greenfoods with this species. Once the chickweed has finished flowering, the birds eat the seed pods. A well-planted flight is necessary to allow them seclusion. Once they have been properly acclimatized, you can keep them in a sheltered outdoor aviary throughout the year.

BREEDING Given suitable vegetation, a pair will build a strong nest together, the cock bird often assuming the responsibility for collecting the nesting material. Spice Finches prefer green stems, such as thick stalks of grass, rather than dried material; they line the interior of the nest with softer items, including feathers and moss, if they can find them.

TRI-COLORED NUN (CHESTNUT MUNIA)
Lonchura malacca

Tri-colored Nuns, generally sleek and immaculate in appearance, are Asian finches found in open countryside in the wild. They are often available and are easy to care for. If you hope to breed them, it is best to concentrate on keeping a group of them together. The likelihood of obtaining at least one pair is greater then, and their breeding instincts will be stimulated.

> ## CHARACTERISTICS
> LENGTH: *11.5cm (4½in).*
> AVERAGE LIFESPAN: *5 years.*
> SEXING: *Scientific sexing required; cocks sing.*
> BREEDING DETAILS: *Incubation lasts 12 days; fledging occurs 21 days later.*
> YOUNG BIRDS: *Similar to adults, but duller in overall coloration.*

HEAD The black head distinguishes this bird as one of the black-headed group of munias.

FEMALE PLUMAGE The coloration of the wings is sometimes slightly lighter in hens.

UNDERPARTS Initially creamy in color, the underparts tend to become paler as the plumage ages.

FOOD & HOUSING A foreign finch seed mix plus millet sprays suits these birds well. Tri-colored Nuns also eat greenfood, and forage for insects, such as greenfly, in their aviary. They take seeds from grass, using stems to make nests. Acclimatized birds are quite hardy, but in temperate areas you may prefer to overwinter them in a heated birdroom. If so, keep them in a flight rather than a cage, where they will be less nervous.

BILL Magpie Mannikin cock birds usually have larger bills than the hens.

BREEDING It is said that if you add bamboo to the aviary you will encourage Tri-colored Nuns to breed, probably because they nest in clumps of bamboo in the wild. If you offer soaked seed and small livefood you may also encourage birds to breed, a measure that works with related munias. Often, however, when they are kept in a group, only relatively few pairs breed; reducing numbers in the flight may help to overcome this problem.

VARIETY *The black and white plumage of the African Magpie Mannikin (L. fringilloides) gives the bird its common name.*

MAGPIE MANNIKIN COCK

CUT-THROAT FINCH
Amadina fasciata

Being naturally bold and inquisitive, these sociable finches from Africa make attractive aviary occupants. In their native territory, they often live near villages and towns, frequently nesting under the eaves of buildings. Caring for them presents no particular problems, and since they can be sexed easily and are usually reliable parents, you can obtain breeding results without difficulty. The other member of this genus, the Red-headed Finch *(A. erythocephala)*, is equally easy to sex, because the cock birds have red heads. They are rarer in aviculture than Cut-throat Finches, and though they have similar requirements, they may not be as hardy.

CHARACTERISTICS

LENGTH: 11.5cm (4½in).
AVERAGE LIFESPAN: 5 years.
SEXING: Cocks have red throat plumage.
BREEDING DETAILS: Incubation lasts 12 days; fledging occurs 21 days later.
YOUNG BIRDS: Similar to adults; young cocks have paler red throat plumage than adults.

THROAT The red markings on the cock's throat give rise to the name of Cut-throat Finch for these birds.

ABDOMEN The chestnut-colored markings on the abdomen are a feature of cocks, although you may sometimes find a trace on the hens.

FEMALE PLUMAGE Hens are a paler shade of brown than cocks.

FOOD & HOUSING Offer these finches a diet of millets and other smaller cereal seeds, and some greenfood. Also offer livefood regularly, although pairs sometimes rear chicks without it. The birds will thrive in a planted aviary with a shelter. They tend to be aggressive, so do not house them in the company of smaller birds, such as waxbills. Larger birds, such as weavers or whydahs, are more suitable companions.

BREEDING To prevent any squabbling between pairs in the breeding season, provide finch nestboxes and open-front boxes in a variety of sites around the aviary. They may prefer to build their own nests. Watch hens carefully. They can be susceptible to egg-binding.

PARADISE WHYDAH
Vidua paradisaea

The spectacular breeding plumage of the cock birds characterizes the whydah group of finches. A number of species are represented in aviculture but, because of their specialized nesting habits, breeding success in captivity is relatively rare. Paradise Whydahs were brought initially from the African port of Widah by Portuguese sailors, hence their common name. They are also known as widow birds, because of the cock's black plumage.

NECK The ocher coloration extends around the neck, and is usually a shade darker on the chest.

PLUMAGE Cocks have streaky plumage when they are out of color (O.O.C.).

BREEDING Paradise Whydahs do not rear their own chicks. Instead, hens lay their eggs in the nests of various waxbills, who then hatch the eggs and rear the chicks alongside their own. Cock whydahs molt into their magnificent plumage at the start of the mating period. House a cock with several hens, and keep them in the company of pytilia species for breeding purposes. The Melba Finch *(Pytilia melba)* is the natural host of this species, but whydah chicks have also been reared by Fire Finches *(Lagonostica s. senegala)*.

TAIL The Paradise Whydah holds its tail almost horizontally in flight. The long plumes of the tail are easily damaged, so position perches where cocks can turn around without catching their tails on the mesh.

FOOD & HOUSING Offer Paradise Whydahs a diet of a foreign finch mixture with additional millet sprays, and also some greenfood and livefood. Whydahs need a large planted aviary, since they are active birds by nature. They are hardy once acclimatized, so you can house them in an aviary. Alternatively, you can keep them in a large indoor flight. Avoid housing them with the foster waxbills out of the breeding season, as they may bully them. When Paradise Whydahs are out of color (O.O.C.), you may have difficulty separating the sexes. If so, you should be able to distinguish a cock from a hen by the slightly longer tail and the darker markings on its body.

CHARACTERISTICS

LENGTH: 13cm (5in) out of color, cocks are 40cm (16in) during the breeding season.

AVERAGE LIFESPAN: 10 years.

SEXING: Hens have duller plumage than cocks; they also have no tail plumes.

BREEDING DETAILS: Incubation lasts 14 days; fledging occurs 14 days later.

YOUNG BIRDS: Similar to adults; they are reared by foster waxbills.

ORANGE WEAVER (RED BISHOP)
Euplectes orix

Found over an extensive area of the African continent, from south of the Sahara to South Africa, a number of slightly different forms of Orange Weaver exist, which differ in their coloration. The cocks also have a spectacular change at the start of the breeding season, when the chest and head turn a vivid orange. The birds are well known in aviculture, but breeding results are not commonly achieved, though cocks readily weave elaborate nests with strands of dried grass. They even produce nests if kept on their own, provided suitable material, such as discarded millet sprays, is available.

BILL When cock birds are in breeding condition, their bills darken to black.

BREAST The depth of the orange plumage can be intensified by color-feeding the cock prior to the molt.

IN FULL COLOR This cock bird is described as being "in full color," often abbreviated to I.F.C.

CHARACTERISTICS
LENGTH: 12.5cm (5in).
AVERAGE LIFESPAN: 7 years.
SEXING: Hens have no black plumage, nor the orange coloration of the cock in full color.
BREEDING DETAILS: Incubation lasts 14 days; fledging occurs 15 days later.
YOUNG BIRDS: Plumage is paler than in adults.

OUT OF COLOR Cocks out of color (O.O.C.) resemble hens, but may retain darker markings.

FOOD & HOUSING Offer a diet of small cereal seeds, and supplementary greenfood and livefood, especially if there are chicks. These weavers are easy to manage, and can usually be kept without heat through the winter months in temperate countries, once they are properly acclimatized. They are boisterous by nature, so do not house them with smaller finches, such as waxbills. Cockatiels are suitable companions for them.

BREEDING For breeding purposes, you need to house a cock with several hens, since they are polygamous by nature. A cock makes a nest out of dried grass and then mates with one hen, who takes over the rest of the breeding process, before he moves on to another partner in the flock. The cock is not involved in the incubation process, and also leaves the hens to rear the chicks on their own. If you keep the cock with just one hen, there is a risk that the cock will persecute his sole mate. Breeding success is then most unlikely.

NAPOLEON WEAVER (GOLDEN BISHOP)
Euplectes afer

The Napoleon Weaver is found over the same vast territory in Africa as the Orange Weaver. In the wild it frequents reedbeds, and often builds its nest in the reeds, where it is relatively safe. In the vicinity of large nesting colonies, however, crocodiles may lurk and seize young birds as they emerge from their nests – a hazard the breeder does not face! Breeding results in captivity have not been frequently obtained, but if you decide to specialize in these birds, there is no reason why you should not succeed. The Napoleon and the Orange Weaver require identical care.

FOOD & HOUSING Offer Napoleon Weavers a diet of a foreign finch mix, plus greenfood and insects, as chicks are unlikely to be reared without suitable livefood. Soaked seed can also be helpful in rearing chicks. Appropriate color feeding at the onset of the molt will intensify the yellow coloration of the cock birds. They are hardy once acclimatized, but need a snug shelter in cold weather. Separate them from waxbills, who they are likely to bully.

ECLIPSE PLUMAGE This cock Napoleon Weaver in eclipse plumage is starting to become more colorful.

BILL A stocky bill is essential for cracking seed husks, for weaving, and for squabbling.

HEAD Bright yellow coloration covers the cock's head and extends down to the breast.

MARKINGS Black streaking merges with yellow feathering to create an individual pattern of markings.

CHARACTERISTICS
LENGTH: 12.5cm (5in).
AVERAGE LIFESPAN: 7 years.
SEXING: Hens have heavier streaking than cocks out of color.
BREEDING DETAILS: Incubation lasts 14 days; fledging occurs 15 days later.
YOUNG BIRDS: Upper parts are browner, and streaking is less prominent than in adults.

BREEDING Start with at least two cock birds and four hens, assuming that you can obtain birds in color. It may well take a year for them to settle fully, but then the cocks will compete with each other to attract the hens, by singing and displaying to them. In this situation, there is no serious risk of fighting. In order to encourage nesting, plant stands of bamboo in the aviary, taking care to choose a variety that will not grow too tall.

GOLDEN SONG SPARROW
Passer luteus

Though the name is appealing, it is inaccurate, as Golden Song Sparrows are not really songsters, and only the cock bird is yellow. The cock's song is simple, yet pretty, and is made up of a series of cheeps, similar to those of house sparrows. Golden Song Sparrows are easy birds to maintain and are happy when kept in a small flock – breeding is most likely under these circumstances. Alternatively you can keep a pair of Golden Song Sparrows indoors in a box-type cage fitted with a finch front. Acclimatize Golden Song Sparrows properly when you first buy them. They should be kept in a heated birdroom during cold weather.

FEMALE PLUMAGE
The hens are easy to recognize by their dull, brownish plumage.

BILL The cock's bill is normally a pale horn color; during nesting it darkens to black.

MALE PLUMAGE
The depth of the cock's yellow coloration varies between individuals. You can deepen it with color feeding.

FOOD & HOUSING Golden Song Sparrows eat a variety of small seeds and spray millet, as well as livefood, such as whiteworm and small crickets. After careful acclimatization, you can house these birds in a planted aviary. Alternatively, keep one or two inside in a box-type cage with a finch front. Keep them separate from waxbills, since these sparrows can be rather boisterous, especially in a group.

BREEDING For successful breeding, house Golden Song Sparrows in a well-planted aviary and provide them with nestboxes. Suspend chunks of gorse in their enclosure to encourage them to breed. As they nest in thorn bushes in the wild, they readily build their nests in aviaries under the protection of the sharp spikes of gorse.

CHARACTERISTICS
LENGTH: 12.5cm (5in).
AVERAGE LIFESPAN: 5 years.
SEXING: Hens have brown coloration.
BREEDING DETAILS: Incubation lasts 12 days; fledging occurs 14 days later.
YOUNG BIRDS: Resemble hens, but are paler on their underparts; odd gray feathers are also present on the back of the head.

BLUE-HEADED PARROT FINCH
Erythrura trichroa

Although initially costly, Blue-headed Parrot Finches can prove very prolific under favorable conditions – one pair I know reared nearly 40 youngsters in a period of less than 18 months! The best breeding results are likely to occur in a well-planted aviary, where these somewhat nervous birds can feel secure and settle down. Blue-headed Parrot Finches rarely settle well enough in cage surroundings to nest, as they require more privacy.

FOOD & HOUSING A foreign finch mix, plain canary seed, and paddy rice, augmented with suitable livefood, suits Blue-headed Parrot Finches well. House them in an indoor flight and suspend conifer branches from the top to provide the birds with extra seclusion; this seems to reassure them.

HEAD Deep blue head markings are a distinguishing feature of this species. The blue and green areas of plumage are clearly divided. The bird's common name comes from its similarity of plumage to parrots.

WINGS Like other finches, Blue-headed Parrot Finches are quick on the wing and agile in flight.

TAIL The tail feathers are noticeably pointed at their tips.

PLUMAGE The green plumage covering most of the body provides natural camouflage for this bird.

CHARACTERISTICS
LENGTH: 11.5cm (4½in).
AVERAGE LIFESPAN: 7 years.
SEXING: Hens have smaller and duller blue patches on their faces than cocks, although this depends to some extent on individual birds.
BREEDING DETAILS: Incubation lasts 14 days; fledging occurs 21 days later.
YOUNG BIRDS: No blue coloration on the heads; their bills are yellow.

MUTATION *The Red-headed Parrot Finch (Erythrura psittacea) originates from Samoa and other nearby islands in the South Pacific, and is quite well established in aviculture. A prolific species, one man managed to breed these birds to 30 generations in his lifetime.*

RED-HEADED PARROT FINCH COCK

BREEDING Although they will live quite happily in the company of other finches of similar size, you should not house more than one pair together, as they may fight, and so disrupt any chances of nesting. Provide breeding pairs with a nestbox.

GREEN SINGING FINCH
Serinus mozambicus

Talented songsters, these Green Singing Finches are related to the wild ancestor of the domesticated canary, and have similar requirements. Green Singing Finches occur over a wide area of Africa, south of the Sahara, so regional variations occur in the bird. One variety you may encounter is the larger St. Helena Seed-eater or Giant Green Singing Finch (*S. flaviventris*). Sometimes these African seed-eaters are confused with those of the unrelated New World genus, *Sporophila*. The New World seed-eaters can be identified by their much broader bills.

BREEDING Provide hens with canary nestpans. Give pairs fresh canary-rearing food each day, and then provide small livefoods from just before the chicks are due to hatch, right through the rearing period, until the chicks fledge. Cocks are best kept apart, because they may be aggressive toward one another, but you can safely keep and breed a single pair of Green Singing Finches in the company of other waxbills.

FOOD & HOUSING Offer these finches a canary seed mix supplemented with additional plain canary seed. Though relatively hardy once acclimatized, you may prefer to overwinter these birds indoors in temperate climates.

HEAD Cocks have bright yellow patches on the face, whereas hens are duller and have blackish spots on the throat.

BACK Greenish gray in color, with yellowish underparts.

RUMP A definite shade of yellow in this species, but the rump is greenish in the Giant Green Singing Finch.

VARIETY *The Gray Singing Finch (S. leucopygius) is duller than the Green Singing Finch, but needs identical care.*

GRAY SINGING FINCH COCK

CHARACTERISTICS
LENGTH: 12.5cm (5in).
AVERAGE LIFESPAN: 12 years.
SEXING: Hens are duller than cocks; blackish spots on their throats may merge into a band.
BREEDING DETAILS: Incubation lasts 14 days; fledging occurs 14 days later.
YOUNG BIRDS: Like hens; heavier streaking.

MELBA FINCH (GREEN-WINGED PYTILIA)
Pytilia melba

Pytilias form a distinctive group of four species of waxbill, one of which is the Melba Finch. Pytilias are slightly larger in size than the related estrildids (see pages 33, 35, 36). All pytilias need to be carefully acclimatized and are best kept indoors during damp weather. The Aurora Finch (*P. phoenicoptera*) is another popular member of the pytilia group of finches, needing identical care.

CHARACTERISTICS
LENGTH: 12.5cm (5in).
AVERAGE LIFESPAN: 6 years.
SEXING: Hens' heads are entirely gray.
BREEDING DETAILS: Incubation lasts 12 days; fledging occurs 21 days later.
YOUNG BIRDS: The rumps and tails have orange rather than red coloration.

FEMALE PLUMAGE Hens are duller overall in coloration, making it easy to recognize a pair.

MALE PLUMAGE Melba Finch cocks are instantly recognizable by their red heads. They can be particularly aggressive toward birds with similar markings that share their quarters.

BILL They use their strong bill, which is far more robust than that of the smaller waxbills, to break open termite mounds and eat the exposed insects.

FOOD & HOUSING Offer Melba Finches a diet of foreign finch mix, and augment this with suitable livefood, which is required in greater quantities when they start to breed. A densely planted flight suits them well. They are best housed on their own, especially when breeding, otherwise they can become aggressive to other birds.

FEET Surprisingly, the coloration of the feet is much duller than the bill.

BREEDING Pairs often prefer to construct their own nests, rather than using a nestbox. They position their nests at a low height in a suitable shrub, such as box. They favor dried grass for building nests, and occasionally use feathers to line it. The pair may nest two or three times during the summer months. Remove chicks once they are feeding on their own as the parents might want to nest again.

FLANKS Several different races of Melba Finch are recognized. The barring on the flanks may vary between the races.

BORDER FANCY CANARY
Serinus canaria

This canary breed was developed on the borders of England and Scotland toward the end of the nineteenth century. The birds were originally known as Cumberland Canaries in England, although in Scotland they were known simply as Common Canaries. In 1890, at a meeting held at Hawick, in Cumbria, the new name "Border Fancy Canary" was agreed as a compromise. This name is now used internationally.

HEAD The Border Canary's head is quite small and rounded, and the eyes are always positioned centrally.

PLUMAGE A Clear Yellow Border Canary should have a pure and even depth of coloration.

TAIL In this breed of canary, the tail is rounded and quite narrow.

BODY Both the back and chest are rounded; the wings meet at their tips.

FOOD & HOUSING Offer Border Fancy Canaries a canary seed mixture and greenfood, plus egg food through the breeding period. These birds are hardy and can be kept in an aviary throughout the year. They are often recommended for beginners, as they are easy to care for and to breed. They do not need to be color-fed, but it is a good idea to provide them with a plentiful supply of greenfood such as spinach, an excellent source of the natural yellow coloring agent, lutein. Well-trained Border Fancy Canaries are lively, and hop readily from perch to perch. There is now a smaller form of this bird, known as the Fife Fancy, which has become very popular during recent years.

BREEDING Provide hens with a nestpan. Correct size is an important feature in this breed, and the Border Canary is traditionally referred to as the "wee gem." When pairing birds, it is important to avoid mating the coarse-feathered buffs to each other. Mate buffs with the so-called yellow birds, which have softer plumage.

CHARACTERISTICS
LENGTH: 14cm (5½in).
AVERAGE LIFESPAN: 10 years.
SEXING: Scientific sexing required; cocks sing.
BREEDING DETAILS: Incubation lasts 14 days; fledging occurs 14 days later.
YOUNG BIRDS: Similar to adults.

PLUMAGE This "lightly variegated" bird has mainly light-colored plumage.

BUFF VARIEGATED COCK

MUTATIONS *The Border Canary has numerous color mutations, which include white, cinnamon, green, and variegated forms.*

GLOSTER FANCY CANARY
Serinus canaria

This relatively new arrival on the canary scene owes its origins to crosses made between crested Roller Canaries and small Border Fancy Canaries. A breeding program with these two birds was begun in the English county of Gloucestershire, and the new breed was first exhibited at a major show in 1925. Since the Second World War, Gloster Fancy Canaries have gained popularity, and are widely available. The terms "buff" and "yellow" do not refer to the bird's coloration, but rather to its feather type. Buff birds have coarser feathers, and appear slightly larger. They have recently become more common. Gloster Fancy Canaries with crests are described as coronas, while those without are referred to as consorts.

CREST The crest is reasonably compact. Unlike other canaries it does not extend over the eye. The feathers are even in length.

NECK The thick neck matches the relatively broad head.

PLUMAGE The combination of dark and light plumage gives this bird the alternative name of Variegated Gloster.

CHEST The chest is rounded in shape, and the well-laid plumage contributes to the bird's sleek appearance.

FOOD & HOUSING A standard canary seed mix, plus greenfood and softfood, suits Gloster Fancy Canaries well. You can also offer them greenfood on a regular basis, with chickweed being a popular choice. They are quite hardy, and can be housed in a snug outside aviary throughout the year. This canary does not need to be color-fed, and good quality stock is usually available at realistic prices, so keeping these birds presents few problems.

BREEDING Provide hens with a nestpan. As explained on page 187, it is vital that you do not pair coronas together. Also, repeated pairings of buff-type birds have led to an increased incidence of feather cysts in this breed. The cysts reoccur at each molt, usually appearing over the bird's back. Monitor your breeding program closely, and use yellow-feathered birds to prevent these incurable cysts.

SCOTCH FANCY CANARY
Serinus canaria

Being one of the so-called type breeds, the Scotch Fancy Canary is judged on its shape. It was immensely popular in its native Scotland during the last century but, since then, its fortunes have waned. However, the breed has recently undergone a revival, and good stock has again become more widely available. Aside from their posture and type, these birds have another important attribute, which is essential for success on the show bench. The bird's movement is described as "traveling," as it moves back and forth from perch to perch. It should hop, without the use of its wings, turn, and, without hesitation, adopt its characteristic stance in front of the judge. Sadly, it seems that the time needed to train these birds was one of the factors that led to their decline.

FOOD & HOUSING Offer a diet of canary seed mix, greenfood, and softfood throughout the year. These birds are hardy and can be housed in an aviary throughout the year.

BREEDING Provide hens with a nestpan for breeding purposes. Although hardy, Scotch Fancy Canaries are usually bred inside cages in a birdroom to ensure the chicks' parentage.

HEAD The bird holds its head forward and its long neck emphasizes the curved posture of this breed.

PLUMAGE This is a buff feather-type yellow bird. The plumage is slightly paler than the equivalent yellow form.

POSTURE The back of the Scotch Fancy Canary has an obvious curve. Because of this posture, this bird is sometimes called "the bird o'circle."

TAIL This bird's long tail should curve under the perch.

BUFF VARIEGATED SCOTCH FANCY COCK

VARIETIES It is thought that Scotch Fancy Canaries descend from the Belgian Fancy Canary. The miniature Japanese Hoso is now bred, but is still rare.

CHARACTERISTICS
LENGTH: 17cm (6¾in).
AVERAGE LIFESPAN: 10 years.
SEXING: Scientific sexing required; cocks sing.
BREEDING DETAILS: Incubation lasts 14 days; fledging occurs 14 days later.
YOUNG BIRDS: Similar to adults, but they will fledge with shorter tails.

ROLLER CANARY
Serinus canaria

A breed developed essentially for its singing skills, the Roller Canary was already well-known in Germany in 1675 and was very popular in the area of the Harz Mountains. For competitions, Roller Canaries are trained to sing set passages, called tours and rolls, and they are judged on their singing performance. The exhibition Roller Canary has a pure-sounding, melodic song, which can range over nearly three octaves. Yet even top-class birds cannot master the full range of tours and rolls. New birds used to be taught by a "schoolmaster" bird, but now they are often taught with a cassette tape.

FEET Like other finches, canaries use three toes to grip the front of the perch, and one behind.

FOOD & HOUSING It is usual to offer these canaries a diet of a standard canary seed mix, augmented with German rubsen rapeseed, which is said to encourage their singing skills! Also give them some greenfood, such as chickweed, and softfood. If you want to keep Roller Canaries as pets, keep two cock birds in the same room, though in separate cages to prevent fighting. This encourages the birds to sing in competition with one another. Alternatively, once properly acclimatized, these birds are hardy enough to remain in an outdoor aviary throughout the year.

CHARACTERISTICS

LENGTH: 12.5cm (5in).
AVERAGE LIFESPAN: 10 years.
SEXING: Scientific sexing required; cocks sing.
BREEDING DETAILS: Incubation lasts 14 days; fledging occurs 14 days later.
YOUNG BIRDS: Similar to adults.

BILL The cock bird keeps his bill virtually closed when singing.

POSTURE When singing, as here, the cock Roller Canary adopts an upright stance, and keeps his head raised.

BREEDING Provide hens with a nestpan for breeding. Although hardy, canaries are usually bred in a birdroom in cages to ensure parentage. Increase the amount of greenfood and softfood from the time breeding starts until the chicks fledge.

PLUMAGE This bird is a variegated yellow Roller Canary. However, for show purposes, color is not significant, as the birds are judged mostly on their singing abilities.

LIZARD CANARY
Serinus canaria

The Lizard Canary is probably the oldest surviving breed of canary. Whether it has a cap or not, the bird's unusual pattern of markings distinguishes this breed. Canaries resembling Lizard Canaries were first described as long ago as 1709. Although the breed's fortunes have fluctuated since then, this canary has recently undergone a revival, and is quite common nowadays. Feathering is a vital feature of Lizard Canaries. They must turn around readily when exhibited so that the judge can closely inspect the crescent-shaped spangles on their backs.

BREEDING Provide hens with nestpans for breeding. The terms "gold" and "silver" are used instead of "yellow" and "buff" to describe the feather types in these canaries. To obtain the best breeding results, pairs should consist of one bird of each form. Also, breeders rarely pair two clear cap Lizard Canaries together because their chicks frequently have caps that are too large. Instead, mate a clear cap with one of the other cap forms, although broken cap Lizard Canaries can be paired together quite successfully.

HEAD This clear cap gold Lizard Canary has the typical oval-shaped cap on the top of his head, running from the bill to the base of the skull.

PLUMAGE The plumage of Lizard Canaries has a silky appearance, and the markings on the sides of the body, called "rowings," should form distinct lines.

FEET AND LEGS Lizard Canaries should have dark feet and legs in all forms.

BROKEN CAP COCK

HEAD The clear plumage on the head is broken by dark plumage.

VARIETIES Besides the clear and the broken cap Lizard Canary, it is possible to have non-capped Lizard Canaries, which have no clear head markings.

CHARACTERISTICS
LENGTH: *12.5cm (5in).*
AVERAGE LIFESPAN: *10 years.*
SEXING: *Scientific sexing required; cocks sing.*
BREEDING DETAILS: *Incubation lasts 14 days; fledging occurs 14 days later.*
YOUNG BIRDS: *Similar to adults.*

FOOD & HOUSING Offer a canary seed diet plus greenfood and softfood. Exhibition birds must also be color-fed, which should start just before the molt, to ensure even coloration. The plumage and markings of this breed are of critical importance. They are hardy birds, and can be kept in an outdoor aviary year-round.

YORKSHIRE FANCY CANARY
Serinus canaria

In the Yorkshire coalfields, where this breed was first developed in the 1860s, it used to be said that these canaries were so slim that they could slide through a wedding ring. Today, Yorkshire Fancy Canaries have become larger, but they still rate as one of the slimmer breeds. The extinct Lancashire Canary, Belgian Fancy Canary, and the Norwich Fancy Canary all contributed to this breed's development. Yorkshire Fancy Canaries are exhibited in cages with a single perch, since they are not expected to move during judging. The training needed to adopt the necessary posture is demanding.

HEAD The head should be well rounded, with the eyes located centrally.

BREEDING Breeding Yorkshire Fancy Canaries to a high standard is a relatively difficult task. As with other canaries, hens tend to be left on their own to incubate and rear the resulting chicks, with breeders transferring their mates to separate accommodation. It is best to provide a deep nestpan for the chicks, as they seem to need the extra security. The difficulty in breeding is that birds of a good size are often afflicted with coarse feathering. As a guide, you can pair a fairly small hen with good type and feather quality to a big cock bird. This should produce good quality offspring, without such distinctive flaws in the feathering but, inevitably, some will be better than others.

POSTURE This bird makes the most of its length, being quite erect in stature.

PLUMAGE This variegated Yorkshire Canary has buff-type plumage. The wings are fairly long and extend right down the center of the back, but do not cross at the tips.

CHARACTERISTICS
LENGTH: 17cm (6¾ in).
AVERAGE LIFESPAN: 10 years.
SEXING: Scientific sexing required; cocks sing.
BREEDING DETAILS: Incubation lasts 14 days; fledging occurs 14 days later.
YOUNG BIRDS: Paler than adults, until molting their nestling tail and flight feathers.

FOOD & HOUSING
Offer a diet of a good canary seed mix and greenfood, as well as softfoods for rearing chicks. Regular color feeding is necessary when these canaries begin to molt, otherwise their appearance will be spoiled until the next molt. Breeders often house these hardy canaries in tall breeding cages, as they have a tendency to hunch. Good posture is very important, because an upright stance is required in the show cage.

NORWICH FANCY CANARY
Serinus canaria

Due to their squat looks, Norwich Fancy Canaries are sometimes described as the John Bull of the Canary Fancy, after the stocky figure of British folklore. They were introduced to East Anglia by Flemish weavers fleeing religious persecution at the end of the seventeenth century, and the birds have had a loyal following ever since. The Norwich Fancy is closely related to the rare Crested Canary.

FOOD & HOUSING A regular canary diet suits Norwich Fancy Canaries well. Coloration is an important feature in exhibiting, so they must be color-fed if you wish to show them. These birds are quite hardy, and can be housed in aviaries even during cold weather, provided that they have snug roosting quarters. As their demeanor suggests, these canaries are rather sluggish.

PLUMAGE The yellow plumage is actually a deep orange. The color must be even, and the feathers must be fine and silky.

HEAD The large, broad head contributes to the bird's stocky appearance.

BODY Stocky in shape, the chest and back are broad.

TAIL The short tail emphasizes the stocky build of the Norwich Fancy Canary.

VARIETY *Variegated yellow canaries have a pattern of light and dark plumage, which is variable.*

VARIEGATED YELLOW COCK

CHARACTERISTICS
LENGTH: 16cm (6¼in).
AVERAGE LIFESPAN: 10 years.
SEXING: Scientific sexing required; cocks sing.
BREEDING DETAILS: Incubation lasts 14 days; fledging occurs 14 days later.
YOUNG BIRDS: Similar to adults.

BREEDING Provide a nestpan when a pair is placed in their breeding quarters. It is important to appreciate that these canaries are not as prolific as some of the smaller breeds. In addition, following extensive double-buffing to increase their size, which was carried out in the 1920s, Norwich Fancy Canaries may have a higher than average incidence of feather lumps.

RED FACTOR CANARY
Serinus domestica

During the 1920s, a breeding program to produce a genuinely red canary, which involved the Black-hooded Red Siskin, resulted in Red Factor Canaries. In the past, there has been a tendency to overlook the type of these birds and judge them only by their color; now, however, the type is becoming more significant in exhibition circles.

EYES The dark eye coloration contrasts well with the bright body color.

PLUMAGE The color of the plumage varies, depending on the bird's diet through the molt. Color-feeding is only effective when the feathers have a blood supply.

WINGS The wing tips are often paler than the body.

TAIL In this bird, the tail is much paler than the rest of the body.

FOOD & HOUSING
Because these birds must be color-fed, their diet needs to be monitored carefully, especially during the molt. Avoid sources of lutein, such as greenfood, egg yolk, and rape seed, which will add too much yellow to their coloring. Red Factor Canaries are normally offered a diet of groats and niger seed during the molt, along with grated carrot and a special softfood, with no egg food. This diet is necessary to retain their coloring, or else they become more orange than red. Using a suitable coloring agent is also essential, to show these birds at their best. They are hardy birds once acclimatized, and look most attractive when housed outdoors, under natural light.

BREEDING Provide breeding pairs with a nestpan, and breed them in cages to ensure parentage.

VARIEGATED INTENSIVE COCK

CHARACTERISTICS
LENGTH: 12.5cm (5in).
AVERAGE LIFESPAN: 10 years.
SEXING: Scientific sexing required; cocks sing.
BREEDING DETAILS: Incubation lasts 14 days; fledging occurs 14 days later.
YOUNG BIRDS: Similar to adults.

VARIETY *Instead of the terms "yellow" and "buff," breeders use "non-frosted" and "frosted" for the Red Factor Canary feather type, since buff birds have whitish tips to their plumage, which makes them paler.*

ZOSTEROPS
Zosterops palpebrosa

Zosterops are widely distributed throughout Africa and Asia, with 85 recognized species of these small softbills. They are regarded as pests by fruit farmers in many areas, causing considerable damage by eating ripening fruit. However, they are also helpful since they consume troublesome insects. Zosterops are among the most popular of all softbills as they are attractive and sociable, and can be kept safely together in groups, or alongside other small birds, even waxbills.

FOOD & HOUSING Offer a wide range of diced fruit, with berries in season if possible, and sprinkle it with softbill food. You can also use canned fruit if necessary. They also need small livefoods, particularly when breeding, and a nectar solution every day. Do not be tempted to house zosterops outside unless their plumage is in good condition, since they become chilled easily. Lightly spray them with tepid water each day, or provide them with a shallow bath.

EYE-RING A white area around the eyes is a characteristic of zosterops, and has led them to also be known as "White Eyes."

BILL The bill is narrow and pointed, allowing the bird to peck into fruit and flowers, and to catch insects.

BREEDING Provide suitable material when a pair seems ready to breed; cocks often sing when in breeding condition. They prefer to nest in shrubbery, so a planted aviary is ideal accommodation for this species. In temperate regions, you must be prepared to provide them with warm winter accommodation, as they are not entirely hardy.

PLUMAGE All zosterops tend to be greenish yellow. Distinguishing the different species can be very difficult.

FEET The feet are delicate, so provide fresh, supple perches for zosterops, and replace any branches that become sticky.

KIKUYU ZOSTEROPS COCK

VARIETIES *Kikuyu Zosterops* (Zosterops kikuyuensis) *can be distinguished from other zosterops by its broader eye-ring. They originate from Africa.*

CHARACTERISTICS
LENGTH: 17.8cm (7in).
AVERAGE LIFESPAN: 10 years.
SEXING: Scientific sexing required; cocks sing only during the breeding period.
BREEDING DETAILS: Incubation lasts 14 days; fledging occurs 14 days later.
YOUNG BIRDS: Similar to adults.

FIRE-TUFTED BARBET
Psilopogon pyrolophus

Barbets inhabit an extensive area of the world, occurring in tropical parts of Asia, Africa, and the Americas and are found in both open country and forests alike. The Fire-tufted Barbet is a jungle species, originating from the dense forests of Malaysia and Sumatra. As a result, it settles best in a well-planted aviary.

CHARACTERISTICS

LENGTH: *25cm (10in).*
AVERAGE LIFESPAN: *8 years.*
SEXING: *Scientific sexing required.*
BREEDING DETAILS: *Incubation lasts 14 days; fledging occurs 20 days later.*
YOUNG BIRDS: *Duller plumage than in adults.*

FACE These unusual feathers around the bill are characteristic of all barbets, but here they are particularly pronounced.

THROAT The yellow patch on the throat, and the stocky bill, are reminiscent of toucans, to which barbets are related.

FOOD & HOUSING The Fire-tufted Barbet is one of the more frugivorous barbets, so offer it a good selection of diced fruits and berries every day. You can supplement the fruit with soaked mynah pellets sprinkled with softbill food, but do not rely on these prepared foods, as the diet will then be too rich. Also provide some livefood, such as mealworms, on a regular basis. Always have a pot of clean water available for the birds to bathe. However, initially check that, in their enthusiasm, they do not become waterlogged and unable to fly after a bath, or they will be vulnerable to chilling, particularly in an outside aviary. Fire-tufted Barbets are not really hardy, so it is best to bring them inside during cold weather. House barbets in individual pairs, as they often prove to be aggressive birds.

PLUMAGE Barbets that come from forests have greenish bodies; those from open country often have darker coloration.

FEET The scaling on the feet indicates that this is a mature bird.

BREEDING Offer barbets a nestbox, or a hollow log, which they will often prefer, hammering away at the inside with their powerful bills. Watch the cock bird, as he may be aggressive to his mate.

VARIETY The speckled D'Arnaud's Barbet (Trachyphonus vaillanti) *is typical of the more insectivorous species, needing more invertebrates in its diet. It differs in breeding too. Rather than using a nest-hole, pairs may excavate a breeding tunnel in the aviary floor. If so, watch closely for flooding during heavy or extended periods of rainfall.*

D'ARNAUD'S BARBET COCK

RED-EARED BULBUL
Pycnonotus jocosus

Bulbuls are popular and easy-to-manage softbills. There are about 120 different species, of which perhaps a dozen or so are well-known in aviculture. Those that originated from Asia are more common than the bulbuls from Africa. The Red-eared Bulbul itself ranges from India eastward to parts of southeast Asia and China. Although none of them are brightly colored, they are attractive, personable birds and have appealing songs. Some, as in the case of the Red-eared Bulbul here, also have striking head crests.

CREST This bird holds its conspicuous crest erect at all times.

BILL The shape of the bill is well adapted to plucking berries, and seizing small insects in the undergrowth.

PLUMAGE The upper parts of this species are brownish gray and the lower parts are mainly white, apart from the red feathering close to the tail.

CHEEKS Another mark that identifies this species is the red patches on the face, explaining why this species is also known as the Red-whiskered Bulbul.

FOOD & HOUSING Offer bulbuls fruit and softbill food, with soaked mynah pellets and some livefoods. They feel at home in a planted aviary and, once acclimatized, can overwinter in it if they have snug, dry roosting quarters. To prevent chilling, keep any birds in poor feather indoors in cold weather until they have molted and have a covering of feathers in good condition.

BREEDING Bulbuls are social birds by nature, and live happily in groups. The best way to recognize a pair, therefore, is simply to house a group together in a flight and keep watch for birds pairing up to breed. Provide plenty of bushes under cover in the flight. Among them, the bulbuls are likely to build their cup-shaped nests, using grass stems, feathers, and leaves. A typical clutch has four eggs. Pairs are generally good parents, but avoid any unnecessary disturbance at this stage, as this could cause them to abandon their nest.

VARIETIES Scientific sexing is necessary in all bulbul varieties, but cock birds often sing to attract their mates, and display the red plumage of their underparts.

RED-VENTED BULBUL COCK

CHARACTERISTICS
LENGTH: 22.5cm (9in).
AVERAGE LIFESPAN: 8 years.
SEXING: Scientific sexing required.
BREEDING DETAILS: Incubation lasts 14 days; fledging occurs 20 days later.
YOUNG BIRDS: Duller plumage than in adults.

GREATER HILL MYNAH
Gracula religiosa

Being one of the clearest mimics in the avian world, the Greater Hill Mynah has been a popular pet for centuries throughout its extensive range in Asia. However, it has always proved difficult to breed in captivity. With the advent of new sexing methods, more breeders are now being attracted to these personable birds. Their lively, brash personalities are easy to enjoy in aviary surroundings.

CHARACTERISTICS
LENGTH: *30cm (12in).*
AVERAGE LIFESPAN: *8 years.*
SEXING: *Scientific sexing required.*
BREEDING DETAILS: *Incubation lasts 14 days; fledging occurs 20 days later.*
YOUNG BIRDS: *Duller than adults; their wattles are also relatively inconspicuous.*

WATTLE The bare area of fleshy skin is more prominent in certain races of mynah.

FOOD & HOUSING Offer mynahs a diet of diced fruit and softbill food, along with mynah pellets and invertebrates, such as mealworms. Kept in cages, mynahs are prone to obesity, so try to provide them with a large flight unit rather than a standard box-type cage. Do not keep mynahs with smaller birds, as they may actually eat them. Although relatively hardy outdoors, these mynahs hate damp, foggy weather. Regular bathing is essential, especially for mynahs housed indoors. Also wash or replace their perches as necessary, to minimize the risk of any foot infections developing.

PLUMAGE The Greater Hill Mynah's black feathering is highly iridescent under sunlight, and can show hues of purple and green.

WINGS There is a white patch of plumage on the flight feathers.

BREEDING Provide pairs with a nestbox; twigs and other nesting material may be used to form a lining for the eggs. Livefood is very important once the chicks hatch. Watch closely when the chicks leave the nest, in case the parents decide to breed again, as they may attack their offspring.

PURPLE GLOSSY STARLING
Lamprotornis purpureus

These strikingly attractive birds are quite easy to maintain in aviary surroundings, where you can appreciate the beautiful iridescence of their plumage in the sunlight. Other very similar species are available, such as the Long-tailed Glossy Starling (*L. purpuropterus*), which requires identical care. They can be aggressive, especially toward smaller birds and, for breeding purposes, pairs should be kept on their own.

PLUMAGE Iridescence may create a variable bronzy-purple color over the wings, depending on the light. •

EYES A startling feature, the eyes are an intense yellow.

FOOD & HOUSING Offer these birds a diet of diced fruit, softbill food, soaked mynah pellets, and some livefood, such as tebos or mealworms. These hardy birds are happy housed in individual pairs in a planted aviary. They like to bathe, which helps keep their plumage in good condition. If you transfer Purple Glossy Starlings to an outdoor aviary, check that they do not become waterlogged when it first rains. If you keep them indoors, spray them with water to help maintain their natural waterproofing.

BREEDING When the birds are ready to breed, provide a nestbox lined with twigs. Remove chicks as soon as they are feeding themselves, or their parents may attack them.

FEET Purple • Glossy Starlings are prone to losing claws, and they are also at risk from frostbite, so encourage them to use the shelter in the aviary for nesting.

PLUMAGE The Malabar Mynah's plumage is an attractive combination of soft, muted shades. •

MALABAR MYNAH COCK

CHARACTERISTICS
LENGTH: 22.5cm (9in).
AVERAGE LIFESPAN: 10 years.
SEXING: Scientific sexing required.
BREEDING DETAILS: Incubation lasts 16 days; fledging occurs 21 days later.
YOUNG BIRDS: Duller plumage than adults.

VARIETY *The Malabar Mynah (Sturnus malabaricus), an Asiatic species, requires identical care to the Purple Glossy Starling. Again, it is not possible to sex Malabar Mynahs visually with any degree of certainty, but other sexing methods are available. This should ensure that you have a breeding pair.*

PEKIN ROBIN (RED-BILLED LEIOTHRIX)
Leiothrix lutea

Pekin Robins are not actually robins at all but members of the thrush family; Pekin Robin cocks have an attractive song, which is heard mainly in the breeding period. The cock's song also provides a distinctive means to distinguish between the sexes. This bird is common over much of southern Asia, ranging from India to China. Occasionally, you may find the related Silver-eared Mesia *(L. argentauris)* available, which needs similar care to the Pekin Robin. In an aviary, Pekin Robins can become quite tame if you offer them a treat, such as mealworms, each time you enter the aviary. They will soon expect such offerings, and become bold in your presence. It is best not to mix them with smaller birds, as they have been known to steal eggs in aviary surroundings.

CHARACTERISTICS

LENGTH: *15cm (6in).*

AVERAGE LIFESPAN: *10 years.*

SEXING: *Scientific sexing required; hens may have grayer lores.*

BREEDING DETAILS: *Incubation lasts 14 days; fledging occurs 14 days later.*

YOUNG BIRDS: *Duller plumage.*

BILL The bill is darker at its base than at its tip.

LORES Hens are often grayer around the lores.

WINGS The gold and tawny colors on the wings are evident even when the wings are held closed.

PLUMAGE The yellow coloration on the throat and breast may vary in depth. However it is not an indication of the bird's sex.

BREEDING If you place container-grown fir trees in the aviary and arrange them in circles, you may encourage a pair to build their open, cup-shaped nest, or they may choose to nest in a Budgerigar nestbox. In either case, they often line their nest with moss and leaves. The eggs are greenish blue and are speckled with darker markings. Both sexes share the incubation and rearing of the chicks. Egg food and small livefoods are likely to be required in increasing quantities once the chicks have hatched. After the chicks fledge, the parents may nest again.

FOOD & HOUSING These softbills eat not only the usual diet of fruit, invertebrates, and prepared foods, but also a little canary seed. They will also eat soaked millet sprays. Since they are forest dwellers, Pekin Robins are more likely to breed in an aviary if given adequate cover. They may need additional warmth during the cold weather.

WHITE-CRESTED JAY THRUSH
Garrulax leucolophus

The White-crested Jay Thrush, one of the laughing thrush group, is an attractive songster with a lively character. This mountain forest bird is happiest housed in a densely planted aviary. The birds are found over a wide area, from southeastern Asia to southern parts of China.

CREST The crest is nearly always held erect.

EYE-STRIPE Black primarily, but eye-stripes may have a brownish tinge in some cases.

PLUMAGE The White-crested Jay Thrush has predominantly brown plumage.

BREEDING For breeding purposes, you can have pairs sexed either chromosomally or surgically. If you want to encourage these birds to nest, house them in a well-planted aviary. Any conifers in their quarters are often popular breeding sites, since the birds build a cup-shaped nest in the branches of such trees in the wild. Keep disturbances to a minimum during the breeding period, otherwise they may desert the nest or even eat their chicks. They may have up to four chicks in a nest. A plentiful supply of livefood is essential for rearing purposes. Scatter this on the aviary floor, so that the parents are forced to hunt for it. This should prevent them from becoming bored and attacking their young.

FOOD & HOUSING
Offer White-crested Jay Thrushes and any other laughing thrushes softbill food and soaked mynah pellets, as well as diced fruit, some seeds, and a variety of invertebrates. They are easy birds to maintain, and hardy once acclimatized. If you plan to keep laughing thrushes in a small group and allow them to pair off, watch for signs of bullying. Laughing thrushes tend to be aggressive, especially when they are breeding, so remove weaker birds before they are harmed.

CHARACTERISTICS
LENGTH: 30cm (12in).
AVERAGE LIFESPAN: 10 years.
SEXING: Scientific sexing required; hens may be distinguished by their smaller, grayer crests.
BREEDING DETAILS: Incubation lasts 13 days; fledging occurs 21 days later.
YOUNG BIRDS: Duller plumage than adults.

HARTLAUB'S TOURACO
Taurus hartlaubi

Touracos are native to Africa, with Hartlaub's Touracos found in Kenya and Tanzania. These brightly colored softbills make spectacular occupants for an aviary, and pairs often attempt to breed if their aviary surroundings are suitable.

CREST In this group of birds, the crest varies significantly in shape and coloration between different species.

EYE-RING The eye-ring may vary somewhat in its depth of coloration.

BREEDING Keep pairs separate for breeding purposes. They will require a nesting platform, such as an open wicker basket, where the hen can lay. This they line with twigs and similar material. Ensure that the hen is not chased relentlessly by her intended mate prior to egg-laying. If this is the case, you may need to clip his wings to give the hen some peace. Each clutch is likely to consist of just two eggs, although pairs may nest twice in a season.

VARIETY *The White-cheeked Touraco (T. leucotis) has, as its name suggests, white patches on its cheeks.*

WHITE-CHEEKED TOURACO COCK

BILL The bill's broad shape enables touracos to pluck berries. They also have a wide gape, which lets them swallow fruits whole.

CHARACTERISTICS
LENGTH: 40cm (15¼ in).
AVERAGE LIFESPAN: 12 years.
SEXING: Scientific sexing required.
BREEDING DETAILS: Incubation lasts 20 days; fledging occurs 28 days later.
YOUNG BIRDS: Bills are dark; plumage is duller than in adults.

WINGS The red coloration present on the wings results from a copper pigment that is found only in touracos.

TAIL In this species the tail feathers are green. Violet-blue is the predominant color of some other touracos.

FOOD & HOUSING
Provide touracos with a varied diet of diced fruit, and greenfood sprinkled with softbill food, with some softbill pellets as well. These birds tend to dislike livefood. Provide them with plenty of flying space in a large aviary, at least 3.7m (12ft) long. They tolerate cold weather, but ensure that they roost under cover, because their claws are susceptible to frostbite.

WHITE-COLLARED YUHINA
Yuhina diademata

All ten species of yuhina (pronounced "you-hina") are found in Asia. They are lively little birds, and settle down well in aviary surroundings. Although they are not colorful, they are attractive aviary occupants, frequently displaying their distinctive crests. Cock birds also have a pretty song. Though they mix well with small finches and other softbills, they are not very sociable with their own kind, so pairs should be kept apart.

FOOD & HOUSING Offer White-collared Yuhinas a diet consisting of diced fruit and berries, sprinkled with a fine insectivorous softfood, and small livefoods, such as aphids. They also feed on nectar every once in a while, so you can add small amounts of finely ground pollen granules to their food. In the wild, yuhinas help to fertilize flowers by transferring pollen from flower to flower as they search for nectar. For housing, they need a well-planted aviary. Include annuals, such as nasturtiums, in their aviary to attract aphids. The birds are not hardy however, so provide warm indoor accommodation for them in cold weather.

CREST Yuhinas' crests are usually pointed at the front. This bird has white feathering behind the crest.

BILL The narrow bill is ideal for extracting nectar.

PLUMAGE Their muted gray, brown, and white coloring camouflages the birds while they forage in undergrowth.

STRIATED YUHINA COCK

VARIETY *The Striated Yuhina (Yuhina castaniceps) has a less prominent crest than other varieties of yuhina.*

CHARACTERISTICS
LENGTH: 13cm (5in).
AVERAGE LIFESPAN: 7 years.
SEXING: Visually difficult; hens have somewhat shorter crests and they sing less than cocks.
BREEDING DETAILS: Incubation lasts 13 days; fledging occurs 15 days later.
YOUNG BIRDS: Duller plumage than in adults.

BREEDING When a pair looks likely to breed, you should provide grasses and moss so that they can build their own cup-shaped nest. A clutch normally consists of three or four eggs. Maintain a good supply of small livefoods throughout the rearing phase to ensure that the chicks fledge successfully. When the chicks are feeding independently, remove them to their own separate accommodation.

BLUE-NECKED TANAGER
Tangara cyanicollis

Ranging from Canada through to Argentina, tanagers comprise some 200 species. Because of their coloration, tangara tanagers are extremely popular birds in aviculture. The Blue-necked Tanager occurs in northern South America. They are easy to maintain, especially once they are established, but, in cold weather, you must provide heated accommodation.

FOOD & HOUSING Offer tanagers a varied diet of diced fruit and berries, and sprinkle it with a good-quality softbill food. They also appreciate nectar, especially recently acquired birds. Live-food is also important, particularly if a pair nests. House tanagers in a planted flight. Some birds are naturally shyer than others, so if you keep them in a small group, watch for any signs of bullying. Once a pair has formed, you may have to remove other tanagers from the aviary, since the pair is likely to become quite aggressive. Tanagers enjoy frequent bathing to keep their plumage immaculate.

HEAD The color of this bird's head has led them to be described as Blue-headed Tanagers.

WINGS The wing color varies from pure yellow to greenish yellow. The seven sub-species of this tanager differ in this feature.

BREEDING
Provide a good selection of nesting sites, ranging from bushes, where the birds can build their own nests, to hollow logs. Offer grasses, moss, and leaves as nesting material, and avoid disturbing them when they are breeding. Tanagers may produce two or even three clutches in quick succession. Do not rely on coloration differences between individual birds for sexing purposes, although their care is similar in all cases.

FLANKS Blue coloring is not confined just to the head, it also appears on the flanks.

VARIETY Ranging from Central America southward into northern South America, the color of Bay-headed Tanagers varies considerably.

BAY-HEADED TANAGER COCK

CHARACTERISTICS
LENGTH: 12.5cm (5in).
AVERAGE LIFESPAN: 8 years.
SEXING: Scientific sexing required.
BREEDING DETAILS: Incubation lasts 14 days; fledging occurs 20 days later.
YOUNG BIRDS: Plumage is duller in coloration than that of adult birds.

VARIABLE SUNBIRD
Nectarinia venusta

Few birds are more striking or colorful than sunbirds. They are the Old World counterparts of hummingbirds, although they lack their ability to hover. Nevertheless, they are very agile in flight, and can perch close to a flower on a stem or branch, and use their narrow bills to extract nectar.

BILL The bill is slightly curved and pointed, for extracting nectar from flowers. The tongue is longer than the bill.

MALE PLUMAGE
Variable Sunbird cocks have iridescent feathers, especially on their heads and backs.

FEMALE PLUMAGE
Compared to cock birds, hen sunbirds look drab, which may make distinguishing between the different species difficult.

BREEDING When breeding, Variable Sunbirds may use fine grasses and cobwebs to build their own nest. Keep pairs on their own during the breeding season, because cocks are usually aggressive toward one another.

FOOD & HOUSING Sunbirds need nectar and a regular supply of insects, such as fruit flies. Asiatic sunbirds are generally more insectivorous than those from Africa. Also offer finely diced fruit, and a fine-grade softbill food, to add variety to their diet. Scarlet-chested Sunbird cocks require color-feeding. Although it may be possible to keep them in an outside aviary for some of the year, they need to be inside during cold weather.

VARIETY The Scarlet-chested Sunbird (N. senegalensis) is one of the easiest species of the sunbird both to keep and to breed.

CHARACTERISTICS

LENGTH: 10cm (4in).
AVERAGE LIFESPAN: 7 years.
SEXING: Hens are much duller than cocks; plumage is predominantly olive-gray.
BREEDING DETAILS: Incubation lasts 14 days; fledging occurs 14 days later.
YOUNG BIRDS: Similar to adult hens.

SCARLET-CHESTED SUNBIRD COCK

RED-BILLED TOUCAN
Ramphastos tucanus

The toucan's massive bill gives the bird a somewhat comical appearance and a rather top-heavy stance. Surprisingly, the bill itself is quite light, having a honey-combed structure. The bill contains a long, narrow, fringed tongue. The bill may help the toucan to reach fruits that would be out of its reach otherwise, and lets it snap up small animals to eat. Occasionally, toucans may fight with their bills, but the primary reason as to why this enormous bill evolved remains unclear.

CHARACTERISTICS
LENGTH: *45cm (18in).*
AVERAGE LIFESPAN: *10 years.*
SEXING: *Visually difficult; hens may have smaller bills than cock birds.*
BREEDING DETAILS: *Incubation lasts 19 days; fledging occurs 50 days later.*
YOUNG BIRDS: *Duller plumage than adults.*

BREEDING A large, hollow log is ideal for nesting, but it should fit securely in place, so that it cannot be dislodged, causing the loss of eggs and even chicks. Toucans may also use a large nestbox. See that a cock does not harry the hen when breeding, and provide a choice of sites, where she can feed unmolested.

BILL Massive and colorful, the toucan's bill is a distinguishing feature of this species. It may be blunted if the bird hammers with it.

FACE The blue coloration that surrounds the eyes extends down and onto the bill itself.

FOOD & HOUSING Offer Red-billed Toucans a diet of diced fruit with softbill food, and pellets. Supplement this with a regular offering of large invertebrates, such as mealworms, locusts, or even pinkies. These large and lively birds need a spacious aviary, which has adequate protection against the cold. Fix perches so that the birds can land and turn around easily, without any risk to their bills. House toucans on their own, as they have been known to eat smaller birds. Prolonged exposure to damp, foggy weather may lead to respiratory problems.

PLUMAGE The light breast is a characteristic of the ramphastos toucans. Apart from the breast and rump, the rest of the plumage on the body is a glossy black.

TAIL Toucans usually sleep with their tails held vertically so that, in the wild, they can fit into small tree holes for safety from predators.

LIGHT GREEN BUDGERIGAR
Melopsittacus undulatus

The native Budgerigar form is known today as the light green Budgerigar. The earliest color Budgerigar mutations appeared in the second half of the last century, and interest in exhibiting these birds began in earnest during the 1870s. Through the development of judging standards, today's domesticated Budgerigars have grown to be significantly larger than their wild counterparts in Australia. The Budgerigar is now the most popular pet bird in the world, with a population that numbers many millions, with thousands of possible color combinations.

HEAD Adults have yellow foreheads, but those of chicks are barred.

BREEDING To produce specific colors, or develop your own exhibition strain, breed pairs in cages, rather than on a colony system, as this ensures the chicks' parentage. Budgerigars can be fickle, so a cock may mate with several hens. They will be mature enough to breed by the age of one year. When you first introduce a pair to a breeding cage, close the entrance to the nestbox for a week to ensure that mating occurs, preventing the hen from disappearing into the box. Also avoid adding new birds to an established nesting colony during the breeding season, as this is one time they can be aggressive.

BREAST The coloration on the breast is the palest shade of green.

FOOD & HOUSING Offer these birds a mixture of millets and plain canary seed, greenfood, and sweet apple. Give them an iodine block, to ensure that their thyroid glands function properly. Social birds by nature, Budgerigars live well in groups and rarely fight. Provide plenty of fresh branches as perches.

MUTATIONS The emergence in France in 1915 of the dark factor in Budgerigars meant that other, darker shades of green could be produced.

CHARACTERISTICS
LENGTH: 18cm (7in).
AVERAGE LIFESPAN: 7 years.
SEXING: Hens have brown cere above the bill.
BREEDING DETAILS: Incubation lasts 18 days; fledging occurs 35 days later.
YOUNG BIRDS: Eyes are black without a white ring, the mask is smaller, and the forehead is barred. Recently fledged chicks may have dark marks on the upper bill.

DARK GREEN BUDGERIGAR COCK

LUTINO BUDGERIGAR
Melopsittacus undulatus

The yellow forms of these Budgerigars are color mutations. The lutino Budgerigars first emerged during the 1870s, however the genetics of this mutation were not then fully understood, so these colorful birds were not easily established. The problem arose partly from the fact that all of the yellow birds had a tendency to be hens, and pairing these with with light green Budgerigars meant that, frequently, no yellow offspring were produced (see page 185).

FOOD & HOUSING Offer these birds either a Budgerigar seed mixture or your own combination. As a rule, Budgerigar mixes that contain more millets are cheaper than those with a higher proportion of canary seed. Soaked millet sprays and softfood are valuable extras when there are chicks in the nest. If you feed Budgies a diet of greenfood, offer them this regularly rather than just occasionally in large amounts, or they may gorge themselves to excess, and scour. Fresh chickweed or seeding grasses are popular with Budgies. These birds are hardy once acclimatized, and so can be housed in an outdoor aviary.

THROAT Because of the absence of melanin, which is responsible for black plumage, the throat spots are absent.

PLUMAGE The body should be an even, rich yellow, with no traces of a green sheen.

WINGS The coloration of the flight feathers is paler than the rest of the body.

DARK-EYED YELLOW COCK

CERE In cocks, the cere is purplish rather than blue.

MUTATION The dark-eyed yellow mutation is easily distinguishable by the solid and dark eye coloration. This variety originated from Danish recessive pieds in the 1940s. Such birds are still much rarer than lutino Budgerigars, but can be sexed in an identical fashion.

CHARACTERISTICS

LENGTH: 18cm (7in).
AVERAGE LIFESPAN: 7 years.
SEXING: Hens have brown cere above the bill.
BREEDING DETAILS: Incubation lasts 18 days; fledging occurs 35 days later.
YOUNG BIRDS: Eyes are red, with no eye-ring. The depth of their yellow coloration is also paler than in adult birds.

BREEDING When a pair is ready to breed, you should remove them from the aviary and place them in a breeding cage with a nestbox attached in order to ensure parentage of the chicks. Eggs can be anticipated within 14 days, so be sure to provide adequate cuttlefish bone at this stage, to ensure that the hen has enough calcium for the eggshells. The hen usually incubates alone, but the cock may at times join her in the nestbox.

GRAY-WINGED SKY BLUE BUDGERIGAR
Melopsittacus undulatus

Changes to the basic coloration of the Budgerigar have been accompanied by various alterations to the markings on the wings. In the case of the gray-winged sky blue mutation, which occurred in 1918, the dark markings are paler than normal, thus showing as gray rather than black. Other similar variants of this type include the cinnamon Budgerigar, where brown markings have occured instead of black, and the yellow-winged Budgerigar, a green rather than blue series bird with prominent yellow markings over the wings.

FOOD & HOUSING Offer these Budgerigars a standard Budgerigar diet of Budgie seed mixture or your own combination, small amounts of greenfood, and soaked millet sprays and softfood when rearing birds. You can house Budgerigars in an outdoor aviary throughout the year in temperate climates, if they have adequate shelter. But, if the temperature drops very low, provide heating.

WINGS The gray markings on the wings give this mutation a pleasing, mottled appearance.

TAIL Like the wings, the tail is a clear shade of pale gray.

BREEDING When they are ready to breed, put a pair in a breeding cage with a nestbox. Avoid pairing gray-winged sky blue Budgerigars together regularly, because the markings of the chicks may become darker, and lose their distinguishing patterning. The only solution under these circumstances is to pair lightly and darkly marked birds together, in the hope of producing chicks with the desired intermediate markings. There is likely to be some variation apparent however, even between chicks from the same nest.

HEAD The head is usually white in blue Budgies, but it is also possible to breed them with yellow faces.

BREAST The bird's breast coloration is sky blue, the palest of the existing shades of blue. This color arose early in the history of the Budgerigar, first recorded in Belgium around 1880, and immediately became very popular.

CHARACTERISTICS
LENGTH: 18cm (7in).
AVERAGE LIFESPAN: 7 years.
SEXING: Hens have brown cere above the bill.
BREEDING DETAILS: Incubation lasts 18 days; fledging occurs 35 days later.
YOUNG BIRDS: Eyes are black with no white ring, the mask is smaller, and the forehead has a barring pattern, reaching the cere.

CRESTED OPALINE COBALT BUDGERIGAR
Melopsittacus undulatus

It is not just changes in coloration that have occurred during the domestication of the Budgerigar. There are also three distinct crested mutations, of which the full-circular is the most distinctive. The other two are the half-circular and the tufted. All these crested variants can be combined with any color or marking, so the breeding potential is huge. Crested Budgerigars were initially reported by Australian breeders in the 1920s, but they have not become very popular because they are difficult to breed. However, if you want to see some there are usually a variety on view at the major shows. Crested birds represent a considerable challenge for exhibition breeders because of their additional feature.

BREEDING These Budgerigars have a lethal factor in their genetic make-up (see page 183) so never pair full-circulars with each other. Provide breeding pairs with a nestbox. Pair full-circulars with good quality birds with no crests. This pair will produce a percentage of crested offspring.

CREST The flat, even crest is well placed on this Budgie.

PLUMAGE The cobalt coloration is the single dark factor form of the sky blue. It has always been a popular color.

MUTATION Note the even crest feathers in this full-circular crested Budgie. This crest form is the most desirable among exhibitors yet is the hardest to breed to exhibition standard.

CREST DETAIL

MARKINGS The plumage has an opaline patterning, so the head is more lightly marked than normal, with wing markings also affected.

CHARACTERISTICS
LENGTH: 18cm (7in).
AVERAGE LIFESPAN: 7 years.
SEXING: Hens have brown cere above the bill.
BREEDING DETAILS: Incubation lasts 18 days; fledging occurs 35 days later.
YOUNG BIRDS: Eyes are black with no white ring, mask is smaller, and forehead has a barring pattern, reaching the cere.

FOOD & HOUSING Offer these birds a standard Budgerigar seed mixture. Crested Budgerigars are quite straightforward to look after. However, for show purposes, the crest may benefit from a light grooming with a small brush, such as a clean soft toothbrush. These Budgies are hardy once acclimatized and can be housed in an outdoor aviary.

GRAY BUDGERIGAR
Melopsittacus undulatus

There were once two forms of the gray Budgerigar, which could be distinguished only on genetic grounds. Now, however, it seems that only the dominant form, which emerged in Australia during the 1930s, still survives. The separate recessive mutation from England first appeared in 1933, but declined in popularity, probably because it reproduced at a slower rate. It became extinct in the 1940s.

EYES As with most adult Budgerigars, the eye has a white iris encircling the pupil.

HEAD The broad head is a typical feature of an exhibition Budgerigar. Generally, exhibition birds are larger than pet or aviary birds.

MASK This bird's mask has been trimmed to emphasize the markings, which show a well-defined series of spots.

CHARACTERISTICS

LENGTH: 18cm (7in).
AVERAGE LIFESPAN: 7 years.
SEXING: Hens have brown cere.
BREEDING DETAILS: Incubation lasts 18 days; fledging occurs 35 days later.
YOUNG BIRDS: Black eyes have no white ring; smaller mask, and barred forehead, reaching the cere.

BREEDING These birds' breeding requirements are identical to those of other Budgerigars. If you are planning an exhibition stud, it is best to keep fewer pairs of greater quality, rather than a number of inferior birds. Provide birds with a nestbox and make sure that they have plenty of space, which should help to keep them fitter and raise their fertility. Color combinations involving gray Budgerigars are quite common. An attractive yellow-faced, a cinnamon, and a white-winged opaline gray form are all possible. The visual gray Budgerigar, as shown here, is basically a blue series bird. Crossing one with a light green Budgerigar yields gray greens. These are similar to the olive Budgerigar, but are easily discernible by their black rather than deep blue tail feathers.

FEET The gray coloration of the feet enhances the overall appearance of the bird.

FOOD & HOUSING Gray Budgerigars are straightforward in their feeding requirements. Give these birds a regular Budgerigar diet, but as always do not provide carrot prior to a show as the juice may stain their facial plumage. Budgerigars are social birds and enjoy living together in groups. Once acclimatized, they are quite hardy and can be kept in an outdoor aviary year round without artificial heating, provided that they have a snug shelter. If you breed them during cold weather, however, some heating is likely to be necessary.

RECESSIVE PIED VIOLET BUDGERIGAR
Melopsittacus undulatus

The recessive pied Budgerigar, one of the smaller varieties, is always attractively marked. This pied mutation, originating from Scandinavia, is a variety first exhibited in Denmark in 1932. The birds are unusual in that the spots that form the mask vary in number, and, sometimes, may even be totally absent. They can be produced in any of the usual pied combinations.

FOOD & HOUSING Offer these birds a standard Budgerigar diet of Budgerigar seed mix and greenfood. As with all Budgies they are quite hardy, but benefit from heating and lighting if you want to breed them in a birdroom during the winter in temperate areas.

EYES The eyes are a solid plum color in a good light, and have no clearly evident irises.

MARKINGS Pied markings on the body vary. Their color is usually a shade of blue and white, or green and yellow.

CHARACTERISTICS
LENGTH: 18cm (7in).
AVERAGE LIFESPAN: 7 years.
SEXING: Hens have brown cere above the bill.
BREEDING DETAILS: Incubation lasts 18 days; fledging occurs 35 days later.
YOUNG BIRDS: Eyes are black with no white ring, mask is smaller, and forehead has a barring pattern, sometimes reaching the cere.

BREEDING When a pair seems ready to breed, move them from the aviary to a breeding cage that has a nestbox. Recessive pieds can be produced in the usual pied combinations, and other mutations, such as crests, can be introduced as well. Adult cocks have purplish rather than blue ceres. Hens not in breeding condition have pale brown ceres, which darken as the time for egg-laying approaches. It is impossible to predict the pattern of pied markings of chicks by looking at their parents. Some colorful birds may have predominantly white offspring and vice versa.

PLUMAGE This cock's violet plumage is considered by breeders to be one of the most attractive colors possible.

MUTATION The opaline yellow-faced cobalt Budgerigar is one of the many attractive Budgerigar color combinations that can now be bred. The combination of the yellow face with the blue body is unusual in Budgerigar mutations.

OPALINE YELLOW-FACED COBALT HEN

OPALINE DOMINANT PIED BUDGERIGAR
Melopsittacus undulatus

This attractive Budgerigar mutation was first recorded in aviaries in Sydney, Australia in 1935, but it was not until 1956 that such birds were seen in Europe and North America. Being the result of a dominant mutation, these birds have proved quite easy to breed. Other combinations are also possible, involving cinnamon, or dark green, for example. They are now very popular and are bred in large numbers. In North America they are known as harlequins.

CHARACTERISTICS

LENGTH: 18cm (7in).
AVERAGE LIFESPAN: 7 years.
SEXING: Hens have brown cere above bill.
BREEDING DETAILS: Incubation lasts 18 days; fledging occurs 35 days later.
YOUNG BIRDS: No white eye-ring; smaller mask; possible barring pattern on forehead.

MASK Dominant pieds should have three spots either side of the face.

MARKINGS The pied markings vary. Green coloring sometimes predominates, as in this light green. Dark green and olive colors are also possible.

EYES White eye circles can help to distinguish mature birds from their recessive counterparts.

MUTATION *This sky blue and white dominant pied cock results from combining a pied mutation with a blue series bird.*

BREEDING Provide nestboxes for breeding pairs. Only one pied parent is necessary to produce a percentage of pied chicks. Most of these Budgerigars are available as single factor birds (see page 186), producing pied and normal offspring. Double factor birds can be more valuable, because pairing them with light green Budgerigars, for example, results only in pied offspring. No visual difference exists between single and double factor birds, but they can be told apart by breeding results.

FOOD & HOUSING Offer the usual Budgerigar diet, plus an iodine nibble, grit, and cuttlefish bone. Often more placid than their recessive counterparts, they make good pets. House these hardy birds in an outdoor aviary with an attached shelter.

DOMINANT PIED SKY BLUE COCK

SPANGLE LIGHT GREEN BUDGERIGAR
Melopsittacus undulatus

At present, the spangle light green Budgerigar is the newest of the Budgerigar mutations. It first appeared in Victoria, Australia, in 1972. An Australian breeder brought these birds to Switzerland in the early 1980s, when he emigrated. Since then, the mutation has become widely established in collections around the world. This particular mutation primarily affects the markings, rather than the body coloration. The impact of the spangle shows to best effect in birds with darker markings.

NECK The pattern of barring on the neck remains fairly distinctive.

THROAT The pale center of the spot is clearly visible.

WINGS The wings show hardly any of the usual markings.

CHARACTERISTICS

LENGTH: 18cm (7in).
AVERAGE LIFESPAN: 7 years.
SEXING: Brown cere above hen's bill.
BREEDING DETAILS: Incubation lasts 18 days; fledging occurs 35 days later.
YOUNG BIRDS: Black eyes lack white eye-ring; smaller mask; possible barring pattern on the forehead, reaching the cere.

BREEDING Although the spangle Budgerigar is a dominant mutation, it is possible to distinguish visually between single and double factor birds. With single factor birds, the usual patterning is reversed, rather like that of the pearl Cockatiel, with the markings showing as lighter centers with darker borders. In the case of double factor birds, however, their wing markings are virtually absent, because the melanin has been diluted even more. You can pair spangle Budgerigars in exactly the same way as dominant pied Budgerigars, with the effects perhaps being most noticeable in the case of gray birds, although markings are evident on any birds with dark wing markings.

FOOD & HOUSING Provide a good quality Budgie seed mix. Rearing food is helpful during the breeding period, if you can persuade the parent birds to sample it. Provide youngsters with softfood on fledging. House these hardy birds in an outside aviary with an attached shelter.

MUTATION *The spangle pattern can be combined with blue series Budgerigars, as with this cobalt blue spangle, with similar effects, except, of course, that the wings are whitish rather than yellow.*

COBALT BLUE SPANGLE COCK

COCKATIEL
Nymphicus hollandicus

A native of Australia, the Cockatiel was first seen in Europe during the 1840s and, like the Budgerigar, it was soon breeding freely in collections. The cheerful natures of Cockatiels, and their quiet and gentle dispositions have meant that they are now avicultural favorites around the world, both as pets and as aviary birds. Furthermore, they are gentle enough to house safely in a mixed collection, even alongside small finches, such as waxbills.

CREST The distinctive crest is held more vertically when the birds are displaying or excited, as here.

FACE Adult cock birds have brighter facial coloration than hens.

CHARACTERISTICS
LENGTH: 30cm (12in).
AVERGE LIFESPAN: 18 years.
SEXING: Hens have duller facial coloration than cocks; they also have barring on the underside of the tails.
BREEDING DETAILS: Incubation lasts 18 days; fledging occurs 28 days later.
YOUNG BIRDS: Similar to adult hens.

BREEDING Cockatiels are prolific breeders, and may attempt to breed at any time of the year. Remove nestboxes during the colder months to discourage them from breeding, since their rate of breeding success is significantly reduced by low temperatures. Replace nestboxes in the aviary as the weather starts to become warm again.

TAIL The underside of the hen's tail feathers is barred.

FOOD & HOUSING
Offer Cockatiels millets and plain canary seed, some apple, sunflower, and greenfood. You can house these hardy birds in aviaries made of 19 SWG mesh, and they are are not too destructive on the wood-work. Deworm all newly acquired birds, as they can have a heavy burden of roundworms. It is much easier to eliminate these parasites first, before releasing the birds into the aviary.

LUTINO COCKATIEL
Nymphicus hollandicus

Color variants of Cockatiels have only appeared recently. The pied Cockatiel emerged in California during the 1940s, and the lutino was first documented in the late 1950s. The lutino form was developed by a Florida breeder called Mrs. Moon, which led to such birds first being known as "Moonbeams." The lutino has since become the most popular color form of Cockatiel, but cinnamon, white-faced, silver, and even pure white albino Cockatiels are all established now.

FOOD & HOUSING A diet of the smaller cereal seeds augmented with sunflower, greenfood, and fruit suits lutinos well. They are hardy birds. You can keep and breed these and other Cockatiels in a colony in an aviary. Avoid buying lutinos that show a prominent lack of feathering behind the crest. This is a genetic fault, the bald patch being more prominent in some strains of Cockatiel than others.

BREEDING Provide pairs with a nestbox. Breeding results tend to be better when pairs are housed individually, because hens often lay in the same box, and some of the eggs become chilled. Feather-plucking of chicks in the nest is not unusual, and you should remove chicks as soon as they are feeding independently.

CREST The Cockatiel can raise and lower its crest at will.

HEAD Although the yellow coloration on the head may vary from bird to bird, it is impossible to distinguish the two sexes by this difference.

PLUMAGE The depth of coloration on the body varies, depending on the strain. The darkest lutino birds are sometimes described as "golden" or "buttercup."

MUTATION The pearl Cockatiel was first reported in Germany in 1967. Its scalloped pattern can be combined with other colors, including the lutino.

MARKINGS The pearl markings may vary considerably.

PEARL COCKATIEL COCK

CHARACTERISTICS
LENGTH: 30cm (12in).
AVERAGE LIFESPAN: 18 years.
SEXING: Hens have barring on the undersides of their tails.
BREEDING DETAILS: Incubation lasts 18 days; fledging occurs 28 days later.
YOUNG BIRDS: Similar to adult hens but recognizable by their shorter tails.

TURQUOISINE GRASS PARAKEET
Neophema pulchella

Ranked among the most popular of the parakeets, these birds are an ideal choice for a garden aviary. They are easy to sex, colorful, and free-breeding, with inoffensive calls and a nondestructive nature. Furthermore, a number of color mutations are now widely bred.

FOOD & HOUSING Offer a diet of the smaller cereal seeds, with a little sunflower, greenfood, and seeding grasses if possible. Pairs must be housed separately to prevent fighting. Screen new stock for intestinal roundworms.

BREEDING Provide pairs with a nestbox. You can anticipate two, or even three, clutches of eggs from a pair over the course of a summer. Remove youngsters as soon as they are feeding independently. If left with their parents too long, young cocks, in particular, may be attacked by the father. It is also a good idea to screen the end of the flight so that young birds do not attempt to fly through the mesh, which can cause injuries.

• **MALE PLUMAGE**
Reddish wing patches easily distinguish the cock from the hen.

• **FEMALE PLUMAGE**
The hen is slightly duller in coloration than her mate. She has less blue on her face, and a greener breast.

TAIL •
During the breeding season, the cock may fan his tail when displaying to his mate.

YELLOW MUTATION COCK

MUTATION The yellow form is one of the most attractive of the new colors being bred. These birds can be sexed in the same way as other mutations.

CHARACTERISTICS
LENGTH: 20cm (8in).
AVERAGE LIFESPAN: 12 years.
SEXING: Hens have no red wing patches; plumage is duller.
BREEDING DETAILS: Incubation lasts 19 days; fledging occurs 28 days later.
YOUNG BIRDS: Similar to adult hens; plumage is duller.

SPLENDID GRASS PARAKEET
Neophema splendida

For many years, this beautiful bird was an avicultural rarity, but, over the years, it has proved very willing to reproduce in aviaries, and stock is now widely available. Like the other popular grass parakeets, Splendid Grass Parakeets are eminently suitable for newcomers to bird-keeping.

EYES The eyes of Splendid Grass Parakeets are relatively large. This enables the birds to be active at dusk.

HEAD The blue head coloration of this cock bird is more intense than in hens and is also more extensive.

WINGS Powerful wings make the Splendid Grass Parakeet very agile in flight. This can make them difficult to catch in an aviary.

BREAST The area of scarlet plumage on the breast identifies this as a cock bird.

BREEDING Pairs will nest readily, but sometimes the cock can be rather persistent in chasing his mate. A nestbox located under cover in the flight is ideal for breeding pairs. The hen sits alone, emerging only for short periods each day. Splendid Grass Parakeets are prolific breeders and are likely to produce more than one clutch of chicks during the breeding period. Remove youngsters from their parents as soon as they are feeding independently.

FOOD & HOUSING Millets and plain canary seed, with a little sunflower seed and groats, form the basis of their diet. Also give them greenfood and sweet apple regularly. A pair can be housed in a flight 2.7m (9ft) long, but they will not settle in the confines of a cage. In an aviary, these hardy birds can become quite tame and confiding. Their soft calls are unlikely to disturb neighbors.

CHARACTERISTICS

LENGTH: 19cm (7½in).
AVERAGE LIFESPAN: 12 years.
SEXING: Cock birds have red breasts.
BREEDING DETAILS: Incubation lasts 19 days; fledging occurs 28 days later.
YOUNG BIRDS: Similar to adult hens.

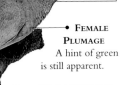

FEMALE PLUMAGE A hint of green is still apparent.

BLUE MUTATION HEN

MUTATIONS In the blue mutations, the cock's breast is much paler than normal, varying from pale pink to white.

BLUE MUTATION COCK

CRIMSON ROSELLA
Platycercus elegans

These colorful parakeets from Australia make a delightful addition to any birdkeeper's collection. They breed freely, and may even nest twice in succession. Several color mutations now exist, of which the blue form is the most common. Start your collection of Crimson Rosellas with a proven pair, if possible, or else with young birds that have not bred before, rather than odd adult birds, because this can increase the chances of the parakeets proving to be compatible. An established pair can prove to be very prolific, breeding regularly for a period of twenty years or more. Crimson Rosellas are grouped with other broad-tailed rosellas, primarily because of their distinctive tails.

PLUMAGE The vibrant coloration of these birds does not depend on color-feeding.

BODY The rich body color usually fades just prior to molting.

WINGS The scalloping pattern on the wings is characteristic of all rosellas.

FOOD & HOUSING
Offer plain canary seed, millets, groats, and a little sunflower seed, along with greenfood and apple. House these hardy birds in an outdoor aviary with a 3.7m (12ft) flight, where their vivid coloration shows to good effect.

BREEDING
Provide pairs with a deep nestbox and soft wood, for lining. Watch that the cock does not drive his mate too fiercely, as some cocks prove much more aggressive than others. If he does, you may have to remove him from the aviary for a period, or clip one of his wings. Also watch for the adults feather-plucking their youngsters, and if they do, apply powdered aloes to the chicks' backs as a deterrent. Remove chicks once they are feeding, or they may be attacked if the adults want to nest again.

TAIL The individual tail feathers are broad, even at the tips.

CHARACTERISTICS
LENGTH: 36cm (14in).
AVERAGE LIFESPAN: 25 years.
SEXING: Scientific sexing required; hens may have smaller heads than cocks.
BREEDING DETAILS: Incubation lasts 21 days; fledging occurs 35 days later.
YOUNG BIRDS: Generally plumage is greenish, but some are almost entirely red.

GOLDEN-MANTLED ROSELLA
Platycercus eximius

The Golden-mantled Rosella, which is sometimes abbreviated to G.M.R., comes from the southeastern corner of Australia, and Tasmania, and is actually a more colorful form of the Eastern Rosella. This species is the most popular rosella with aviculturists around the world. A variety of color forms are now being bred, including a rare but stunning lutino form, which has a yellow and white body, and a red head.

CHARACTERISTICS

LENGTH: 30cm (12in).

AVERAGE LIFESPAN: 15 years.

SEXING: Hens are duller than cocks, with less red on the head and breast.

BREEDING DETAILS: Incubation lasts 21 days; fledging occurs 35 days later.

YOUNG BIRDS: Similar to adult hens, but the back of the head has a green patch.

BILL The bill is evenly colored on the G.M.R. The bills of Eastern Rosellas are light on the upper part, and darker underneath.

CHEEKS Cocks have pure, snowy white cheeks; hens' cheeks are grayer.

BREAST The way that the red feathering merges with the yellow on the breast is an individual characteristic, which differs from one bird to the next.

BACK The yellow plumage on the back is a darker shade in the Golden-mantled than the Eastern Rosella.

WINGS This species has blue on the outer edge of the wings.

FOOD & HOUSING
Give these birds a diet similar to that of the Crimson Rosella. They are equally hardy in the same type of aviary. For both varieties, check new stock for intestinal roundworms, which are common in this group of parakeets. By screening new birds, you will, hopefully, avoid these troublesome parasites becoming established in your aviary.

TAIL The width of the tail shows why rosellas are sometimes called broadtails.

BREEDING Provide a deep nestbox and soft wood, which the birds will gnaw and use for lining. Although these rosellas may breed at just 11 months old, do not encourage them to nest until they are at least 18 months old, and more mature. There is no point in rushing these birds to breed because they should have a reproductive life of over 10 years in aviary surroundings. They do not settle well in the home, being rather nervous birds by nature.

PRINCESS OF WALES' PARAKEET
Polytelis alexandrae

The subtle, pastel colors of Princess of Wales' Parakeets have assured the lasting popularity of these birds. Although hard to substantiate, it is believed that they are becoming quite scarce in their native Australia, where they are essentially nomadic, moving from one area to another, and sometimes not reappearing until years later. This species is well established in aviculture, however, and pairs nest readily, to the extent that both blue and lutino mutations have appeared in captive strains. Some breeders also double-clutch pairs successfully. They can become quite tame in an aviary, but are sometimes noisy.

THROAT This species is sometimes called the Rose-throated Parakeet because of the pink color under the bills.

CHARACTERISTICS
LENGTH: 45cm (18in).
AVERAGE LIFESPAN: 15 years.
SEXING: Hens have grayer crown and rump than cocks.
BREEDING DETAILS: Incubation lasts 19 days; fledging occurs 42 days later.
YOUNG BIRDS: Similar to adult hens, but plumage is often duller.

WINGS On adult cocks, feather enlargement may occur on each wing at the end of the third flight feather. This is normal.

FEMALE PLUMAGE You can distinguish the hens by their shorter tails.

BREEDING These parakeets can be persuaded to nest in a fairly deep nestbox or suitable hollow log. Egg-eating is common in this species. Suspect it if the birds spend long periods in the nestbox, but no eggs appear; you may find shell fragments. Place a plastic, dummy parakeet egg in the box. The birds will be unable to break this, and may be dissuaded from egg-eating. Also review their diet.

TAIL The central tail feathers are very long, often half the bird's total length. The cock flares his tail when displaying.

FOOD & HOUSING Offer Princess of Wales' Parakeets a mixture of millets and plain canary seed, plus some sunflower seed, greenfood, and diced apple. Once acclimatized, house them in an aviary with a long flight, as this allows pairs to show to best effect. Make sure that the floor is easy to clean, since these birds spend long periods foraging on it, leaving them susceptible to intestinal worms.

BARRABAND (SUPERB) PARAKEET
Polytelis swansonii

The strikingly colored Barraband Parakeet is a wonderfully graceful bird, which soon becomes tame in aviary surroundings, rapidly taking tidbits from your hand. Furthermore, Barraband Parakeets are neither destructive nor noisy by nature. Yet, in spite of their engaging habits, their active nature largely precludes them from being kept as pets indoors. Instead, house pairs in a long aviary.

FOOD & HOUSING Offer these birds plain canary seed, millets, some apple, and greenfood and a flight at least 3.7m (12ft) long to keep them in good condition. They are hardy, so can be housed outdoors year round. They are prone to upper respiratory tract infections, notably the disease mycoplasmosis, which also affects the eyes, so watch for any signs of nasal blockage. Sudden cases of paralysis are also sometimes recorded, which may be related to unseen head injuries. They may recover gradually over days.

HEAD The yellow plumage here serves to distinguish the cock easily from the hen.

THROAT The vivid red plumage on the throat contrasts with the yellow of the head.

MALE PLUMAGE The green of the underparts is lighter than the green on the wings.

BARRABAND PARAKEET HEN

CHARACTERISTICS

LENGTH: 40cm (16in).
AVERAGE LIFESPAN: 15 years.
SEXING: Hens have no yellow on the head.
BREEDING DETAILS: Incubation lasts 19 days; fledging occurs 42 days later.
YOUNG BIRDS: Similar to adult hens, but have brown rather than orange irises.

BREEDING When a pair looks ready to breed, provide a nestbox about 60cm (2ft) deep and 20cm (8in) square. Try to house two pairs within sight and sound of each other, to increase the likelihood of successful breeding. Young cocks identify themselves by their singing long before they molt into the adult plumage, which happens when they are about one and a half years old.

FACE The hen is easy to distinguish, being far less colorful on the face than her mate. Interestingly, she is also usually heavier.

FEMALE PLUMAGE There are areas of red plumage at the top of the hen's thighs and the tail feathers are tipped beneath with red.

RED-RUMPED PARAKEET
Psephotus haematonotus

Red-rumped Parakeet cock birds have a most attractive song, which makes them a welcome addition to any aviary collection. You can keep and breed these Australian parakeets quite easily, provided that the cock bird does not become aggressive toward his mate or their offspring. If at all possible, start off with young birds, to increase the likelihood of pairs forming, rather than simply placing two adult birds together.

FOOD & HOUSING Feed Red-rumped Parakeets a mixture of plain canary seed and millets, augmented with millet sprays, some sunflower seeds, greenfood, and apple. Avoid feeding them excessive amounts of sunflower seed, however, because it can cause these birds to become obese. House these hardy birds in an outdoor aviary with a long flight so that they have sufficient room to exercise.

BREEDING Provide a nestbox and soft wood. Be sure to remove the chicks as soon as they are feeding independently, otherwise the cock may attack them. Youngsters are usually nervous, so avoid disturbing them. A typical clutch has five eggs, and pairs may nest several times in succession.

FEMALE PLUMAGE •
Hens' plumage is invariably duller, and lacks the red plumage on the rump.

• MALE PLUMAGE
Cocks have red color on the rump, even before leaving the nest.

• TAIL Though dark when seen from above, the lower tail feathers are white.

MUTATIONS The commonest of the mutations at present is the yellow Red-rump. Other known mutations include lutino, pied, and blue variants. These new color variants are now becoming more common.

YELLOW RED-RUMPED COCK

CHARACTERISTICS

LENGTH: 27cm (11in).
AVERAGE LIFESPAN: 15 years.
SEXING: Hens have grayish green plumage.
BREEDING DETAILS: Incubation lasts 19 days; fledging occurs 30 days later.
YOUNG BIRDS: Similar to adults, but plumage is duller.

PLUM-HEADED PARAKEET
Psittacula cyanocephala

Tolerant, not especially destructive, and with a musical call, the Plum-headed Parakeet, which originates from Asia, is an ideal occupant for a garden aviary, even in a relatively urban setting. The only difficulty with Plum-headed Parakeets is obtaining a true pair, as supposed hens can molt out as cocks in the breeding season.

BREEDING Hens can be aggressive to their mates for most of the year and, at breeding time, the cock may be hesitant to approach his mate. If so, swap the birds so that they have new partners. Position the nestbox in a secluded, sheltered area and watch to ensure that the chicks do not become chilled, as hens often stop brooding while chicks are still relatively unfeathered. Even if the first clutch of eggs fails to hatch, or the chicks die, these parakeets rarely nest again in the same year. To compensate for this, Plum-headed Parakeets can breed into their twenties. If searching for a hen, check for plum-colored feathers on the head. These signify that the bird is a cock.

HEAD The characteristic plum coloration on the head is acquired over the course of several molts.

WING A plum-colored patch on the wings distinguishes the Plum-head from the closely related Blossom-headed Parakeet.

MALE PLUMAGE As with other psittaculid parakeets, the body is comprised of various shades of green.

BILL The bill in the adult hen is paler than the cock's bill.

FEMALE PLUMAGE Adult hens can be distinguished easily from cocks by the gray coloration of their head and the lack of the wing patch. Otherwise, hens are mainly green.

TAIL The whitish, rather than yellow, color on the tips of the tail distinguishes this hen from a Blossom-head.

FOOD & HOUSING A parrot mix with cereal seeds, plus fruit and greenfood is a good diet for these parakeets. As with most parakeets, these birds benefit from an aviary with a long flight. Once properly acclimatized, they are hardy and can stay in an outdoor aviary year round.

CHARACTERISTICS

LENGTH: 33cm (13in).
AVERAGE LIFESPAN: 25 years.
SEXING: Hens have gray heads.
BREEDING DETAILS: Incubation lasts 25 days; fledging occurs 50 days later.
YOUNG BIRDS: Similar to adult hens, although they fledge with green heads.

BLUE RING-NECKED PARAKEET
Psittacula krameri

This striking color form of Ring-necked Parakeet was highly valued by the rulers of India, centuries before it was known elsewhere. The Ring-necked Parakeet is the most widely distributed parrot in the entire world, ranging over the Indian sub-continent westward across northern Africa. The usual green form remains the most commonly seen form in aviculture. However, the blue form of the Ring-necked Parakeet is bred in increasing numbers each year, and so are a brilliant lutino, a snow white albino, and a gray form of this bird.

BILL The red upper bill makes an amazing contrast to the body color of Blue Ring-necked Parakeets.

NECK The cock has a collar, which appears when the bird is three years old.

BODY The depth of blue coloration, an autosomal recessive mutation, varies little.

FEMALE PLUMAGE The plumage of cocks and hens is identical, except that hens have no collar.

BREEDING Ring-necked Parakeets usually breed early in the year in northern climates, and should have a nestbox year round. You can house and breed them in a colony but most breeders house mutations on their own, to ensure parentage of chicks.

FOOD & HOUSING Parrot food, cereal seeds (including groats), fruit, and greenfood are ideal. When planning accommodation, bear in mind that these birds can be susceptible to frostbite.

CHARACTERISTICS

LENGTH: 40cm (16in).
AVERAGE LIFESPAN: 15 years.
SEXING: Hens lack the nuchal collar of cocks.
BREEDING DETAILS: Incubation lasts 24 days; fledging occurs 50 days later.
YOUNG BIRDS: Similar to adult hens; may have shorter tails.

NORMAL FORM The Ring-necked Parakeet hen is dominant to her partner outside the breeding period.

INDIAN RING-NECKED OR ROSE-RINGED PARAKEET HEN

RED-FRONTED KAKARIKI
Cyanoramphus novaezelandiae

Now widely kept in aviculture, the Red-fronted Kakariki was at one time in imminent danger of extinction in its native home of New Zealand. However, the New Zealand government set up a breeding program with aviculturists, which proved highly successful. The total number of kakarikis increased from just 103 in 1958, up to a staggering 2,500 in 1964. Since that time, captive-bred kakarikis have been successfully reintroduced to the wild.

HEAD Red markings on the head identify this species, although they are less conspicuous on • young birds.

PLUMAGE The body coloration is primarily • dark green.

FOOD & HOUSING Offer kakarikis a diet of Budgerigar seed, fruit, and greenfood. They also eat mealworms occasionally, especially when they are rearing chicks. As they are hardy birds, you can house them in an aviary. Pay particular attention to keeping the floor of their quarters clean and dry, as they often scratch around on it like chickens, which leaves them susceptible to roundworms.

• FEET Kakarikis have a habit of running up and down the mesh of the aviary.

CHARACTERISTICS
LENGTH: 28cm (11in).
AVERAGE LIFESPAN: 6 years.
SEXING: Hens are smaller than cocks.
BREEDING DETAILS: Incubation lasts 19 days; fledging occurs 42 days later.
YOUNG BIRDS: The head has a reduced area of red plumage; tail feathers are shorter.

HEAD The area • of yellow plumage on the top of the head distinguishes this variety.

YELLOW-FRONTED KAKARIKI COCK

BREEDING Few parakeets are more prolific than kakarikis, and clutches of nine eggs are not unusual. Provide adequate accommodation for the youngsters, as pairs may nest twice during the year. If possible, it is best to prevent hens rearing more than two rounds of chicks in one season, as excessive breeding will weaken them. Several color mutations have been developed in these parakeets, including cinnamon and pied forms.

VARIETY Yellow-fronted Kakarikis (C. auriceps) are less common in aviculture than the Red-fronted Kakarikis, but are very similar in their requirements, although they do not spend as much time on the ground. As with the Red-fronted Kakarikis, the hens are noticeably smaller than the cock birds, and this makes pairs easy to recognize.

CANARY-WINGED PARAKEET
Brotogeris versicolurus chiriri

If you obtain these attractive South American parakeets as youngsters, they will most likely develop into friendly pets. Older birds remain rather shy, but they will settle well in aviary surroundings and may nest, although pairs can be slow to start breeding.

FOOD & HOUSING Offer these birds a diet of parrot food, small cereal seeds, and fruit, as this forms a significant part of their diet in the wild. They will also benefit from a nectar solution, and may take some greenfood as well. Once acclimatized these parakeets are hardy, so house them in a strongly constructed aviary and provide them with a plentiful supply of perches to divert their attention from the wooden framework – they are surprisingly destructive birds for their size.

BILL The bill will become overgrown if the bird is unable to gnaw regularly.

PLUMAGE Light green body color distinguishes this variety from the closely related White-winged Parakeets *(B. v. versicolorus),* which have much darker green coloration.

WING MARKINGS A brilliant shade of canary yellow marks the edges of the wings.

TAIL The long, narrow tail feathers indicate that this bird is a parakeet.

CHARACTERISTICS

LENGTH: 23cm (9in).
AVERAGE LIFESPAN: 15 years.
SEXING: Scientific sexing required; hens may be smaller than cocks.
BREEDING DETAILS: Incubation lasts 26 days; fledging occurs 50 days later.
YOUNG BIRDS: Similar to adults but plumage is duller; they often have shorter tails.

VARIETY *Like other brotogeris parakeets, the Orange-flanked Parakeet from Peru and Ecuador needs scientific sexing.*

ORANGE-FLANKED PARAKEET COCK

BREEDING Keeping these parakeets in a small group often encourages breeding success, but put all the birds in the flight at the same time, as they are likely to attack any newcomers. Position nestboxes in a darkened locality, such as the shelter, and provide a lining of wooden offcuts inside the boxes. The birds whittle these away to form a soft bed for the eggs. Minimize disturbances, as pairs can be quite nervous, especially when breeding for the first time.

LINEOLATED PARAKEET
Bolborhynchus lineola

Although Lineolated Parakeets are not very common in aviculture, the quiet and inoffensive natures of these birds from South America, coupled with their readiness to breed, makes them attractive aviary occupants. Furthermore, they live and breed quite happily together in groups. Some mutations are available, the most stunning of which is a blue variant from the Netherlands. This is, however, very rare at present. A cinnamon variant has also been recorded, but this color form is no longer represented in aviculture.

CHARACTERISTICS

LENGTH: *15cm (6in).*
AVERAGE LIFESPAN: *10 years.*
SEXING: *Scientific sexing required; cocks tend to have heavier barring than hens.*
BREEDING DETAILS: *Incubation lasts 18 days; fledging occurs 35 days later.*
YOUNG BIRDS: *The head has more of a bluish tinge than adults' heads.*

TAIL The tail is relatively short and quite broad, with the feathers tapering to a fine point.

FEET The feet and legs are usually pink, although the claws can often be darker.

WING MARKINGS The black markings on the wings of these birds give rise to their alternative name of Barred Parakeet. Although individuals vary in their markings, do not rely on these differences for sexing purposes.

FOOD & HOUSING Offer Lineolated Parakeets small cereal seeds, millet sprays, sunflower or small pine nuts, greenfood, and fruit, especially berries in season. They may show a preference for sunflower seeds, but encourage them to eat other seeds as well. A supplement with vitamins D and K may also be beneficial. Keep these birds in a secluded aviary, with plenty of cover, as they dislike bright light. Also provide a choice of nestboxes for roosting. If you can obtain a young bird, it will develop into a marvelous pet, rarely attempting to bite. Aviary birds may need additional warmth during very cold weather, although they have been known to bathe in snow, gleefully flapping about in it in their flight.

BREEDING Provide a nestbox and wood chips. If you keep these birds in a colony, put all the nestboxes at the same height to reduce the risk of fighting. Expect clutches of up to eight eggs.

QUAKER PARAKEET (MONK PARAKEET)
Myiopsitta monachus

The Quaker Parakeet is one of the most common and most sociable of all the parakeets, and it can be distinguished from other species by its breeding habits. In the wild, its nests, built from twigs, can be as heavy as 1235kg (2723lb), with each pair having a separate compartment in the huge structure. These birds, therefore, can breed in large numbers, even where there are no tree holes available. Quaker Parakeets make attractive aviary occupants, but their calls can be raucous. There is an attractive blue mutation, first recorded in Belgium after 1945, which has blue plumage in place of green, and a whitish head and chest. There is also a stunning yellow mutation, which, sadly, has always been scarce, and may now be extinct, although there is always a possibility that it could reemerge in the future.

NECK The gray feathering on the neck extends only to behind the eye.

HEAD The forehead is gray, and has a pattern of barring, which is also present over the breast.

WINGS Traces of blue coloring are apparent on the wings, as is the case with many other parakeet varieties.

PLUMAGE The upper parts of the body are a light green. The underparts are paler.

TAIL The tail feathers are a similar green to those of the upper parts, although paler underneath.

FOOD & HOUSING Offer these birds parrot food, cereal seeds, fruit, and greenfood. Keep them in an aviary built of 16 SWG mesh, in order to protect the woodwork from their destructive bills. Introduce the group of parakeets to the aviary together, to minimize the risk of them fighting.

CHARACTERISTICS
LENGTH: 29cm (11in).
AVERAGE LIFESPAN: 15 years.
SEXING: Scientific sexing required.
BREEDING DETAILS: Incubation lasts 25 days; fledging occurs 50 days later.
YOUNG BIRDS: Forehead has a green tinge.

BREEDING For breeding purposes, keep Quaker Parakeets in a group. Provide them with plenty of branches so that the birds can build their own nests. Fix a wire mesh platform under cover in the aviary to form a suitable base for the structure. Fix the platform to a strong wooden framework, which can take the weight of the nest. Alternatively, you can also provide nestboxes lined with twigs for breeding. Hens may lay up to seven eggs in a clutch.

MAROON-BELLIED CONURE
Pyrrhura frontalis

You can recognize the pyrrhura group of conures by the tipped coloration on the feathers of their breast. Because of this marking, these birds are sometimes described collectively as "scaly-breasted conures." They are ideal birds for the garden aviary, since they are quiet and not especially destructive, unlike their aratinga cousins (see page 95).

EYE-RING The eye-ring in this species is a bare area of white skin. In other cases it may be gray.

BREAST The feathers on the breast are tipped with a lighter color, giving the birds a ruffled appearance.

WINGS The primary feathers on the wings are turquoise, which is apparent when the birds fly.

FOOD & HOUSING Offer these conures a mixture of parrot food and smaller cereal seeds. Groats are a particular favorite but they also like sweet apple and carrot. As a general rule, they are less keen on greenfood. With a little coaxing, they may become tame enough to feed from your hand, even in the aviary. These birds are hardy enough to remain in an aviary year round. Avoid housing pairs in adjoining aviaries, as they often bicker fiercely.

UNDERPARTS The reddish coloration on the belly gives rise to the alternative name, Red-bellied Conure.

CHARACTERISTICS

LENGTH: 25cm (10in).
AVERAGE LIFESPAN: 15 years.
SEXING: Scientific sexing required.
BREEDING DETAILS: Incubation lasts 25 days; fledging occurs 49 days later.
YOUNG BIRDS: Duller than adults, with shorter tails.

TAIL The coloration of the tail is maroon on the underside, and green on the top.

BREEDING These conures stalk and sway when displaying, moving in an exaggerated fashion along the perch. This is quite normal, and is no cause for concern. Provide a nestbox when pairs are ready to breed. These birds are prolific, producing about five or six chicks at a time.

PATAGONIAN CONURE
Cyanoliseus patagonus

A spectacular bird, the Patagonian Conure is the largest of the conures and also one of the noisiest. In its native Argentina it is heavily persecuted as a crop pest, and is an easy target because of its unusual roosting habits. These parrots tunnel into limestone cliffs, excavating burrows with nesting chambers at the end. In aviary surroundings, however, they can be persuaded to adopt artificial nestboxes, and may breed on a colony system, although you should watch for any signs of fighting in a colony.

HEAD Above the bill, the head coloring is brownish, but becomes more olive on the sides of the head and down over the wings.

EYE-RING The white, unfeathered eye-ring is more prominent in birds that are in breeding condition.

WINGS The flight feathers are tinged with blue coloring along their length.

BREAST The extent of white feathering on the breast is more pronounced in some birds than others. Here, there is virtually none.

BREEDING Provide breeding pairs with a sturdy nestbox and blocks of soft wood, which these conures will whittle away to provide a deep lining for their nest. The clutch size is relatively small, consisting of two, or possibly three eggs. The hen incubates the eggs alone, but the cock bird may join her in the nestbox.

FOOD & HOUSING Offer conures a diet of parrot food and cereal seeds, especially maize, sweet apple, and spinach beet, which are particular favorites. These conures often prefer the stems of spinach to the leaf itself. They also consume large quantities of cuttlefish bone throughout the year. Always have nestboxes available for roosting purposes, even though these conures are quite hardy and can stay in an outdoor aviary all year round. They do not require artificial heat, provided that they are properly acclimatized.

CHARACTERISTICS

LENGTH: 46cm (18in).
AVERAGE LIFESPAN: 20 years.
SEXING: Scientific sexing required.
BREEDING DETAILS: Incubation lasts 25 days; fledging occurs 56 days later.
YOUNG BIRDS: Upper bills are white.

SUN CONURE
Aratinga solstitialis

These dazzling Sun Conures have become well known in aviculture only since the early 1970s, and at first they commanded a very high price. However, they have since proved to be prolific breeders, and it is now possible to buy captive-bred stock at quite reasonable prices. Pairs usually prove to be reliable parents, and may nest twice in succession. Their only drawback is their harsh calls.

FOOD & HOUSING Provide Sun Conures with good quality parrot mix, smaller cereal seeds, fruit, and greenfood. Sun Conures are hardy once acclimatized and so they can be housed in an outdoor aviary. Like other conures, you should give them a nestbox to roost in throughout the year. However, you should change this after the breeding season, replacing it with a clean box, to prevent the buildup of any parasites.

BREEDING Pairs are usually best housed individually for breeding purposes, in an aviary about 2.7m (9ft) long. Provide a sturdy nestbox and blocks of soft wood, which they will whittle away to provide a deep lining for their nest. Feather-plucking can sometimes be a problem, but affected chicks grow new feathers once they fledge.

PLUMAGE The coloration of the body varies between individuals, with some brighter than others.

WINGS The wings are primarily yellow in adults, while young birds show more green on the wings.

CHARACTERISTICS
LENGTH: 30cm (12in).
AVERAGE LIFESPAN: 15 years.
SEXING: Scientific sexing required.
BREEDING DETAILS: Incubation lasts 26 days; fledging occurs 56 days later.
YOUNG BIRDS: Duller than adults.

VARIETY *The Mitred Conure (A. mitrata) is one of a number of species that are green with variable amounts of red plumage. Their care is identical to that of the Sun Conure.*

MITRED CONURE COCK

PEACH-FACED (ROSY-FACED) LOVEBIRD
Agapornis roseicollis

The Peach-faced Lovebird is a highly popular, small parrot from Africa. It has been bred in a wide range of beautiful colors, and has less disturbing calls than other parrots. If you can overcome the initial problem of sexing the birds, pairs will nest readily in aviaries, frequently rearing two clutches of chicks during the summer months. Young birds develop into delightful pets, especially if hand-reared, and may learn to repeat a few words.

CHARACTERISTICS
LENGTH: *15cm (6in).*
AVERAGE LIFESPAN: *10 years.*
SEXING: *Scientific sexing required.*
BREEDING DETAILS: *Incubation lasts 23 days; fledging occurs 42 days later.*
YOUNG BIRDS: *Bills have dark brown markings; plumage is duller than adults.*

FOOD & HOUSING A mix of plain canary seed, millets, groats, and a little sunflower seed forms the basis of lovebirds' diet. You should also offer them apple and greenfood regularly. Once acclimatized, these birds are hardy and can be housed in an outdoor aviary. Provide a nestbox for roosting. If you keep more than one pair, put up double-wiring between the flights to prevent any injuries from fighting, as pairs will bicker through the mesh.

EYE-RING The eye-ring of bare skin is less prominent in the Peach-faced Lovebird than in other lovebirds.

BILL The bill is normally the color of horn. The pinkish underlay is the blood supply.

FACE The intensity of the pink facial coloration varies between individual birds.

BODY The squat posture emphasizes the compact body shape.

BREEDING Pairs do not need large enclosures – they will nest easily in aviaries with flights just 91cm (3ft) in length. It has proved possible, notably in Australia, to breed these small parrots on a colony system. To do this though, all the birds must be introduced simultaneously to the aviary, and nestboxes must be positioned at the same height, to minimize fighting. Provide branches of hazel or elder, preferably fresh, so the birds can tear off pieces of bark to use as nesting material. The birds usually carry these strips tucked in among the body feathers to the nest, enabling them to carry more than one length at a time.

TAIL A distinctive characteristic of these lovebirds is their short, rounded tail feathers.

PASTEL BLUE PEACH-FACED LOVEBIRD
Agapornis roseicollis

This attractive blue mutation of the Peach-faced Lovebird was first bred in 1963 by the Dutch breeder, P. Habats. Since that time, this color has become extremely popular, and nowadays it is widely kept around the world.

FACE The facial area often shows traces of a slight salmon-pink suffusion.

PLUMAGE The body color of the blue mutation is a greenish blue. Although not a real blue (in which case the bird's face would be pure white, on a blue body), some are a better shade than others.

BREEDING Mutations have identical breeding requirements to the normal form. Strains of pastel blues vary in their coloration, with selective breeding having some effect on this feature. Among other varieties, the coloration of the pastel blue pieds, resulting from a cross with the pied mutation, is a variable pale lemon against pastel blue. You can breed further colors by combining the pastel blue and lutino mutations, in order to create the cremino. This mutation has predominantly pale lemon plumage, with a contrasting, pale pink face.

FOOD & HOUSING Color variants of these lovebirds need similar care to that of normally colored individuals; they are no harder to care for. All lovebirds need adequate protection in cold weather, otherwise they may suffer from frostbite, which could result in the loss of toes. Provide a nestbox for roosting.

MUTATION *A deep buttercup yellow body, a reddish facial coloration, and red eyes are features of the lutino Peach-faced Lovebird. This mutation was developed in the United States during the 1970s.*

LUTINO PEACH-FACED LOVEBIRD COCK

CHARACTERISTICS

LENGTH: 15cm (6in).
AVERAGE LIFESPAN: 10 years.
SEXING: Scientific sexing required.
BREEDING DETAILS: Incubation lasts 23 days; fledging occurs 42 days later.
YOUNG BIRDS: Bills have dark brown markings; plumage is duller than adults.

RUMP The lutino Lovebird mutation has a white rump rather than the blue of the normal form.

MASKED LOVEBIRD
Agapornis personata

Ideally suited to suburban surroundings, these attractive little parrots are popular aviary occupants because their calls are not harsh, and pairs breed readily. Their nesting habits are fascinating as well, since, in contrast to most parrots, these lovebirds build a nest inside their nestbox. Their behavior provides the most reliable means of sexing, as hens alone carry the nesting material. Their chicks are unusual in that they are covered in reddish down when they hatch.

EYE-RING The prominent white eye-ring is used to classify this subgroup of lovebirds.

FOOD & HOUSING Offer Masked Lovebirds a basic diet of cereal seeds, sunflower, fruit, and greenfood. Pairs are best kept on their own to prevent squabbling, so adjoining flights must be properly double-wired to keep different pairs at a distance. Masked Lovebirds are hardy once acclimatized, but, because they are susceptible to frostbite, always provide a nestbox for roosting purposes. You should locate this in the aviary shelter during cold weather.

HEAD Their black plumage gives rise to the alternative name of Black-masked Lovebird.

BILL Lovebirds with white eye-rings signify a subgroup of lovebirds, all of which carry nesting material in their bills.

BREEDING Give these lovebirds fresh branches so that they can strip the bark to form their nest, which is bulkier and more domed than the nests of the Peach-faced Lovebird. Remove chicks as soon as they are feeding independently, so that the pair can nest again.

MUTATIONS The blue Masked Lovebird mutation is unusual because it was recorded first in the wild in 1927. It has since become quite common in aviaries. Yellow and white varieties are also now bred.

BLUE MASKED LOVEBIRD COCK

CHARACTERISTICS
LENGTH: 14cm (5½in).
AVERAGE LIFESPAN: 10 years.
SEXING: Scientific sexing required.
BREEDING DETAILS: Incubation lasts 23 days; fledging occurs 42 days later.
YOUNG BIRDS: Duller plumage than adults.

MADAGASCAR LOVEBIRD
Agapornis cana

Since these little lovebirds can be sexed visually, the problem of obtaining a true pair for breeding purposes is greatly simplified. They may prove nervous at first, but they settle well in an aviary that offers them adequate seclusion. Furthermore, their calls do not cause close neighbors any offense, nor do they damage the woodwork in their quarters.

FOOD & HOUSING Offer Madagascar Lovebirds a mixture of the smaller cereal seeds, such as millet sprays, plain canary seed, and paddy rice. They may also crack sunflower seeds, and eat fruit and greenfood. These birds are susceptible to air-sac mites, which can cause wheezing and respiratory distress. Watch for this when assessing stock, since treatment may prove difficult.

HEAD The gray head confirms that this bird is a cock.

MALE PLUMAGE Cocks' wings are always a darker shade of green than the rest of the body.

FEET The feet are grayish in color, with sharp pointed claws.

FEMALE PLUMAGE Adult hens are predominantly green. Their bills distinguish them from young birds, which have lighter bills.

CHARACTERISTICS
LENGTH: 13cm (5in).
AVERAGE LIFESPAN: 8 years.
SEXING: Hens have green heads.
BREEDING DETAILS: Incubation lasts 23 days; fledging occurs 42 days later.
YOUNG BIRDS: Bill paler with black base.

BREEDING These lovebirds need inside winter accommodation, since most pairs seem to prefer to breed at this time of year. Ideally, they like a nestbox with cork bark around the entrance, suspended at the rear of the flight. These birds prepare a simple nest, often made up mainly of feathers, for their clutch of four eggs. Avoid any unnecessary disturbance while the eggs are being incubated, as there is a risk that the eggs will become chilled. These birds may spend periods during the day roosting in their nestbox, even when they are not breeding, though this is not a cause for concern. Provide artificial lighting in the birdroom, controlled by a dimmer switch, so that when chicks hatch, the adults will have longer to acquire food for them.

BLUE-FRONTED AMAZON PARROT
Amazona aestiva

Amazon parrots are a group of 27 different species, which are widely distributed throughout the New World. Those that live on some of the Caribbean islands rank among the most endangered parrots in the world. The majority are mainly green, with a range of different head colors. They are talented mimics, although they are often noisy by nature.

FOOD & HOUSING Provide these parrots with a good quality parrot mix, a daily supply of fruit, and greenfood. Blue-fronted Amazon Parrots need a sturdy aviary as, like most parrots, they gnaw at the woodwork. It is also a good idea to keep them confined in the shelter in the mornings and evenings, since they tend to call loudly for a time at first light, and then again at dusk, which can be disturbing to neighbors as well as to you.

BREEDING It is important that the birds are well settled in their quarters before you attempt to breed them. Blue-fronted Amazons have a fairly fixed breeding season, and start to nest in the early summer in the northern hemisphere. They rarely produce two rounds of chicks, unless the first clutch is removed for hand-rearing. On average, a pair will have three or four youngsters.

FACE Do not rely solely on the blue facial patch to identify this species. Other Amazons have similar blue markings. •

HEAD Each bird develops an individual • pattern of markings.

SHOULDER It is the red shoulder markings that identify this bird as a Blue-fronted Amazon. In some cases, though, the red may be absent.

FEET The feet are usually dark in color, but if a claw has been lost, for example, the surrounding area of skin may appear paler.

TAIL These parrots • have moderately long and broad tail feathers, with rounded tips.

CHARACTERISTICS
LENGTH: 37.5cm (15in).
AVERAGE LIFESPAN: 40 years.
SEXING: Scientific sexing required.
BREEDING DETAILS: Incubation lasts 28 days; fledging occurs 65 days later.
YOUNG BIRDS: Plumage is duller than adults; irises are brown.

YELLOW-FRONTED AMAZON PARROT
Amazona ochrocephala

Yellow-fronted Amazon Parrots are found over a wide area, ranging from Central to South America. A number of different forms are recognized, all of which differ according to the extent of yellow plumage on their heads. They may also show some variation in size. This parrot is highly valued, both as a companion and as a mimic. Before purchasing one of these parrots, check that the nostrils are an even size, and show no sign of discharge or of being enlarged or blocked. These signs will usually indicate a respiratory infection to which these parrots are susceptible, and which is often difficult to cure.

CHARACTERISTICS
LENGTH: *35cm (14in).*
AVERAGE LIFESPAN: *40 years.*
SEXING: *Scientific sexing required.*
BREEDING DETAILS: *Incubation lasts 28 days; fledging occurs 65 days later.*
YOUNG BIRDS: *Irises are brown.*

HEAD The extent of yellow coloration on the head varies, depending on the race and age of the bird.

EYES The orange iris shows that this is an adult. Young birds have brown eyes.

PLUMAGE The body coloration is mainly green, like other Amazon parrots.

FOOD & HOUSING Give these birds parrot food, fruit, and greenfood each day. Also offer them parrot pellets, and sprinkle a food supplement over the fruit occasionally, to keep these parrots in top condition. House them in a spacious aviary or cage.

BREEDING It is not possible to sex these birds by the amount of yellow plumage on their heads because hens are sometimes more brightly colored than cocks. Provide them with a relatively deep nestbox for the best results when breeding. Watch the birds carefully, as a pair may become aggressive.

VARIETY The yellow plumage on the Yellow-naped Amazon Parrot (A. o. auropalliata) is confined to the nape of the neck. It is found from Mexico to Costa Rica and Honduras.

YELLOW-NAPED AMAZON PARROT COCK

ORANGE-WINGED AMAZON PARROT
Amazona amazonica

Although somewhat similar to the Blue-fronted Amazon Parrot, this species is significantly smaller. It ranges across northern South America from the eastern side of the Andes. Orange-winged Amazon Parrots are popular as pets, as young birds develop into marvelous companions. Recently, this species has become more appreciated among breeders, although, despite their size, these parrots are no quieter than other Amazons. Color variants among them are scarce, but a lutino Orange-winged Amazon Parrot was kept at Paignton Zoo in Devon, England, during the 1960s.

CHARACTERISTICS

LENGTH: 33cm (13in).
AVERAGE LIFESPAN: 40 years.
SEXING: Scientific sexing required.
BREEDING DETAILS: Incubation lasts 27 days; fledging occurs 50 days later.
YOUNG BIRDS: Irises are brown.

FACE
Markings on the face differ from one bird to another.

WINGS The orange feathering on the wings is most apparent when the wings are held open. This and the lighter color of the bill are distinctive to this species.

FOOD & HOUSING Offer these birds parrot food, fruit, and greenfood. Encourage them to sample parrot pellets as well, to add variety to their diet. Provide an ample supply of perches for them to gnaw, or their bills may become overgrown. House these and other Amazon parrots in a sturdy, spacious aviary or cage.

BREEDING A breeding pair can be housed satisfactorily in an aviary measuring about 3.7m (12ft) in length. When breeding, Amazons are likely to prove destructive, so safeguard exposed woodwork in their aviary or cage. Hens usually lay clutches of three or four eggs. A varied diet is essential if the chicks are to be reared successfully by their parents. It takes two to three years for the young birds to mature.

FEET The feet of the Orange-winged Amazon are often lighter in color than the Blue-fronted Amazon Parrot.

BLUE AND GOLD MACAW
Ara ararauna

In spite of their large size, these stunning members of the parrot family can become very tame if you obtain them as youngsters. Ranging from Central America southward to Bolivia and Paraguay, individuals may show a natural variation in size, depending on their origins. Housing these lively macaws in the home can prove difficult, unless you acquire a purpose-built flight cage, which gives them ample room.

CHARACTERISTICS

LENGTH: *82.5cm (33in).*
AVERAGE LIFESPAN: *50 years.*
SEXING: *Scientific sexing required; hens may have narrower heads.*
BREEDING DETAILS: *Incubation lasts 28 days; fledging occurs 90 days later.*
YOUNG BIRDS: *Similar to adults but irises are dark instead of light.*

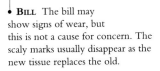

PLUMAGE The body coloration has led this species to be also called the Blue and Yellow Macaw.

BREEDING Macaws can be prolific, often double-clutching readily. A sturdy and well-protected nestbox is essential, so that it remains intact through the breeding period, a time when macaws are particularly destructive. In view of its weight, you may want to use brick pillar supports.

HEAD Blue and Gold Macaws always have a patch of green plumage on the head. •

MASK There are usually three rows of dark feathers below the eyes. When the bird is excited or annoyed, the increased bloodflow causes the whitish bare skin here to become redder. •

HEAD DETAIL

• **BILL** The bill may show signs of wear, but this is not a cause for concern. The scaly marks usually disappear as the new tissue replaces the old.

FOOD & HOUSING Offer these birds a diet of a good quality seed mixture, large nuts, parrot pellets, fruit, and greenfood. Macaws are more adventurous in their feeding habits than many parrots, especially hand-reared youngsters, and can be persuaded to sample a wide range of foods. For them to be comfortable indoors, house them in a spacious, purpose-built flight cage. A pet macaw may be noisy, and certainly needs plenty of attention if it is not to become bored in the home and develop vices, such as feather-plucking. Supervise macaws closely to prevent them from damaging your furniture with their powerful bills.

GREEN-WINGED MACAW
Ara chloroptera

These large parrots range from parts of Central America southward to Bolivia, Paraguay, and possibly Argentina. Young birds can become very táme, and compatible pairs usually nest readily. You must take care when introducing unfamiliar birds to each other as it can take several months before they accept one another. Although their calls are rather loud and raucous, Green-winged Macaws are not usually given to prolonged periods of screeching during the day.

BREEDING Provide a solidly built nestbox for breeding pairs, and house them on their own until the chicks have fledged. A typical clutch contains two or three eggs. Once a pair have started to nest successfully, they usually prove to be reliable breeders, and may do so for decades.

BILL While macaws' bills are particularly strong, they are gentle birds by nature.

FACE The feathering on the face varies greatly from one individual to another.

PLUMAGE The body is a rich, crimson red in both adults and youngsters.

WINGS The green coloration on the wings distinguishes these macaws from the Scarlet Macaw (*A. macao*), which has a noticeable area of yellow plumage on the wings.

FOOD & HOUSING Offer these birds a diet of parrot food, greenfood, and fruit. They also appreciate a regular supply of a variety of nuts. With their powerful bills, they can crack even the hardest nuts, such as Brazils, without any difficulty. Provide robust accommodation, and a supply of branches for gnawing. They are then less likely to use their bills to damage their quarters. Green-winged Macaws are hardy, and can be housed in an outdoor aviary or indoors.

CHARACTERISTICS
LENGTH: 90cm (36in).
AVERAGE LIFESPAN: 50 years.
SEXING: Scientific sexing required; hens may have smaller heads than cock birds.
BREEDING DETAILS: Incubation lasts 28 days; fledging occurs 90 days later.
YOUNG BIRDS: Irises are darker than in adults; some of the feathers running across the bare face are maroon rather than red.

HAHN'S MACAW
Ara nobilis

The smallest of the ara species, Hahn's Macaws are actually more reminiscent of conures than macaws, but the prominent area of largely bare skin that encircles the eyes and extends to the bill leaves no doubt about their correct identification.

Being smaller, they are significantly easier to accommodate than their larger relatives, either in aviaries or as companion birds in the home. Chicks that are hand-reared are delightfully tame, and many learn to talk without too much difficulty.

BILL The bill is black in this subspecies, but brown with just a black tip in the subspecies known as the Noble Macaw. •

FACE The prominent area of bare skin on the face is a feature of all ara macaws. The face is usually white.

HEAD Cocks often have a more rounded, larger head than hens.

PLUMAGE When they are perched, the plumage appears to be mostly green, but the underwing area is red.

FOOD & HOUSING Offer these parrots a diet based on a good quality parrot mix, augmented with a selection of fruit and vegetables cut into manageable pieces. They are fond of dry or soaked millet sprays, and pomegranates in season are also popular. You can house these birds in a solidly built, wooden-framed aviary, but protect the framework properly from their powerful bills. Provide a nestbox throughout the year, as pairs like to roost in them at night, even when not breeding. They are quite hardy once acclimatized, but do not allow them to remain in the open part of the aviary on cold, frosty nights, as their feet may begin to suffer from frostbite.

BREEDING Social by nature, two pairs can be bred successfully in one aviary if their quarters are suitably spacious. However, watch for any signs of aggression, especially when you first introduce them. With a sturdy nestbox, pairs may rear more than one clutch of chicks during the breeding season. Taking away the first chicks as soon as they are feeding on their own encourages the parents to nest again, although it has been known for the first brood to remain in the aviary without any problems. Expect about four eggs per clutch as Hahn's Macaws are more prolific than their larger relatives.

CHARACTERISTICS

LENGTH: 32.5cm (13in).
AVERAGE LIFESPAN: 20 years.
SEXING: Scientific sexing required.
BREEDING DETAILS: Incubation lasts 25 days; fledging occurs 55 days later.
YOUNG BIRDS: Plumage is duller than adults; heads have a little blue plumage; wings have a little red plumage when the chicks fledge, although in some cases this may be absent.

SEVERE MACAW
Ara severa

MASK The bare areas of skin present on the mask are a characteristic of ara macaws.

PLUMAGE The coloration of the body is a dark shade of green. Watch for any bald patches, as this could indicate feather-plucking.

WINGS The wing edges are a prominent shade of red. This coloring is most obvious when the bird is in flight.

The Severe Macaw is one of the dwarf varieties and ranges in the wild from Panama down through most of northern South America. It can be identified by its significantly smaller size and mainly green plumage. They are not common in aviculture, but caring for them is straightforward, provided that you allow for their destructive habits.

CHARACTERISTICS

LENGTH: 40cm (16in).
AVERAGE LIFESPAN: 30 years.
SEXING: Scientific sexing required.
BREEDING DETAILS: Incubation lasts 25 days; fledging occurs 60 days later.
YOUNG BIRDS: Irises are dark.

FOOD & HOUSING Provide Severe Macaws with a good quality parrot food, cereal seeds, fruit, and greenfood, such as spinach beet. These macaws are hardy once acclimatized and can be housed in an outdoor aviary year round.

TAIL The tail is long, and composite in color, like that of other dwarf macaws.

BREEDING Compatible pairs nest quite readily. Provide a sturdy nestbox when a pair looks ready to breed. Watch carefully when a pair breeds for the first time, as inexperienced birds may neglect their chicks, with fatal results. It is better to give the chicks additional food rather than removing them from their parents, in the hope that the parents soon learn what the chicks require.

VARIETY Yellow-naped Macaws *(A. auricollis) are an attractive species from the southern part of South America, and are naturally talented mimics.*

YELLOW-NAPED MACAW COCK

ECLECTUS PARROT
Eclectus roratus

First discovered in the 1500s, the Eclectus Parrot ranges over many islands from Indonesia and New Guinea south to Australia. Up to ten forms of these birds are recognized, with hens showing the greatest variation. The diversity in coloration is so great that the sexes were originally thought to be two separate species.

FOOD & HOUSING Provide parrot food and generous amounts of greenfood, fruit, corn-on-the-cob, and carrot each day. These parrots have a long digestive tract, and therefore need a high amount of dietary fiber. Once acclimatized, they can be housed in aviaries.

HEAD Eclectus Parrots have broad, rounded heads, and a curved bill.

COLLAR The bluish coloration of the collar is also present over much of the hen's abdomen.

PLUMAGE Coloration on hens is reddish with variations depending on each race. The cock is mainly a bright, emerald green.

CHARACTERISTICS
LENGTH: 35cm (14in).
AVERAGE LIFESPAN: 30 years.
SEXING: Cocks are green, and hens reddish.
BREEDING DETAILS: Incubation lasts 30 days; fledging occurs 75 days later.
YOUNG BIRDS: Irises and bills are dark.

BILL The cock's bill does not turn completely orange until three years of age.

MARKINGS Red markings extend down the sides of the cock's body and under the wings.

ECLECTUS PARROT COCK

BREEDING Hens are usually dominant outside the breeding period, and can be quite spiteful toward their mates. Provide a breeding pair with a sturdy nestbox. Eclectus Parrots may nest at almost any time of the year, with two eggs being usual. You can sex the offspring by the color of their plumage before they leave the nest – red birds are hens and green birds are cocks. Eclectus Parrots sometimes have chicks that are all of the same sex, for reasons that are still unclear. One pair at Chester Zoo in England produced one hen out of 30 young birds. Nothing can be done to prevent such occurrences.

CELESTIAL (PACIFIC) PARROTLET
Forpus coelestis

If you only have limited space available, these lively little parrots are an ideal choice as they will normally breed quite well in either cages or a small aviary. A striking blue mutation has recently been seen in Europe and, doubtless, such birds will become more common in the near future as their numbers increase.

CHARACTERISTICS
LENGTH: 12.5cm (5in).
AVERAGE LIFESPAN: 20 years.
SEXING: Hens have duller plumage, and lack the blue coloration of cocks.
BREEDING DETAILS: Incubation lasts 18 days; fledging occurs 42 days later.
YOUNG BIRDS: Duller plumage than in adults; young cocks have smaller blue areas; lower back is bluish green, not blue as in adult cocks.

HEAD The blue markings on the head indicate that this is a cock. Hens' heads are mainly green.

WINGS Cocks can also be identified by the blue feathering on the wings.

BILL Be wary of their bills, as they can inflict a painful nip in spite of their small size.

PLUMAGE Apart from the patches of blue coloration on the head, back and wings, Celestial Parrotlets are predominantly green.

BREEDING Provide a sturdy nestbox for breeding. If you have more than one pair, breeding results may be improved if you have a large gap between their flights, so that the pairs are not distracted. Remove chicks as soon as they are feeding on their own, or their parents are likely to attack them. Celestial Parrotlets generally nest twice in rapid succession. Breeding starts when they are one year old.

FOOD & HOUSING Offer Budgerigar seed mix, or millets and plain canary seed, with some sunflower seeds, greenfood, and fruit. Celestial Parrotlets are hardy, so you can house them in an aviary all year round, but they benefit from having a nestbox to roost in throughout the year. These parrots are aggressive to their own kind, so if you have more than one pair, put up double-wiring between their aviaries and ensure that it stays taut, so that the birds cannot reach each other and injure their neighbors' feet. Alternatively, you can erect a wooden partition so that they cannot see each other.

BLUE-CROWNED HANGING PARROT
Loriculus galgulus

These small parrots originate from south-east Asia, with related forms found on many of the islands to the north to the Philippines. The term "hanging parrot" describes their habit of roosting upside down on a perch.

HEAD The distinctive blue spot on the cocks is much less obvious in hens.

THROAT Red feathering on the throat is normally only seen in cock birds.

FOOD & HOUSING Unlike most other psittacines, these parrots require nectar; put it in a closed container or they will try to bathe in it, and end up with sticky, saturated plumage. Also offer them greenfood, fruit, and smaller cereal seeds, such as plain canary seed and millet sprays. Hanging parrots thrive in a planted aviary and do not inflict great damage on the plants. They need warmth during cold months, but messy feeding habits mean that they are not suited to cages. Gentle birds, they can be housed with finches or small softbills.

BREEDING Provide a Budgerigar-type nestbox in the spring when the birds are ready to breed, and they should soon start to line the interior of the box. If they are housed in a planted aviary, they may slice off some leaves when preparing their nests, carrying these to the nest site tucked among their feathers.

WINGS This golden-brown area on the wings is more pronounced in cocks than hens.

CLAWS Check that the claws do not become overgrown, or the parrot can be caught up as it climbs around its quarters.

VARIETY *Nine different species of hanging parrot are recognized; all have similar care requirements. Vernal Hanging Parrot cocks have white, not brown, irises.*

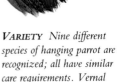

VERNAL HANGING PARROT COCK

CHARACTERISTICS

LENGTH: 12.5cm (5in).

AVERAGE LIFESPAN: 15 years.

SEXING: Hens lack the scarlet throat coloration of cocks, and are duller overall.

BREEDING DETAILS: Incubation lasts 20 days; fledging occurs 35 days later.

YOUNG BIRDS: Similar to adult hens but their plumage is duller.

BLUE-HEADED PARROT
Pionus menstruus

The pionus parrots are a group of eight species, which occur in Central and South America. None of them are gaudily colored, but in the sunshine their subtle hues and the iridescence in their plumage stand out clearly. The Blue-headed Parrot is one of the best-known species in aviculture. Compared to other parrots, they are neither particularly noisy nor destructive. Hand-reared chicks develop into very affectionate companions, and learn to talk well with regular training.

FOOD & HOUSING A standard parrot mix, with fruit and greenfood, keeps these parrots in good health. Also provide grit and cuttlefish bone. They can be housed outdoors year round but they need a solid aviary that will withstand their gnawing. When selecting pionus parrots, pay particular attention to their breathing. They are susceptible to the fungal disease aspergillosis. Labored or noisy breathing and weight loss are symptoms of this disease.

BREEDING Locate these birds' nestbox in a quiet part of the aviary to minimize any unnecessary disturbance, especially around hatching time, since nervous pairs sometimes attack their chicks if they are upset during this period.

HEAD The rich blue coloration on the head indicates that this is a mature cock. Youngsters' heads are greener.

EYE-RING Watch for swelling of the eye-ring, as this is often linked to a nasal blockage.

BILL The bill varies in color, and may be flaky through wear, though this need not be a cause for concern.

BODY Blue-headed Parrots have vivid contrasting coloration on the body.

CHARACTERISTICS
LENGTH: 27.5cm (11in).
AVERAGE LIFESPAN: 25 years.
SEXING: Scientific sexing required.
BREEDING DETAILS: Incubation lasts 26 days; fledging occurs 70 days later.
YOUNG BIRDS: Not as blue.

SENEGAL PARROT
Poicephalus senegalus

The poicephalid parrots originate in Africa, where nine species can be found. The Senegal Parrot is the commonest in aviculture, and is an attractive aviary occupant, although adult birds can be rather nervous. They are not noisy, but they attack the aviary woodwork on occasion, especially just prior to the breeding period. Individuals may differ in the depth of their yellowish orange plumage, but they cannot be sexed reliably on this basis.

FOOD & HOUSING Offer Senegal Parrots a mixture of parrot food, small cereal seeds, greenfood, and fruit. Peanuts are a favorite with these birds. Like most other parrots, Senegal Parrots are quite hardy once properly acclimatized, but they must have adequate protection against wet and cold weather. A dry, snug shelter in their aviary will keep them comfortable. House pairs separately to prevent any bickering.

EYES The bright yellow eyes provide an easy means of identifying adult birds.

BREAST The extent of green plumage on the breast varies from bird to bird.

FEET The dark feet have sharp claws. As a result, their grip is quite painful.

CHARACTERISTICS

LENGTH: 25cm (10in).
AVERAGE LIFESPAN: 30 years.
SEXING: Scientific sexing required.
BREEDING DETAILS: Incubation lasts 28 days; fledging occurs 85 days later.
YOUNG BIRDS: Irises are dark.

BREEDING These parrots require a fairly deep nestbox, located in a darkened corner of the aviary. Some pairs choose to nest outdoors, and this creates problems during cold weather. You may need to remove the eggs or chicks if they risk getting chilled. Hand-raised chicks can develop into very tame and confiding pets, and may even learn a few words.

MEYER'S PARROT COCK

VARIETIES Meyer's Parrot (P. meyeri) comes in various forms, which differ slightly in their coloration.

AFRICAN GRAY PARROT
Psittacus erithacus

As one of the best-known and most talented of the parrots kept as pets, the African Gray has been bred in ever-increasing numbers during recent years. If you are seeking a pet bird this means that a good choice of hand-raised birds is usually available. The African Gray Parrot should develop into a superb companion for you, although it may take six months after you acquire it before it starts talking.

FOOD & HOUSING Offer a good-quality parrot mix, augmented with pellets, fruit, and greenfood. Gray Parrots are not particularly noisy, so you can keep them in an aviary or indoors. However, do not expect birds acquired as adults to become tame, especially in aviary surroundings. If you live in a temperate climate, and your parrot is not used to being outside over winter, bring it into a flight in a heated birdroom for the first winter.

CHARACTERISTICS
LENGTH: *32.5cm (13in).*
AVERAGE LIFESPAN: *50 years.*
SEXING: *Scientific sexing required.*
BREEDING DETAILS: *Incubation lasts 29 days; fledging occurs 90 days later.*
YOUNG BIRDS: *Irises are dark.*

BREEDING Provide pairs with a sturdy nestbox. Compatibility is important in breeding African Gray Parrots. Obtain a pair that have nested before, or that are spending time together and preening each other. Cocks are sometimes recognizable by their darker backs, but this can also denote the bird's origins. It is best to house pairs separately during the breeding season.

PLUMAGE The shade of gray varies from pale to dark. Birds with the lightest color are known as "silvers."

EYES The adult's yellow eye coloration distinguishes it from the young bird's dark eye coloration.

TAIL African Gray Parrots always have red tails, except in the Timneh race *(P. e. timneh)*, which is distinguished by its dull maroon-colored tails.

GREEN-NAPED LORIKEET
Trichoglossus haematodus

The many different forms of Green-naped Lorikeet vary slightly in their coloration. Like other lories and lorikeets they originate from islands off the coast of Asia, as far south as Australia. Pairs are usually eager to nest, and prolific.

FOOD & HOUSING Offer Green-naped Lorikeets a nectar solution or dry nectar diet. Also offer them fruit, such as diced apple and grapes, plus some greenfood and seed, such as soaked millet sprays. If you adjust their diet, do so slowly, to minimize disturbances to their digestive tract. You can house them outdoors year round once they are acclimatized. Make sure that the accommodation for these and other nectar-feeding parrots is easy to clean, because they have messy feeding habits, and liquid droppings. If you keep the birds indoors, offer them bathing facilities each day.

BREEDING Provide a sturdy nestbox and remove the chicks once they are feeding independently. Some pairs pluck their offspring, but the feathers soon regrow once the chicks are housed on their own and are not prone to attacks by their parents.

VARIETIES *Goldie's Lorikeet (Trichoglossus goldiei) is just 19cm (7in) long, making it ideal for the smaller aviary. It may need extra heat in cold weather.*

NECK The green area of plumage at the side of the neck is a characteristic of this species.

BODY The barring pattern on the body varies according to the race.

ABDOMEN The subtly colored abdomen contrasts well with the brighter coloration of the breast.

TAIL The tail is long and the feathers are pointed, a characteristic of lorikeets.

GOLDIE'S LORIKEET COCK

CHARACTERISTICS

LENGTH: 20cm (8in).
AVERAGE LIFESPAN: 25 years.
SEXING: Scientific sexing required.
BREEDING DETAILS: Incubation lasts 25 days; fledging occurs 70 days later.
YOUNG BIRDS: Similar to adults, but they can usually be identified by their darker bills.

CHATTERING LORY
Lorius garrulus

Stunningly attractive, these colorful birds prove lively and inquisitive, and soon become tame even when housed in an aviary. The only drawback with Chattering Lories is their loud calls. Pairs normally nest quite readily, as is the case with most brush-tongued parrots, and prove to be good parents.

BREEDING Provide a sturdy nestbox as these birds are rather destructive. Also provide plenty of softwood battening for them to whittle into a nest lining, which will absorb the young birds' liquid droppings. If the interior of the nestbox becomes very wet, add to this or replace it with coarse shavings from a pet store. To minimize disturbance, fix the box so it is easy to clean.

> ## CHARACTERISTICS
> *LENGTH: 30cm (12in).*
> *AVERAGE LIFESPAN: 25 years.*
> *SEXING: Scientific sexing required.*
> *BREEDING DETAILS: Incubation lasts 28 days; fledging occurs 80 days later.*
> *YOUNG BIRDS: Similar to adults in appearance; bills and irises are dark.*

EYE-RING A bare area of grayish-white skin surrounds the eyes, but is separated from the cere by feathering.

BILL Mainly orange in adults, but young birds have dark markings extending down to the tip of the bill.

BACK The yellow patch on the back identifies this bird as belonging to the Yellow-backed race *(L.g. flavopalliatus)*.

WINGS The green coloration on the wings has a slight iridescence.

FEET The feet and claws are gray in Chattering Lories.

FOOD & HOUSING
Chattering Lories need a fresh solution of nectar once or twice a day, always in an enclosed drinker, along with fruit, greenfood, and a little seed. They may sample mealworms, especially when there are chicks in the nest. Also provide grit, although they may take it only rarely. They are hardy birds. Chattering Lories, and other lories of similar size, need a flight about 3.7m (12ft) in length. Try not to house pairs in adjoining aviaries, as they often squabble relentlessly. Check that the perches do not become sticky with nectar and droppings; wash or replace them as necessary. The birds gnaw their perches to keep their bills trim.

DUIVENBODE'S LORY
Chalcopsitta duivenbodei

The coloration of this lory is very unusual, because few parrots are predominantly brown. When in flight, the brilliant yellow plumage under the wings is clearly visible, and contrasts strikingly with the body feathering. Duivenbode's Lory has never ranked among the best-known species in aviculture, but, recently, it has become increasingly common, as more pairs breed.

FOOD & HOUSING Duivenbode's Lories need nectar, fruit, greenfood, and a limited amount of seed. They are relatively easy birds to care for, but can become aggressive when nesting. House them in a solidly built aviary so that their strong bills cannot do too much damage. They are hardy so can stay outdoors year round.

BREEDING Provide pairs with a nestbox. Pairs may decide to breed during the colder months of the year, with a reduced chance of success. Have an incubator and brooder available.

FACE The color of the face can vary between individuals.

NECK The feathers on the neck taper to points, which the bird can raise slightly, like hackles, when displaying, or showing aggression.

CHARACTERISTICS
LENGTH: 32cm (12½in).
AVERAGE LIFESPAN: 20 years.
SEXING: Scientific sexing required.
BREEDING DETAILS: Incubation lasts 24 days; fledging occurs 80 days later.
YOUNG BIRDS: Plumage is duller than adults' plumage; white skin encircles the eyes.

FEET Grasping with its feet, this species hops and struts along its perch.

TAIL Yellow tail markings are evident.

UMBRELLA COCKATOO
Cacatua alba

Sometimes also called the Great White Cockatoo, these majestic birds are truly spectacular when kept in spacious aviary surroundings. However, you should bear in mind that they do have quite loud and penetrating calls, which could lead to complaints from near neighbors. The Umbrella Cockatoo can be found on the northern and central Moluccan islands of Indonesia and ranks among the largest of the cockatoos.

FOOD & HOUSING Offer cockatoos a diet of good quality parrot mixture, fruit, greenfood, and invertebrates, such as mealworms. These birds need a strong aviary, which offers spacious surroundings and is able to resist their powerful bills. Maintain a constant supply of soft wood pieces in the bottom of the nestbox to deflect the birds' attention away from the structure of the nestbox itself. Once acclimatized, these birds are hardy and stay outdoors year round.

BREEDING Provide a breeding pair with a sturdy nestbox. Adult birds often tend to be nervous, so try to leave them alone as much as possible when they are breeding. Otherwise, they may neglect or even attack their chicks. Hand-raised Umbrella Cockatoos are delightful birds, but they need constant attention, and tend to become rather aggressive once they mature.

CREST The crest is white, like the rest of the body, but broad in shape, giving rise to the name of Umbrella Cockatoo.

EYE-RING The eye-ring is a bare area of white skin.

PLUMAGE The body is completely white, with slight traces of yellow only apparent on the lower surfaces of the flight and tail feathers.

FEET The grayish coloration of the feet and bill contrasts notably with the plumage.

CHARACTERISTICS

LENGTH: 30cm (12in).

AVERAGE LIFESPAN: 40 years.

SEXING: The eye coloration of hens is a dark reddish brown.

BREEDING DETAILS: Incubation lasts 28 days; fledging occurs 80 days later.

YOUNG BIRDS: Similar to adults, but eyes are grayer and the bill is whitish.

LESSER SULFUR-CRESTED COCKATOO
Cacatua sulphurea

Found on various Indonesian islands, it is not surprising that several distinctive forms of this cockatoo have evolved, the most recognizable being the Citron-crested Cockatoo (*C. s. citrinocristata*). These and other cockatoos can prove to be rather highly strung, but young birds should develop into good companions. When purchasing cockatoos, remember that the disease PBFD is closely associated with them. You should avoid purchasing a bird from any group where one or more of the birds displays the characteristic signs of this infection, such as loss of feathers and abnormalities of the bill. Even starting your collection with hand-reared chicks is not entirely safe, as the virus spreads in the rearing room. Work to produce a vaccine is now well-advanced, however, so this problem could soon be virtually eliminated.

CREST The orange feathering on the crest identifies this bird as the Citron-crested Cockatoo, from the Indonesian island of Sumba.

CHEEKS This variety has orange ear coverts. The crest and coverts are yellow in other races of the Lesser Sulfur-crested.

HEAD DETAIL

CREST When resting, the crests are laid back. They only raise the crest when excited or alarmed. •

BREEDING If you want to breed cockatoos successfully, obtain a compatible pair. Cocks, otherwise, can suddenly turn on prospective mates with great savagery. The young may also be attacked once they have left the nestbox, so you should remove them from the aviary as soon as possible, especially if there are any signs of aggression.

LESSER SULFUR-CRESTED COCKATOO COCK

NORMAL FORM The Lesser Sulfur-crested Cockatoo, often abbreviated to "L.S.C.," has yellow feathering on its crest and cheeks; otherwise it is mainly white.

FOOD & HOUSING Offer these cockatoos parrot food, pellets, fruit, and greenfood, although some of this may be spurned, as their eating habits are conservative. These birds are hardy. House them in a strong, spacious aviary and protect woodwork from their bills.

CHARACTERISTICS
LENGTH: 30cm (12in).
AVERAGE LIFESPAN: 40 years.
SEXING: Cocks invariably have darker eyes than hens.
BREEDING DETAILS: Incubation lasts 28 days; fledging occurs 70 days later.
YOUNG BIRDS: Similar to adults; the lores are pink.

GOFFIN'S COCKATOO
Cacatua goffini

These Indonesian cockatoos became available to aviculturists in the 1970s, at the time when their native islands were cleared for timber. They have a rather limited area of distribution, being confined just to the Tenimber islands. With the widespread destruction of their habitat, their future is uncertain. Therefore, every effort should be made to breed them.

BREEDING A robust nestbox is essential for breeding pairs, otherwise the birds could destroy the box, which would result in the loss of eggs and possibly even chicks. It is advisable to keep a discreet watch on young birds to ensure that they are being adequately fed in the nest.

CREST The white crest is relatively small and inconspicuous in this particular species. •

EYE Sexing these cockatoos on their iris coloration is possible but difficult; the cock's is black, and the hen's a • dark reddish brown.

LORES The pink of the lores varies in depth between birds. It is not an indication • of the gender.

FOOD & HOUSING A standard parrot mixture, with added fruit and greenfood suits these birds well, although some may be rather conservative in their feeding habits. Persevere, persuading them to take a varied diet, and use a supplement to augment their food intake. This species is destructive and is adept at stripping mesh from aviary framework and using the bill to extract netting staples, so inspect their quarters regularly. When possible, place staples out of their reach, as they can cause injury if swallowed. Goffin's Cockatoos are hardy once they are properly acclimatized.

• **PLUMAGE** These birds should have dense, sleek plumage. Check for any signs of PBFD prior to purchase.

CHARACTERISTICS
LENGTH: 30cm (12in).
AVERAGE LIFESPAN: 40 years.
SEXING: Cocks have darker irises.
BREEDING DETAILS: Incubation lasts 28 days; fledging occurs 70 days later.
YOUNG BIRDS: Lack salmon-pink lores.

GALAH COCKATOO (ROSEATE COCKATOO)
Eolophus roseicapillus

With a population that numbers in the hundreds of millions, this cockatoo is one of Australia's commonest birds. Yet it is one of the more costly cockatoos in aviculture, because the numbers available for captive-breeding outside Australia are quite small. However, Galah Cockatoos tend to be more prolific in captivity than other cockatoos.

BREEDING Some pairs like to use material such as old millet sprays as a lining in their nestbox. They may lay up to five eggs in a clutch. Chicks grow and develop quite rapidly, compared with the offspring of other cockatoos, and a pair may produce two clutches of chicks in a season. You should remove the first round of youngsters once they are feeding themselves, as they may be attacked otherwise.

CHARACTERISTICS
LENGTH: 35cm (14in).
AVERAGE LIFESPAN: 40 years.
SEXING: Cocks have darker eyes; hens have reddish brown irises.
BREEDING DETAILS: Incubation lasts 25 days; fledging occurs 50 days later.
YOUNG BIRDS: Irises are dark gray.

CREST The whitish crest is broad and quite short.

EYES The eyes provide a means of sexing these birds. The blackish eye here indicates a cock bird.

WINGS The depth of gray coloration on the wings varies from bird to bird. In some cases, it can be almost white.

FOOD & HOUSING Diet is very important with these birds, because they are prone to fatty tumors called lipomas. Offer them a low-fat diet, concentrating on cereal seeds, augmented with some sunflower, as well as fruit and greenfood. A good-sized aviary with plenty of flying space gives these hardy birds the opportunity to exercise. Also offer plenty of fresh branches for them to gnaw. They are not especially destructive birds, but branches should divert attention away from the aviary structure.

BREAST The pinkish red plumage of the breast is sometimes flecked with gray feathering.

CHAPTER THREE

PRACTICAL
MATTERS

BLACK-CAPPED LORY *(above) These colorful birds nest readily and they are also playful by nature. But, because of their dietary needs, they can be rather messy, especially when housed indoors.*

PEACH-FACED LOVEBIRDS *(left) These are just two of the many color forms of the Peach-faced Lovebird now being bred. Lovebirds generally are popular aviary occupants, being quiet and not especially destructive when housed in a garden aviary.*

Choosing a Bird

Birds are naturally lively and alert, so any that appear dull and unresponsive are unlikely to be in good health. Young birds tend to be less active than adults, and they may perch with their feathering slightly ruffled. This is not necessarily a cause for concern, although in older birds it may indicate illness.

── The Points To Consider ──

Although it is difficult to gain an accurate impression of a bird's overall state of health simply by observing it, you can look for a number of points. Before purchasing a bird, check its head, plumage, and feet. Starting with the head, check that the nostrils are clear and of even size. Blocked nostrils may indicate a localized infection, perhaps caused by mycoplasmas. These microorganisms are present in the upper part of the respiratory tract and normally cause few problems. If the bird is stressed, however, they can cause breathing difficulties. In a long-standing infection, the affected nostril can erode and the entrance hole is then likely to become enlarged.

In more extreme cases, the infection will affect the sinuses and cause the area around the eyes to become swollen. This is most likely to occur in Amazon parrots, and can be linked to a vitamin A deficiency. Check the eyes for any sign of discharge. In the case of red-eyed birds, such as lutino Budgerigars, inspect the eye more closely, since these birds are more prone to cataracts and blindness than dark-eyed individuals.

Breathing

You will also need to check a bird's breathing. Listen for any signs of wheezing, which could be indicative of a range of problems from parasites to a fungal disease. Certain species of bird are more vulnerable than others. The Gouldian Finch, for example, suffers from debilitating air-sac mites. You can assess the bird's breathing by noting its tail movements, which should be barely perceptible when the bird is resting.

It is also important to check the bill for any deformities. Young Budgerigars may suffer from an undershot upper bill – the upper part curves round and, instead of fitting over the lower bill, tucks into it. Since there is no cutting surface, the lower bill grows at an abnormal angle. With such a bird, you will have to cut the bill from time to time if it is to eat without difficulty.

Overgrowth of the top bill is more common, and, in parrots, often results from a lack of gnawing opportunities. Some species, such as brotogeris parakeets and pet Budgerigars, are especially susceptible. By providing suitable wood for the birds to gnaw, you can often correct the problem without cutting the bill. Once you start cutting, the bill grows at a faster rate and therefore needs more frequent trimming.

Scaly face mites, a common parasitic problem, may be evident on the bill of some Budgerigars. Check for these mites before making a purchase, as they spread rapidly within a collection of birds. Early signs of infection are usually apparent across the upper bill as small, snail-like tracks, which scar this area. In more severe cases, you will see small swellings at the sides of the bill and around the eyes.

IRIS COLORATION IN YOUNG BIRD

IRIS COLORATION Note the dark iris, which distinguishes this young African Gray Parrot from its parent below. A similar distinction exists in other species, and this is the clearest indication of age.

IRIS COLORATION IN 4-YEAR-OLD BIRD

Provided there is no evident distortion of the bill, these mites are easy to eliminate, but you will need to keep affected birds on their own for a month or possibly more. The infection responsible for scaly face may also spread to the legs, which may often result in swelling under the rings. However, this condition is also treatable.

PLUMAGE

The condition of a bird's feathering is generally not that important. Recently imported birds may have slightly tatty plumage, but any damaged feathers will be replaced when they next molt.

A HEALTHY PARROT The alert demeanor of this Yellow-fronted Amazon Parrot is quite apparent. Its clear nostrils, bright eyes, and sleek plumage are all indications of this bird's healthy condition.

NOSTRILS Generally unfeathered and of an even size, the nostrils should normally be unblocked and free from discharge. •

GENERAL ALERTNESS A healthy bird should respond when you are close to it. •

PLUMAGE The plumage should be glossy, with no bald patches or areas of stunted growth. •

EYES The eyes should normally be bright, and there should be no signs of swelling or discharge around the eyes or lids.

BILL The top and lower bill should meet, with no signs of deviation. •

BILL DEFORMITIES Undershot bills are often related to poor nest hygiene, while the upper bill can become overgrown due to the lack of opportunity to gnaw branches. Regular trimming may be necessary in both cases. Bill deformities are most common in Budgerigars.

UNDERSHOT BILL IN BUDGIE

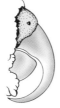

OVERGROWN UPPER BILL IN BUDGIE

The plumage of parrots, cockatoos and Budgerigars is of more significance, however. Cockatoos are susceptible to a progressively debilitating and ultimately fatal condition known as psittacine beak and feather disease (PBFD). Although PBFD has been reported in a wide variety of psittacines, it has been most commonly found in cockatoos.

The effects of French molt, a feather ailment associated with Budgerigars, are less severe, but this virus can, like PBFD, devastate a breeding stud. The symptoms become apparent in birds when they are about five weeks old. The flight and tail feathers are liable to be shed, although the extent of feather loss is variable. Always check the flight feathers for evidence of French molt by holding the wing open. Any gaps here in youngsters are likely to indicate the disease; in older birds, traces of dried blood in the feather shafts are highly suggestive of past infection.

In some cases, feather loss is likely to be the result of self-mutilation.

PBFD

Affected birds have stunted and twisted feathers, with bald areas developing over their bodies. In the latter stages, the tissue of the bill and claws is also affected. PBFD is now known to be caused by a virus, and research toward developing a vaccine is still continuing. At present there is no cure, and afflicted birds die within a year or so, often as the result of a secondary bacterial infection.

Vasa Parrot with PBFD

When new plumage develops, the bird pulls it out as it starts to emerge through the skin. It is unwise to purchase any parrots that are removing feathers because this behavior is very difficult to prevent once it is established. Feather-plucking in finches is less of a problem, however, and often results from overcrowded conditions.

Leg Rings

Aluminum rings are often used on canaries and Budgerigars. If the ring is a closed band it guarantees the bird's age, because it can be applied to chicks only for a short period while the foot is small enough for the band to be slid over the toes.

Stainless-steel bands are used for larger parrots, as they can cut through aluminum with their bills. Split celluloid rings are used on canaries and finches, frequently

Signs of Illness
Huddled-up, with eyes closed, this Bengalese Finch is clearly sick.

for identification purposes – for example, rings can be used to identify a pair. They are simply clipped in place around the leg, and provide no guarantee of age.

TOES AND CLAWS

It is important to check the toes for slipped claws, since this can lead to difficulties in perching. Canaries normally tend to grip with three toes directly forward and one behind the perch. In some cases, however, the hind toe is incorrectly positioned and slides over the top of the perch. Problems during mating are likely to result, because the bird will be less able to support its own weight, or that of its partner. Parrots and Budgerigars have quite a different perching arrangement, with two toes in front and two behind the perch. As a result, they are less prone to this complaint.

You should also check the bird's claws. If they are overgrown, you will need to cut them back. Nuns and weavers typically have long, straggling claws, which need a regular manicure, and those of canaries and Budgerigars may also need trimming.

Once you have carefully looked at a bird, ask the vendor to catch it. Check the bird's breastbone, which runs in the midline from the lower part of the chest to the abdomen. Normally it should be only just noticeable, with the pectoral muscles present on either side. In a bird in poor condition, muscle-wasting will soon be apparent here, and cause the breastbone to become prominent.

WEIGHT LOSS

If you are able to place your fingers on either side of the keel, this is a clear sign of weight loss. It may simply be that the bird has not been receiving an adequate diet. Some softbills, for example, tend to eat only fruit, which has little protein or fat content. Alternatively, there may be a more sinister reason – perhaps the presence of a chronic disease such as aspergillosis. This fungal infection, a particular problem with softbills, often shows few, if any, clinical signs until it is well advanced. Tumors in Budgerigars may also first be suggested by weight loss across the breastbone. As a final check, it is also worthwhile looking at the plumage around the vent for any staining. Fecal deposits here indicate a digestive upset.

TRIMMING CLAWS

Claws can grow in peculiar ways. Regular trimming with nail clippers may be necessary to prevent birds becoming caught up in their quarters. You should carry this out with a strong pair of clippers, in good light, having always located the blood supply first.

NORMAL CLAW

CURLED CLAW

SPINDLY CLAW   **HOOKED CLAW**

OLD BIRDS
Heavy scaling on the legs can indicate old age, and this tanager is over 18 years old.

·MAKING A CHOICE·

The first place to look for birds is at your local pet store. Here you will also be able to find much, if not all, of the equipment you need for their care. Some stores specialize in birds, but the vast majority only have a selection of canaries or young Budgerigars. You will probably find a wider choice during the summer months, since this is the peak time for breeding.

Alternatively, a specialist bird farm may be located near you, where you will find a larger number of species. This is often a better option if you are seeking breeding pairs, because they will have a wider choice. In the case of parrots, you are also more likely to obtain a compatible pair.

WHAT TO LOOK FOR

Watch the birds closely as they move about in a group. Notice if some birds show clear signs of pair-bonding, such as following each other around their quarters,

SELECTING STOCK Before selecting your stock, watch a group of birds carefully. Check physical appearance, and for any pairs that might prove to be compatible.

sitting close together, and preening each other. Always allow yourself plenty of time when buying birds. Never be tempted to rush into a purchase – it could prove disastrous in the long term.

Many bird farms offer sexed pairs, and can arrange confirmation of the gender of birds of your choice for a fee. With the safe and reliable sexing methods that are now available, it is most unwise to purchase expensive birds without such a guarantee.

Hand-reared chicks are also generally available from such sources, although you can contact breeders directly through the advertisement columns of the various bird-keeping publications. It is generally much more satisfactory to obtain a young bird, since it should settle well without problems. An older parrot may prove shy, and it can take you months to win its confidence.

If you are seeking exhibition stock, make your purchase direct from breeders. In this way you will be certain of obtaining reliable advice about the origins of the birds, and the pairings that are most likely to yield quality offspring. The majority of exhibitors are keen to assist newcomers to the fancy, although you may have to be patient to obtain precisely the stock you want. The best time to purchase birds is just after the end of the breeding season, since most fanciers retain some surplus stock until then.

A WORD OF WARNING

Always beware of "bargain" offers of pet parrots. These individuals may turn out to be adult birds that have not settled in the home. They may also be susceptible to feather-plucking, a habit that is difficult to correct once it has become established. Such birds are still suitable for breeding, although feather-plucked birds need careful acclimatization until their plumage has regrown.

EARLY CARE

You can buy birds without seeing them first, and then have them sent to your home by road, rail, or air. It is always best, however, to travel to the breeder or supplier in order to make your own choice. This applies particularly to exhibition birds, because you are the only one who can judge which birds will make the best contribution to your breeding program.

INTRODUCING NEW ARRIVALS

When you intend to purchase birds, go prepared with a container in which to bring them home. A cage may seem an obvious choice, but most birds dislike traveling in the open. A darkened box is a better option.

For small, nondestructive species, such as canaries, a cardboard box is ideal. Punch airholes in the lid and at the top of the sides, and take rubber bands and tape to hold the lid in place. In the case of Budgerigars and parrots, you will need something more substantial, such as a sturdy plywood box.

Transport boxes need to be relatively small so that the birds cannot injure themselves by attempting to fly. They should settle down quietly in these, as they do when they are in a nestbox. It is safest to move them individually, otherwise there is every chance that they will start squabbling in such a confined space.

For a journey lasting just a few hours, no food is usually necessary. However, nectivores, especially hummingbirds, should have a feeder and a convenient perch. For finches and parrots, simply sprinkle some seed on the floor of the box. Fruit can be a good source of water during a journey. However, you

should avoid mushy varieties. The birds will simply trample them underfoot and make a mess of their plumage as a result.

On the way home, do not stop more than necessary, and never place birds in the car trunk, where there may be a shortage of air, and exhaust fumes may penetrate into the compartment. It is much safer to keep the carrying boxes on the floor inside the car. Here they should be relatively cool, and out of both direct sunlight and drafts.

TRANSPORTING BIRDS

Use a suitable container for transporting birds, one with plenty of airholes. A cardboard box is suitable for small, nondestructive birds, and a plywood box for larger species. This should have a strong base and a hinged lid that opens downward, allowing you easy access. A small bolt, or hasp and padlock, fitted on the top will prevent the door from opening accidentally during the journey; this could have devastating consequences if the bird escapes when you are driving. If you have to stop on the way home, remember that on a hot day the temperature inside a car can rise to fatal levels for a bird in a few minutes. If in doubt, never leave the bird in the car.

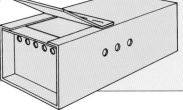

TRAVELING BOX *This type of box is ideal for many bird species, except parrots, which may gnaw their way out.*

SETTLING IN

Try to prepare for the arrival of new birds as much as possible in advance. Ensure that their quarters are clean and equipped with perches. It helps, especially with nectar-feeding parrots and all softbills, if you have a diet sheet from their previous keeper so that you can give them the same food. Recently, probiotic compounds have become popular with bird-keepers to minimize the stress of transportation.

ISOLATING NEW BIRDS

Even if you are introducing just one new bird alongside existing stock, do not be tempted to omit a period of isolation for the newcomer. Although the bird may look

INTRODUCING BIRDS Watch for signs of aggression when introducing birds.

healthy at the time of purchase, it could be incubating a disease that will become apparent after the stress of the journey. You also need to be certain that the new bird is eating properly; transferred straight away to an aviary with other birds, it may be bullied and not be able to feed adequately. A two-week isolation period will also allow you to carry out any routine treatment against external and internal parasites that may be required.

You should treat Australian parakeets, in particular, for roundworms. Lories and lorikeets are susceptible to tapeworms; it should be possible to diagnose an infection of this type from a fecal sample. Your

veterinarian will be able to advise you on this and any necessary subsequent treatment. However, for this purpose, a sample of droppings from each bird is usually required.

INTEGRATING NEWCOMERS

Once past their isolation period, you can release birds into the aviary, but only when you are going to be at home for a couple of days so that you can check on them regularly. This is especially important when adding newcomers to an existing group, as bullying may be a problem. Enclose newcomers in the shelter for a day or so to allow them to find their food and water. Then, when they venture into the flight, they are likely to return to the shelter without any hesitation.

You need to take particular care if you add new birds during the breeding season, as established birds are more likely to be belligerent. To minimize the chances of aggression, take all the existing birds out of the aviary beforehand for a few days. When you return all the birds to the aviary together, the original occupants should have lost their territorial advantage.

Take equal care when introducing a new pet parrot into the home with an already established individual. Parrots can be jealous of other pets, such as dogs, as well as other birds. After a period of isolation, place the newcomer's cage close to the established bird, yet taking care that they cannot reach each other through the bars. Budgerigars and Cockatiels are more amenable than parrots, and usually accept the company of another of their own kind without any problems.

·THE TAMING PROCESS·

One of the main benefits of purchasing parrot chicks that have been hand-raised is that they have little fear of people. Budgerigar chicks, whose nestboxes are cleaned regularly, are similarly accustomed to human attention.

Working with a naturally tame bird is simply a matter of reinforcing this bond. Allow them time to settle down for a day or so, and then encourage them to eat by offering fruit or greenfood by hand.

Accessibility to the bird's quarters is useful during the training period. Ideally, the entire front of the unit should lift off, which is another advantage of purchasing a sectional flight cage rather than a conventional parrot cage (see page 136).

Once the parrot is reasonably tame, you should allow it out of its cage on a regular basis, although you must be present to supervise its movements. Arrange the room in such a way that the safety of your pet is ensured (see page 133).

Do not allow your parrot out of its cage when you are eating, or it is likely to make a nuisance of itself at the dinner table. At first it may be a novelty to have your parrot

---

> ### TAMING YOUR BIRD
>
> • *Win your pet's confidence by offering it fruit to eat from your hand.*
> • *Wear gloves initially with parrots. They may nip, and their claws can be sharp.*
> • *All birds appreciate a routine, so make a point of carrying out training at regular times.*
> • *Persevere with training sessions for five minutes at a time before allowing the bird to rest.*

---

stealing peas from your plate, but this could quickly become a problem. Later, if the parrot does not receive a snack when the family is eating, it may become troublesome. There is also the risk that it could take unsuitable fatty or salty food. Retrieving food from a determined parrot is a difficult task!

Parrots can learn a wide variety of skills. Some seem to enjoy riding on miniature roller skates and similar toys. In all cases, though, be patient with your pet, and do not try to punish it in any way if it fails to respond as you would wish it to. Apart from anything else, this will harm the established bond between you. With patience and kindness, you can build a strong rapport with a tame parrot.

When training parrots, it is also a good idea to involve the whole family. One hopes a parrot will learn to react to children. You should, however, always supervise such a situation closely. Introducing a second parrot later is also a good idea. It will learn by example from the established bird, and this will make the task of training it easier.

FORMING A BOND *Tame parrots enjoy having the back of their necks tickled. This is where parrots would normally preen each other. Once a parrot allows you to stroke it here, you know that it has accepted you.*

·Teaching Your Bird to Talk·

The talking abilities of birds differ significantly, even between individuals of the same species. The African Gray Parrot is accepted as the best natural mimic of all the parrots, but mynah birds tend to have better diction and can be taught to whistle tunes with great clarity. It is also worth bearing in mind that birds generally find it easier to mimic the voice of a woman or a child rather than a man's. Hand-raised parrots that are accustomed to the sound of human speech are likely to start talking much earlier than parent-reared offspring. But there really is no shortcut to persuading a bird to start to talk – it is essentially a matter of patience and repetition. The more time that you can devote to teaching the bird, the more likely it is to learn quickly.

First Steps

The key is breaking sentences and words down into short sections. Once the bird can mimic the first part successfully, you can continue with the next, adding it on to the first and thus building up the word, sentence, or rhyme.

When teaching a bird to talk, ensure that the surroundings are quiet. You can have several teaching sessions each day, starting when you first enter the room where the bird is kept. If you greet your bird each

Talking Birds (above) The ability of many birds to mimic human speech, and other sounds, has fascinated and shocked people down the centuries. Patience and a good teacher are key elements in producing a good talker, as shown in this Victorian illustration.

Talented Talker (right) The victorious Sparkie Williams, with a trophy he won for his talking skills. Some Budgies are better mimics than others.

ENCOURAGING SPEECH

• *Ensure that the surrounding environment is quiet, in order to maintain its attention.*

• *Have several teaching sessions each day, starting first thing in the morning when you enter the room in which the bird is kept.*

• *Encourage the bird to learn its name and its address or telephone number. This can be invaluable if a bird escapes, or is stolen.*

• *Repeat words or phrases constantly and clearly, over a period of about five minutes a session, sitting close to the cage in order to maintain the bird's attention.*

• *Do not rush the bird, otherwise it is likely to become confused, which will only delay the learning process.*

• *Prepare a cassette tape, which contains chosen words and phrases, and play it to the bird as an auxiliary training method. The first signs of success may be when a word or parts of phrases start to appear in the bird's normal chatter. You should then continue emphasizing these words until the bird is able to repeat them readily.*

to retain the sound or word. Another possibility is to cover the cage immediately after hearing the unwanted utterance. The bird will soon come to associate being plunged into darkness with its vocalization. Only cover the cage for about five minutes; a longer period serves no useful purpose.

There is no doubt that one parrot can learn words from another, but if you start off with two birds, it may be more difficult to persuade them to start talking in the first instance. They will prefer to mimic their own natural calls. For training purposes, you may need to use a cassette tape as a regular back-up to reinforce your own training sessions with them. It is also likely to be difficult to persuade an adult bird to start talking, but an established talking bird may add to its vocabulary throughout its life. It is now possible to purchase various cassette tapes that are specifically intended to assist you in teaching your bird to talk. These provide a useful back-up to your sessions, and, of course, you can prepare similar tapes of your own.

TRAINING A PARROT TO TALK No other pet can respond in the same way as a parrot. They make great companions and live for many years.

morning with the same phrase, it will probably soon respond in a similar manner. Later in the day, encourage the bird to repeat its name and its address or telephone number. This is vital if the bird escapes or is stolen. Repeat the details clearly over about a five-minute period, sitting close to the cage. Do not be in a hurry to rush the bird, otherwise it may become confused.

Some repetitive household sounds may be mimicked by birds with no training. A ringing telephone is a typical example, and the bird's accurate intonation may cause you to come running. This can become quite a problem, as may a bird that persistently swears. It is difficult to correct such behavior, but by withdrawing the stimulus of repetition, the bird is less likely

⸺· TOYS FOR YOUR BIRD ·⸺

It is generally only parrot species and, to a lesser extent, mynahs that benefit from toys in their environment. In the past, most toys have been made for Budgerigars.

Many people provide a mirror for a Budgerigar housed on its own, which provides a measure of companionship for these highly social birds. However, problems sometimes arise when a Budgerigar persistently feeds its reflection and attempts to mate with it. If you notice your pet spending an abnormal amount of time playing with its reflection, remove the mirror for a few weeks.

A ladder is a more functional toy, which enables the Budgerigar to scamper up and down. Ladders present a slight risk with young birds, however, whose playful instincts may result in them becoming stuck between the rungs. It is preferable, therefore, to withhold a ladder until your pet is about five or six months old. At first the bird may be nervous of its toys, but within a short period its natural curiosity will win through.

To cater to the destructive nature of parrots, special chews are available. These fit on to the perch, or you can place them on the floor of the cage. They also help to keep their bills in trim.

ADAPTING HOUSEHOLD ITEMS

Simple, ordinary household items will also appeal to your pet. One of the most satisfactory is a Ping-Pong (table tennis) ball. This is light enough for a Budgerigar to push around with its bill and it may also attempt to stand on it, rolling it along as a result. A simple toy for parrots is a wooden cotton-reel. Soak off the labels, suspend it on strong wire, and tie it out of reach. The parrot will readily learn to climb up and grasp it in its bill and slide the reel up and down the wire.

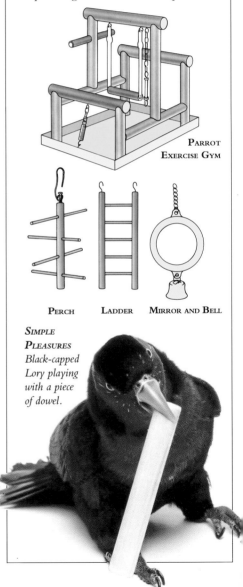

SAFE TOYS

As a general rule, do not buy elaborate toys, since you must be able to clean them. Avoid any item that could have sharp projections. Budgerigars tend to nibble their toys, so avoid any that might be coated with toxic paint.

PARROT EXERCISE GYM

PERCH   **LADDER**   **MIRROR AND BELL**

SIMPLE PLEASURES *Black-capped Lory playing with a piece of dowel.*

⟶ EXERCISE FOR YOUR BIRD ⟵

Periods of regular exercise outside the cage are essential for pet parrots. You will have to supervise these, however, to ensure that the bird does not injure itself.

Try to establish an exercise routine as part of your parrot's life. Before you let the bird into the room, first check that the windows are all closed and screened. If you have a dog or cat, be sure it is not in the room. There are stories of birds and cats sharing their lives, but a cat's instincts have been embedded over centuries, making it unsafe to assume that it will distinguish between wild and pet birds.

With small, tame parrots and Budgerigars, do be certain that you know their whereabouts. This applies especially before settling down in a chair, since a number of cherished pets have been fatally injured by their owners sitting on them. You must also be careful with cups of coffee or other hot drinks in the room, as well as glasses of alcohol. Even a small amount of alcohol can be fatal to a bird.

COMPANIONSHIP

If you are alone, it is sensible to have the telephone in the room with you when you exercise your bird. Then if it rings you will not have to leave the bird unsupervised while you answer it.

Try to allow for your pet's natural needs as part of its exercise requirements. Aside from flying and exploring its environment, the bird must also have companionship. Parrots, in general, are gregarious birds and demand plenty of attention if they are kept on their own. Otherwise, they are quite likely to become bored and develop abnormal patterns of behavior.

INDOORS So that parrots can keep fit, they should be let out of their cage every day, and be allowed to exercise by flying around.

MAKING A ROOM SAFE

Before releasing your pet bird, close all windows and cover the glass with net curtains. Otherwise, the bird might not see the glass. Fireplaces are also a potential danger. Ensure that they are fully screened to prevent the bird slipping inside and entering the chimney.

During its exercise period, your bird will want to rest, so provide perches around the room. To be safe, remove small objects that you prize or are valuable, as well as any poisonous plants. Some examples of plants that should not be in the same room as your bird include amaryllis (Amarylidaceae), dumb cane (Dieffenbachia species), and philodendron (Philodendron species). Hair sprays and furniture polish are also poisonous to birds, although susceptibility varies.

An often unrealized danger comes from aquariums. Cover these to prevent the bird falling in, and to keep it from drinking the water, which often has high bacteria levels, and can give rise to a serious digestive upset.

HANDLING AND HOUSING

Many people are reluctant to handle birds for fear of hurting them but, provided you are careful, there is no reason why you cannot catch and hold a bird safely. In fact, in the case of parrots, it is more likely that they will hurt you if you do not restrain them properly, since these birds have sharp bills and their claws can be painful if they dig into your hand.

──•HANDLING BIRDS•──

There is really no substitute for learning how to handle birds, other than by doing it yourself. It is almost certainly easier to catch a bird in a cage rather than one in an aviary. But in either case, start by covering or removing the perches, and move any pots that could get in the way.

SMALL BIRDS

If you are right-handed, place your right hand inside the cage, using your left to cover the door to prevent any escape. The bird is likely to fly briefly before coming to rest on the floor. Place your hand over it, taking particular care to restrain its neck

gently. Then, all you do is close your hand around it as soon as its wings are closed. Slowly withdraw your hand from the cage, carefully negotiating the door. If you want to examine the bird, move it to your left hand. Ideally, hold its neck between your first and second fingers, with its wings restrained in the palm of your hand. You can then examine its eyes, clip its claws, and even administer medication.

LARGE BIRDS

You can adopt a similar technique with parrots, but use gloves if you are inexperienced. Take extra care, however, since it is easy to press too hard when wearing gloves. Like other birds, parrots will not struggle once restrained, so concentrate on this rather than on trying to grasp the bird tightly.

To handle the very largest species, such as the macaws, you need to wear a second pair of thinner gloves beneath a thick outer pair. If the parrot

HANDLING SMALL BIRDS Finches are restrained more easily than parrots, simply because they are unlikely to bite.

does bite, the simplest way to persuade it to let go is to loosen your grip slightly. You should then be able to restrain it again before it starts to fly free.

USING A NET
Australian parakeets can be elusive – quick in flight, they very rarely allow you to approach closely. For this reason, you may prefer to employ a net.

Select a net with a suitably broad diameter, and a bag sufficiently deep to hold the bird. Most importantly the rim of the net should be well padded. Once you have removed all the perches, the bird is likely to cling on to the mesh, where it will be far easier to net. Do not use too much force – you can still injure the bird by hitting its head, even on a padded net rim.

Bear in mind that this process is stressful for the bird. Should it start to display signs of distress, such as panting with its bill open, then leave the aviary for a period.

Take particular care with recently fledged Australian parakeets, since they have little concept of their environment and may fly directly at the mesh, possibly fracturing their thin skulls as a result.

If the birds are breeding, it is important to minimize any disturbance when trying to catch young birds, otherwise eggs may be damaged or abandoned. Try to catch youngsters early in the morning, so that the adult hen quickly returns to the nest. If she is disturbed during the late afternoon, she may stay off the nest overnight, with fatal consequences for any fertile eggs.

HANDLING PARROTS You should wear a pair of gloves when handling parrots, so that you are not hurt if they bite you. Once it is restrained, the bird will not usually continue struggling, which will help to make an examination of the bird far easier to carry out.

→ SELECTING INDOOR ACCOMMODATION ←

The best way to overwinter the more delicate foreign finches is to move them to a small indoor flight made of mesh panels (see page 145). This does not need to be an elaborate affair, and could fit in a spare bedroom. Indeed, there is no reason why you cannot house and even breed small birds here on a permanent basis.

It is a good idea to draw the design of the flights before you start any carpentry in earnest. The key to any successful housing system of this type is to be as flexible as possible. Working on this basis, design the flight panels around the width of the wire mesh used to cover them. This is normally 90cm (3ft), but larger widths are available. The flight must be high enough to allow you to enter easily, and 180cm (6ft) is usually an ideal height.

Start by assembling the timber outdoors where you will have more space. Lay the frames out on a flat surface and tack the end of the roll of mesh in place. Carefully draw it back over the frame. If you tack the corners in position first, you can make adjustments without too much difficulty.

When you come to cut this length of mesh from the roll, keep the wire-cutters as close as possible to the horizontal strand running across the frame. This will ensure that there are no long strands of mesh that could injure a bird. You will also need a suitable base for the flight, and for indoor use, plywood is best.

If you want something far less elaborate than an indoor flight, you can purchase suitable, spacious indoor enclosures for parrots, complete with a stand. A taller cage is recommended for a macaw, to accommodate its long tail.

It is easier to obtain suitable cages for Budgerigars and canaries. You may have to replace the perches if they are made of plastic, since plastic thwarts the natural desire of many birds to gnaw at wood. Natural perches, which you wash off first, are the best choice. Both ends of the branch may need shaping with a knife in order to fit into the holders intended for the plastic perches in the cage. Secure the perches in place, positioned so that the bird's tail will not catch on the cage's sides.

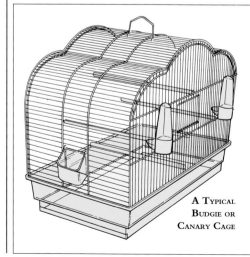

A TYPICAL BUDGIE OR CANARY CAGE

SELECTING A CAGE

Many cages come equipped with swings, but most birds are reluctant to perch on what appears to be a poorly supported branch. If your pet avoids its swing, replace it with a proper perch. You should also check the fastening on the door. Parrots, in particular, are adept at undoing simple catches. The only entirely secure method of restraining a parrot in its quarters is to fit a padlock and chain on the door. You may also need to clamp the feeding bowls in place if you service these from outside the cage. Otherwise they may be tipped out over the floor. A plastic base to the cage will help to prevent seed husks from being scattered.

SITING A CAGE

A flight housing finches or softbills is ideally located in a spare bedroom, where disturbance is minimal, but a pet bird needs a more prominent position in the home. Avoid the kitchen, however, because apart from hygiene concerns, the bird's health can be at risk. Birds are highly sensitive to toxic fumes, which their body absorbs rapidly. A number of fatalities have been recorded in which pets have inhaled polytetrafluoroethylene gas, produced by overheating nonstick pans. In the event of an escape, there is also the risk that a bird may scald or burn itself, and the sudden changes in temperatures common in a kitchen may stimulate irregular molting.

It is much better to keep your pet in the living area of your home. Though risks of injury and poisoning still exist here, you can plan the room to minimize them. The bird must feel secure in its surroundings, so position the cage in a corner where it will be able to watch what is happening, yet be able to retreat to the rear of its quarters without fear of being approached from behind. The height of the cage above the floor is also significant. Ideally, it should be just below eye-level as this enables you to talk directly to the bird and encourage it to feed from your hand. At this height, the bird feels secure, and should respond to you more readily. Support the cage securely on a stand or a piece of furniture, which may be safer if you have children who might pull a stand over, injuring the bird or themselves in the process.

CLEANLINESS

Bear in mind that the area surrounding the cage will become soiled by droppings and food. If the bird decides to bathe, water droplets are likely to be splashed outside the cage. By screening the back and sides of the cage with a clear acrylic surround,

---

SHADING A CAGE

Although many parrot species originate from tropical regions, they are still susceptible to the effects of heatstroke. Therefore, do not position a parrot cage directly in front of a sunny window or in an unshaded, unventilated conservatory in warm weather. The same consideration applies to other birds, since excessive heat can prove fatal. Avoid siting a cage against a radiator, too, since the irregular output of heat may affect the bird's molting behavior. Birds kept inside often shed feathers throughout the year, but this increases greatly when they are actually molting.

---

and by standing the cage on a plastic sheet, such as a tablecloth you use for picnics, you can protect your furniture and walls to a great extent. You can make the screen by sticking pieces of acrylic together with a suitable glue. Allow a gap of about 5cm (2in) around the base of the cage, so that the bird cannot reach the screen and gnaw it. Wipe the acrylic and the tablecloth at intervals with moistened paper toweling, which will not scratch the surface, to pick up the feather dust from the bird's plumage near the cage without scattering it.

Mynah birds are probably the messiest of all birds to keep in the home, and they are usually housed in box-type cages. You will need to protect the front of their quarters, where the water pot is located, because they are inveterate bathers and will splash water far and wide. This is normal, but spraying them with water may help to reduce this urge (see page 160). An indoor flight will be a better environment than the cramped quarters of a mynah cage. Attach plastic sheeting around the rear and sides to keep the room clean.

·THE OUTDOOR AVIARY·

Y̶ou can house all the birds that are covered in this book in an outdoor aviary, for at least a part of the year in temperate parts of the world.

PLANNING

An aviary has two parts: the mesh flight, which is partially open to the elements; and the sheltered area, where you feed the birds and encourage them to roost. The first stage in planning such an aviary is to decide on its location. Choose a sheltered site, out of the prevailing winds, but in sight of the house. It should also be away from overhanging trees, whose branches could damage the structure.

You will need to take the existing layout of the garden into account at the early planning stage. With care, the aviary will

A TYPICAL AVIARY This consists of a flight, shelter, and safety porch. Translucent plastic sheeting attached to the framework of the flight provides the birds with protection against the elements.

FLIGHT Mesh attaches to the flight on the inner surface.

DOOR TO SHELTER Hinged to open outwards for easy access.

GUTTERING AND SLOPED ROOF Directs rainwater away from the flight.

MESH TO DETER CATS Raised to deter cats from walking on the aviary.

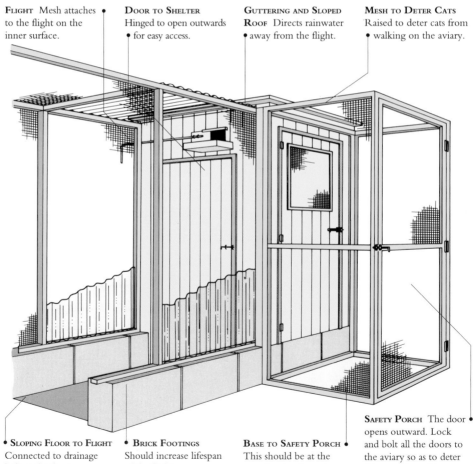

SLOPING FLOOR TO FLIGHT Connected to drainage hole at the front.

BRICK FOOTINGS Should increase lifespan of the flight.

BASE TO SAFETY PORCH This should be at the same level as the aviary.

SAFETY PORCH The door opens outward. Lock and bolt all the doors to the aviary so as to deter thieves and vandals.

any harsh outlines. Freestanding arches smothered with climbing plants are useful for achieving this type of effect.

Another point to consider at the outset is the siting of the doors. A safety porch is also needed to stop the birds escaping as you enter. It is often better to have just a single external door providing access to the shelter where you feed the birds. You will then need a connecting door leading from the shelter to the flight. This should minimize any disturbance to breeding birds, since you will not have to walk past their nest site in order to feed them.

SITING AN AVIARY

✦ *Choose a spot out of prevailing winds, and away from overhanging trees, as far as possible.*

✦ *Avoid a site close to the road, where the aviary would be an easy target for vandals or thieves, and sitting birds could be disturbed by the headlights of passing cars.*

✦ *Choose a level part of the garden, in a spot that will not upset the neighbors.*

✦ *Check that there are no possible planning infringements before building the aviary.*

blend into your garden as an attractive feature. This is particularly the case if you are keeping finches or softbills, which thrive in planted flights. The plants provide natural cover for breeding and attract insects, which help to supplement the birds' diet.

Plant small shrubs, such as box *(Buxus sempervirens)*, which is ideal for nesting cover, or annuals such as nasturtiums *(Tropaeolum majus)*. These will attract aphids, which are valuable for waxbills rearing chicks. You can also train climbing plants up the sides of the aviary, which helps to discourage young birds from flying at the mesh and hurting themselves.

Even so, it is probably worthwhile setting plants in tubs and small containers, and covering the aviary floor with paving slabs or a layer of concrete. This will make it much easier to keep the aviary clean, and prevent the build-up of parasites or disease organisms. Drainage will also be more reliable with a solid base, protecting the floor against waterlogging. At the end of the breeding season, remove the plants, disinfect the floor, and discard the annuals.

Most parrots, with the exception of hanging parrots, will destroy all vegetation in their enclosure, and so the aviary will appear rather sparse. But careful styling around the outer perimeter should soften

AVIARY OPTIONS The type and number of birds you intend to keep will influence the aviary design. Always ensure adjoining flights are double-wired, to prevent injury to the toes of birds in neighboring aviaries.

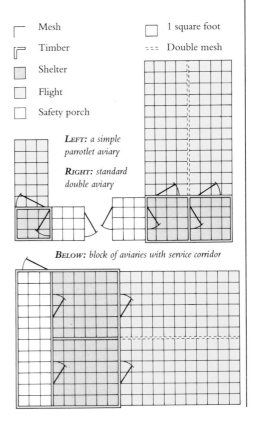

Mesh

Timber

Shelter

Flight

Safety porch

1 square foot

Double mesh

LEFT: *a simple parrotlet aviary*

RIGHT: *standard double aviary*

BELOW: *block of aviaries with service corridor*

Building an Aviary

For many species, apart from the larger, more destructive parrots, a wooden frame is adequate for the flight area of the aviary. The frame for the flight usually consists of lengths of timber about 3.75 – 5 cm (1.5 –2 in) square. Joint these as well as screwing them together for extra stability.

All wood used in the aviary must be treated to prevent rot; tanalized timber, which has preservative forced inside the wood in a vacuum, is ideal. You must ensure, however, that all substances used are nontoxic, since birds will inevitably gnaw at the wood. Once the frame is in place, attach a fine mesh, the mesh size

dimensions of which should be no larger than 2.5 x 1.25 cm (1 x 0.5 in), which will exclude rats and most mice and snakes.

While the aviary flight is usually of a reasonably standard design, you can construct the shelter in various ways. You can even use a converted garden shed.

The provision of windows is vital, since these will actually persuade the birds to use the shelter. A window at the back of the structure will allow you to check where the birds are before entering, and a smaller side window is also recommended. Screen all windows with mesh so that you can open them safely for ventilation.

Sloping Roof The sides should accommodate this slope, with the runoff away from the flight.

Window Cover the window with mesh. A well-lit aviary encourages the birds to enter.

Door The door should have a lock on it, and it should be hinged to open outwards.

Shelter Construct the shelter from weatherproofed, tongued and grooved wood. This can look quite attractive.

Raised Pillars These pillars should be constructed on a solid base, and be able to bear the weight of the shelter. Masonry nails or frame fixers will attach them together. You can also use concrete blocks.

Shelter Types *Depending on the design of your aviary, you may prefer a raised shelter (left), or a full-length shelter (above). It may be cheaper to build a raised shelter, but a full-length shelter is often more convenient, especially in the case of a large structure. Unless you can shut the birds out in the flight, a safety porch around the entrance is recommended.*

ERECTING THE AVIARY

The site for the aviary should be quite flat.
Mark out the area, and then cut away any
turfs. Store these in a shady spot, and keep
them moist if you want to reuse them
later. The foundations of the aviary are
important, to support the structure and to
deter rats from tunneling in. Concrete
building blocks, buried to a depth of at
least 45 cm (18 in), are suitable for this. On
top of the foundations, build up the base of
the aviary to a height of at least 30 cm (1
ft) above ground level. This will raise the
wooden parts of the structure, and prevent
them from rotting prematurely.

To prepare the base, use a 25 cm (10 in)
layer of compressed hardcore topped by a
coarse mix of cement and ballast, in a 1:3
ratio, and add a final layer of sharp sand
and cement in a 1:1 mix. A plastic sheet
between these top two layers of cement in
the shelter section will serve as a damp-
proofing membrane.

Outside, in the flight area, the floor must
be laid in so that it slopes away from the
shelter. This will allow rainwater to run off
toward a drainhole that you will need to
position at the front of the aviary later.

Frame fixers are the most convenient way
of attaching aviary panels to the base. The
panels can be held together with bolts fitted
with well-oiled washers. For extra support,
place the frames on a bed of mortar. Next,
put the roof sections in place so that these
pull the panels together. When the whole
structure is erected, fit the doors in position.

FINISHING OFF

Aside from this shelter, the birds will need
protection from the elements in the flight,
as well as from predators, such as cats. Use
translucent plastic sheeting mounted on
strong wooden supports. This should slope
so that rainwater runs off into a gutter away
from the aviary. The plastic sheeting must
extend for a minimum of 90 cm (3 ft) on
the roof, and a similar distance on the sides,
to provide additional shelter from driving
rain or snow, as well as wind.

CATCH YOUR BIRD

*The purpose of the device shown below is to
confine birds either in or out of the shelter,
when cleaning or feeding them with a door
open. This also makes them easier to catch.
Easy to operate from outside the flight, it is
simply slid across the opening when required.*

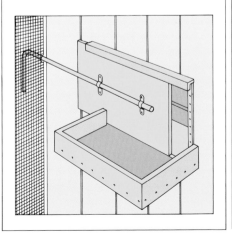

THE SCOPE OF A BIRDROOM

A significant drawback of housing larger parrots in an outside aviary is the noise they make – often commencing at dawn. Not surprisingly, therefore, many breeders now house their stock indoors, where they can soundproof the enclosure to a degree, and also adapt the environment to suit the needs of their birds.

FEATURES OF A BIRDROOM

An indoor structure for housing birds is called a birdroom, and as well as being ideal for parrots, it has long been popular with Budgerigar and canary breeders, too. Within its confines you can include breeding cages, which allows you to supervise activities more closely than would be possible in an outside flight. Other features you can incorporate include training cages for exhibition stock, a food preparation area, and an indoor flight. Here you can also overwinter more delicate species, providing artificial heating and lighting.

Parrots are often housed in suspended cages within a birdroom, because this tends to make cleaning easier. Droppings and discarded food fall through the mesh to the floor below where you can sweep them up at any convenient time.

Keepers of more delicate birds often prefer to incorporate the shelter component of an aviary into the birdroom, since there is then no need to provide separate winter accommodation. Instead, they simply close off access to the outside flight during periods of bad weather.

If you decide to have electricity in your birdroom – which certainly makes it easier to provide heat and light – have a qualified electrician undertake the work to ensure that all electrical wires are boxed in safely.

AIR POLLUTION

A major problem that can arise within the birdroom is a buildup of dust. Probably the most effective means of improving the birdroom environment is to install an air cleaner, which will actively remove airborne dust particles from the atmosphere. These may otherwise be inhaled and cause an unpleasant, tight-chested feeling, especially if you are prone to such chest

VENTILATING THE BIRDROOM Good ventilation is vital in a birdroom. During the summer, open the outer door during the day when the weather is warm. A sturdy, inner mesh door will keep out cats and other predators, while creating a flow of air. A mesh-covered window at the front of the birdroom is also useful, and if you open the outer door at the same time as the window, this will help to create a good through breeze.

ailments as asthma. In addition to dust, an air cleaner will also extract any potentially harmful microorganisms from the air.

Ionizers are now common, and these help to counter a deficiency of negative charges in the air within the birdroom by producing a stream of negative ions. The ions combine with dust particles, which are then drawn to an earthed surface. A layer of dust will build up on the ground, for example, where you can wipe it away.

A further advantage of using an ionizer is that the negative ions will also destroy harmful microorganisms, and reduce the

threat of bird infection. The effects of ionizers can be apparent within minutes in a badly polluted atmosphere, and they are extremely durable units. Even so, you can help to control aerial pollution in the first instance by regular vacuuming. The noise seems to have no harmful effects on the birds, and cock Budgerigars, especially, seem to sing louder in competition with the motor of the cleaner!

A TYPICAL BIRDROOM This offers a great deal of scope, especially for the keen exhibitor or foreign bird breeder. It is also useful for storing equipment and seed, and for training birds for show purposes.

IONIZER This will help to reduce the amount of dust that builds up in the birdroom.

LIGHTING Lighting may be necessary when the days are short.

ENTRY DOOR TO INDOOR FLIGHT Ensure that access is easy.

OUTLET TO OUTDOOR FLIGHT This should be fitted to open outward into the flight.

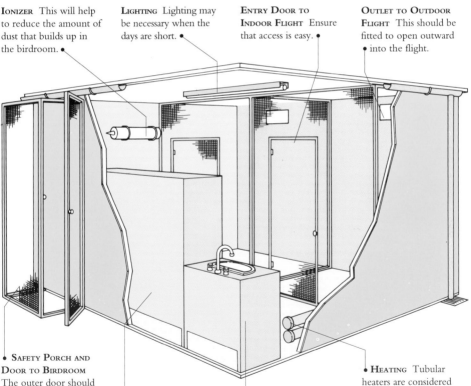

SAFETY PORCH AND DOOR TO BIRDROOM The outer door should secure with locks, and should be fitted so that it can be closed from inside the birdroom. Keep the hinges oiled so that they do not become stiff, and the door difficult to open.

BREEDING CAGES Double breeding cages can be easily converted into stock cages after the breeding season, provided they have a removable center partition.

SINK AND CUPBOARD The sink provides easy access to water, and the cupboard is useful for storing food and cleaning equipment. You should lag all external pipes.

HEATING Tubular heaters are considered the best option when heating your birdroom, as they are the safest and cleanest to use. They are available in a range of wattages and can be regulated by a thermostat.

→HEATING AND LIGHTING←

Daylight is considerably shortened in temperate regions during winter, reducing the birds' opportunity to feed. With smaller species, especially, this can render them vulnerable to hypothermia – their small body mass is relative to a large body area, which causes them to lose heat rapidly. For foreign finches in particular, therefore, heating and lighting in the birds' quarters are important. This also applies to species that tend to breed at this time of year within the confines of a birdroom, such as the Madagascar Lovebird.

Good insulation in the birds' quarters will reduce heating costs and may make the installation of a heating system un-necessary. As well as lining the walls and roof, fit draft excluders around the doors and temporary double glazing over windows as necessary.

VARIABLE LIGHTING

Using artificial lighting not only extends the birds' feeding period, it will also provide you with the opportunity to attend to your stock when it is dark.

A variable lighting control, or dimmer switch, lets you raise and lower the light intensity gradually. Combine this with a time-switch, and you can turn the lights on and off whether or not you are present. Bear in mind, however, that any more than about 12 hours of exposure to light in a day may trigger premature breeding activity. Under no circumstances should you walk into the birdroom and turn the lights on straight away. This causes panic and may result in the loss of eggs and chicks.

If your birdroom is shaded, then a light sensor positioned on a window may be useful. When the level of illumination falls to a predetermined level, the sensor activates a gradual increase in light. In the morning, for example, program the

---

HEATING OPTIONS
* *When deciding on heaters for the birdroom, choose a higher capacity than will normally be required, to provide a safety margin.*
* *Few breeders use oil heaters because toxic fumes can prove fatal and there is no effective means of regulating the heat output.*
* *Fan heaters are very efficient within the confines of the birdroom, but dust is a frequent source of problems.*
* *Tubular convector heaters are widely used. These units are available in a range of wattages and lengths to suit most needs.*
* *Electric heaters are safest and cleanest.*

---

controls so that the lights come on and rise slowly to full intensity by the time you enter the aviary. Similarly, in the evening, the lighting should dim gradually, otherwise hens may be left stranded off their nests, causing them, and other birds, to panic.

LIGHTING TYPES AND SAFETY

Whether you use tungsten bulbs or fluor-escent lighting tubes is a matter of choice. What is essential is to keep electrical apparatus away from the birds. If you have an aviary with a large shelter, you may want to include heating and lighting inside it. In this case, shield the wiring, and screen the lighting units and heat source in wire mesh cages.

While this should be adequate protection for electrical units in enclosures housing finches and smaller softbills, it is harder to protect equipment in a parrot aviary. One viable option is to partition off the rear of the shelter entirely, which will enable you to dispense with a safety porch, and in the intervening gap you can include lighting and heating, along with a control panel.

WINTER ACCOMMODATION

Provided that they are properly protected and acclimatized, many foreign birds can be surprisingly hardy through a temperate winter. There is a tendency to think that all birds from the tropics live in hot conditions. In reality, a number of species are found at high altitudes, where temperatures at night may dip down to freezing or below. You should, however, bear in mind that some of the smaller birds are less able to maintain their body temperatures under such conditions, and usually require additional heating and lighting.

It is also important to persuade larger birds to move under cover at night, due to the risk of frostbite, with certain species being more vulnerable than others. Freezing temperatures combined with damp perches mean that birds could be roosting on ice. If their toes freeze, the blood supply to them is disrupted. Although there is little evidence of this at first, the bird may be reluctant to perch, and traces of blood may be visible on the wood. Within a few days, however, the toes shrivel and ultimately drop off.

Therefore, you should ensure that susceptible birds, such as touracos, hornbills, Peach-faced Lovebirds, and psittaculid parakeets, roost under cover. Some individuals, even though they will feed in the shelter, are reluctant to remain in it at night. Catch these birds regularly before dusk and shut them in overnight.

Alternatively, vary the height of the perches, having them higher in the shelter than in the flight. Birds naturally prefer to roost on the highest perch at night, so this may well lure the birds inside.

UNWELCOME VISITORS

Aside from the cold, you will also need to remain alert during the winter for rodents or foxes. Cats are also a problem, as they may climb on to the aviary and menace the birds from above. However, some manufacturers are now marketing special electric fences, which discourage them from doing this. Alternatively, you could add a false roof to the aviary by attaching vertical uprights around the edges of the roof and then covering this with mesh.

WINTER IN THE BIRDROOM At this time of the year, while you can allow birds out into the flight during the daytime, check that they all return to the shelter at night. Heating and lighting are necessary for a number of species, especially finches and softbills, and controls for any heating and lighting system may normally be pre-programmed. Good insulation will help cut heating costs at this time of the year.

FEEDING

There is a tendency to categorize birds pretty broadly as either seed-eaters or softbills, according to their feeding habits. This is too simplistic an approach. Many finches, for example, do eat seed, but most will also take a wide variety of other foods. The term softbill is even less meaningful, encompassing as it does everything from hummingbirds to crows.

——• TYPES OF BIRD SEED •——

There has been considerable progress in understanding the nutritional requirements of pet and aviary birds during recent years, and a wide range of new products is available. But many bird-keepers rely on seed as the major part of their birds' diet.

Cereal seeds tend to form the main item in the diet of many finches. These contain the highest percentage of carbohydrate, and lesser amounts of proteins and fats. The other group of seeds, known generally as oil-based seeds, primarily contains oil (fat), and its protein content is higher than that of cereal seeds. You can obtain mixtures of seeds for specific groups of birds, such as Budgerigar seed. Unlike most cat and dog foods, however, these products do not contain all the ingredients needed to keep birds in good health. Seeds, for example, are generally deficient in vitamin A, so you need to supplement this by giving special additives.

BUDGERIGAR SEED

FOREIGN FINCH SEED

BLUE MAW (BREEDING)

CANARY SEED

PARROT FOOD

NIGER SEED (BREEDING)

PURCHASING SEED

Bird seed is sold either as a variety of branded products or as loose seed. Branded packets tend to be more expensive, but the quality of this seed is likely to be better than that of loose seed, since it will probably be free from dust and harvesting debris. Some loose seed is also clean, but, as it is often left lying around in pet stores, contamination by water or rodent excrement is a dangerous possibility.

The two most significant cereals used as bird food are plain canary seed and millets. Different types of millet are often available from pet stores, and some are more popular with certain birds than others: pearl white, for example, is a large variety of millet more suitable for Budgerigars than finches; panicum millet is generally acceptable to all birds. Popular oil-based seeds include sunflower seeds (white varieties

contain more protein and less oil than striped ones), and pine nuts, a particular favorite with many species of parrot.

In the wild, some birds do feed on dry grasses, but they prefer ripening, more digestible grains. You can prepare ordinary seed so that it is similar to ripening seed. Soak a day's portion in a bowl of hot water for 24 hours. The seeds will absorb the water and start to swell and soften. The germination process will then begin and the nutritional value of the seed will alter as a result. Its protein level rises, which is one reason why seed prepared in this way is popular with birds rearing chicks. It can also assist in recovery after an illness.

AVIAN FOODSTUFFS *A selection of the seeds and other foods necessary for both seed-eating and softbill birds. Be sure to store all foodstuffs in a dry place, and protect them from rodents. Buy quantities of food on a regular basis, to ensure a fresh supply. This is particularly important with pellets and softbill food, which have the shortest storage lives.*

SOFTBILL PELLETS **PEANUTS** **SPRAY MILLET**

PARROT PELLETS **PINE NUTS** **SOFTBILL FOOD**

FRUIT AND GREENFOOD

Many birds feed on fruit and need a suitable selection each day. You will soon be able to assess the amount of fruit required and so avoid wastage. Bacteria and fungi multiply rapidly on cut surfaces, so discard uneaten fruit the following day.

The choice of fruit depends on where you live and on the time of year. Many bird-keepers rely heavily on apples, as they are constantly available. Like many fruits, apples are mostly water with only traces of nutrients, although they are popular with birds. Buy apples that do not bruise easily; damaged fruit is not suitable as bird food. Check around the core for signs of mold. Softbills, in particular, are vulnerable to the fungal disease aspergillosis, so exposure to any molds should be kept to a minimum. Always wash the skin of fruit thoroughly, and some bird-keepers also peel fruit as a precaution against chemical residues.

FREEZING FOOD

You can preserve and store some fruits by freezing them. Pick only ripe fruit and divide it into batches of a size suitable for an individual day's portion. When you come to thaw it out, wash the fruit under running water and allow it to drain thoroughly before tipping it into the birds' food pots. Many types of vegetable can also be successfully frozen, but, unlike fruit, you usually need to blanch the produce first in boiling water. However, for use as bird food, it is only corn on the cob that is regularly prepared and stored in this fashion.

A Choice of Fruits Offer fresh and prepared fruits, depending on the season. Buy grapes and cherries in bulk, when they are cheap, for freezing. These are especially valuable if you own a collection of softbills.

APPLE

SULTANAS

CHERRIES

ORANGE

GRAPES

RAISINS

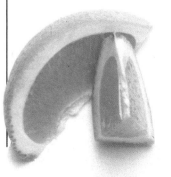

Grapes, which are popular with many bird species, can be offered whole, even if they do contain seeds. In the case of fruit with much larger stones, such as peaches, it is best to section the fruit. Stone cherries as well if you are feeding them to parrots. However, larger softbills, such as toucans, will regurgitate cherry stones once they have absorbed the fruit.

Citrus fruits, such as oranges, may seem an ideal food for birds, especially in view of their vitamin C content, but they tend to be rather acidic. Oranges are popular with parrots, however, but peel them first.

Do not suddenly substitute one fruit for another, since this might trigger a digestive upset. Make changes gradually, so that the different proportions of fruits can be varied over a period of time.

VEGETABLES

Vegetables are acceptable mostly to parrots, but some softbills, notably touracos, can be persuaded to take greenfood on a regular basis. Again, as with fruit, choice will be influenced by where you live and the time of year, but in most parts of the world it is possible to grow perpetual spinach, which is a valuable source of calcium, iron, vitamin A, and some members of the B group. You can also give cabbage of various types during the winter, although it is not universally popular with parrots. Larger parrots can be given whole leaves, but in some cases they prefer the stalk. Cabbage is not recommended for Budgerigars, since it can make them susceptible to thyroid disorders.

One of the best natural sources of vitamin A is carrots. Some strains have higher levels than others, so it is worth finding these if possible. You can feed carrots whole to parrots, but wash or scrub them first. For smaller birds, dice them into small

pieces or shred them lengthways. Many other vegetables are also beneficial and can also be included in a bird's diet, including peas, either loose or in pods. Ripe sweet corn is also very popular, especially with neo-tropical parrots, such as Amazons. Fresh beans and even raw onion may also be taken by some birds. Those that have been hand-reared are most likely to sample a range of such foods.

Sprouting seeds of various types are popular with many parrots. You can purchase these, along with seed-sprouters, from most health food stores. Mung beans, also known as Chinese bean sprouts, are widely used, but others, such as salad alfalfa, are also suitable. Apart from being very nutritious, they crop readily in a matter of days. Check that they are fresh and have not turned moldy, which can happen surprisingly quickly. After rinsing the sprouts, place them in a food container separate to that used for dry seed, since water stimulates the seed to germinate and become moldy.

MUNG BEANS

SWEETCORN

PEAS

CARROT

LIVEFOODS

The feeding habits of birds will change during the year. When waxbills breed, for example, they tend to become far more insectivorous, and the raised level of protein in their diet helps them to sustain the rapid growth of their chicks.

MEALWORMS

The traditional livefood for the avicultural market is the mealworm *(Tenebrio molitor)*, the larval stage of the meal beetle's lifecycle. These are fine for many larger species, such as glossy starlings, but they tend to be too big for small softbills. Mealworms also have a hard, protective outer cuticle of chitin, and this needs to be broken down before they can be digested. Only when the worm is molting can it be digested easily. In nutritional terms, mealworms are about 31 percent fat and 56 percent protein, and are sold by weight, in small containers. They should be spread out in a suitable medium, such as chicken meal, in a large, clean margarine container with air holes in the lid. Provide them with slices of apple for moisture. As with all livefoods, offer only a few at a time, otherwise they might escape.

FRUIT FLIES & MAGGOTS

Fruit flies *(Drosophila)*, a vital part of the diet of hummingbirds and sunbirds, cannot be bought commercially, so you will have to culture them yourself. The usual way of doing this is to place the starter culture in a bucket of banana skins, with muslin over the top, in a warm place, between 21–25°C (70 –77°F). When the flies have hatched, cut a small hole in the muslin to allow them to escape into the aviary.

In the past, maggots were widely used as bird food, but as they feed on putrid meat you could risk an outbreak of botulism. In several cases, almost entire collections of birds have been all but wiped out.

CRICKETS

Crickets have become popular with bird-keepers in recent years, and these insects thrive on a basic diet of cereal and grass. Provide suitable retreats in their quarters - an aquarium with a hood is ideal – such as rolled-up newspaper, and a moist piece of sponge as a water source. Crickets are more nutritional than mealworms, with, on average 13 percent fat and 73 percent protein, although their calcium content is poor. Breeders tend to sprinkle them with a powdered supplement before giving them to their birds. Without additional calcium, the presence of vitamin D_3 serves to withdraw this mineral from birds' bones.

Hatchling crickets are very suitable for smaller softbills, because of their size and soft body casing, and it is possible to breed your own supply. Females have a pointed

LIVEFOODS These items are particularly important in the diets of many softbills and finches, especially during the the breeding season, when they will be needed in increasing quantities once chicks hatch. It is, therefore, important to make adequate provision of livefood well in advance.

MEALWORMS

TEBOS

CULTURES

Not all types of livefoods are available in commercial quantities, and in certain cases you may have to purchase starter cultures and then build up your own stock. Whiteworm (Enchytraeus), for example, is especially popular as a rearing food for young waxbills. Whiteworm and microworms are both easy to keep in a moist, peat-lined plastic container, as long as it has ventilation holes in the lid. Place them on a layer of wholemeal bread moistened with milk. This should meet all their nutritional needs.

OTHER LIVEFOODS

Livefood suppliers are always searching for other potential invertebrates for the avicultural market. A recent introduction has been farmed snails, which are available in varying sizes. Many birds, such as members of the thrush family, feed naturally on snails, but there is a risk attached to feeding them snails gathered from the garden, since these often play host to parasitic worms.

There are livefoods you can collect safely, provided that you do not use insecticides in your garden. Spiders are a favorite of many softbill species, and if you trawl long grass with a deep net you can catch a variety of suitable invertebrates.

The largest softbills, such as toucans, may eat "pinkies," which you can buy from suppliers as snake food. These are dead, day-old mice, usually sold in frozen packs. Allow them to thaw out overnight at room temperature, but do not prepare more than the required quantity.

Although it may seem unpleasant offering birds food of this type, some, such as toucans, eat small mammals in the wild. It is more nutritious than minced meat or ox-heart, for example, as these are deficient in vitamin A and show a serious imbalance in their calcium to phosphorus ratios.

tip to the abdomen, which is used to lay the eggs in containers of moist sand. Eggs need to be kept at about 27°C (81°F), and they take about two weeks to hatch.

LOCUSTS

Locusts are similar to crickets, but grow to be much larger, making them unsuitable for smaller birds. You can house them until required in the same kind of accommodation that is normally used for crickets, and you can feed them on a diet of fresh grass.

CRICKETS

LOCUSTS

HOPPERS *One of the advantages of choosing crickets or locusts is that they are available in various sizes. Obviously, the smallest hoppers are most suitable for the smallest birds. These invertebrates are not difficult to maintain, so you can buy them when they are small, and rear them at home. It is even possible to breed your own supply.*

——→ SUPPLEMENTING THE BASIC DIET ←——

Since birds have no teeth, they depend on their gizzards to crush their food. It is then broken down by enzymes and absorbed through the intestinal wall. Grit has an important part to play in this process. The rough surfaces of the stones grind up the seeds and prevent the particles of food from adhering together in a lump.

There is controversy over the necessity for providing grit but, clearly, it can only be beneficial. It helps to meet the body's need for minerals, such as calcium, which is also broken down. Oyster shell grit tends to be more soluble than mineralized grit, so it is best to provide a mixture. Grit sold for Budgerigars is suitable for canaries, finches, Cockatiels, and smaller parakeets, but pigeon grit is best for larger species.

In addition to grit, birds that are offered seed regularly should also be provided with cuttlefish bone. These white "bones" come from marine mollusks and provide an essential source of calcium. This is more important during the breeding period, when calcium is needed to form egg shells.

CUTTLEFISH FROM THE BEACH

If you live in a coastal area you may find cuttlefish washed up on the beach. Avoid any that are covered in tar or have remnants of the cuttlefish's body still evident. Take the bones home and wash them thoroughly under running water. Then immerse them in a bucket of clean water and soak them to remove excess salt. Change the water in the bucket about twice a day. Then, after a week, rinse the bones again and leave them to dry in a sunny spot. When they are completely dry, transfer them to a plastic bag, where they can be stored indefinitely until they are needed.

For Budgerigars, you should also provide iodine blocks. This trace element is vital to the proper functioning of the thyroid gland, which produces the hormones involved in regulating levels of body activity. Budgerigars appear to have a much higher requirement for iodine than other species.

VITAMIN SUPPLEMENTS

During the last few years, many food supplements for birds have become readily available. Unfortunately, very little scientific work has been carried out into the precise nutritional requirements of birds, and this has made the assessment of accurate supplementation a vexed issue. Indeed, clear evidence of excessive supplementation, notably that of vitamin A and, to a lesser extent, vitamin D_3, has been recorded in some cases.

Before using any supplement, look closely at your birds' diet and assess what could be missing. Cockatoos, which only eat seed, for example, and refuse fresh foods, are likely to have a low intake of vitamin A and calcium, especially if they ignore your offerings of cuttlefish bone.

Vitamin supplements are available in powdered form and as liquids. The latter tend to contain a less comprehensive range of ingredients, and they often lack some of the essential amino acids. However, with a powdered supplement, the problem is often how to administer it to best effect. Simply sprinkling it over seed is generally unsatisfactory, because the powder does not adhere well. Soaked seed (see page 147) is more suitable, because the powder sticks to the damp seed surfaces. But most species discard the outer husk anyway, and the powder along with it.

Rather than using loose powder, you can provide finches and parrots, which are more at risk from nutritional deficiencies than softbills, with impregnated seeds. These have been specially treated by the manufacturer to counter any possible dietary shortages, and the birds find them just as palatable as normal seeds. Always read the packaging instructions supplied with these supplements to avoid the possibility of overdosing. A single incident may not be significant in itself, but repeated, regular overdosing can cause a wide variety of problems, ranging from skeletal changes to diarrhea, weakness, and even death. Bear in mind, too, that although one

supplement can be helpful, the use of two together may double the dose of certain chemicals contained within them.

Other foods may specifically help the birds' vitamin intake. Budgerigar breeders favor cod-liver oil because it contains vitamins A and D. Prepare this by mixing the oil with seed in a ratio of 1 tablespoon of oil, in the form of an emulsion, to a 9-liter (2-gallon) bucket of seed. Take care, however, since rancid cod-liver oil will induce a vitamin E deficiency.

If you use a supplement that is added to water, place the water container away from direct sunlight, since this will rapidly reduce its vitamin content. This is a recommended practice in any event to minimize any algal development.

DIETARY ADDITIONS Grit is needed by seed-eating birds, along with charcoal, cuttlefish bone, and an iodine block. Red pepper is a natural coloring agent, while a food supplement can be of value for all birds.

IODINE BLOCK

POWDERED SUPPLEMENT

PARROT CHEW RING

MINERAL GRIT

RED PEPPER

OYSTER SHELL GRIT

CHARCOAL

CUTTLEFISH BONE

SPECIAL DIETS

There is no single diet that is suitable for softbills. Most softbills are offered a mixture of fruit, insects, and softbill food. Softbill food is available from pet stores and specialist suppliers. Some foods are intended for birds that are more insectivorous in their feeding habits, such as flycatchers, whereas others are geared to the needs of more frugivorous (predominantly fruit-eating) species. Softbill food can be wasteful, however, because few birds will eat it in loose form, with the end result that the birds may not receive enough

SEEING RED Birds like the color red, so special types of drinker have been designed for nectivores, such as hummingbirds. These have red encircling the spout, which attracts the birds, and encourages them to drink from this point.

nutrients, feeding largely on a diet of fruit and some invertebrates. It is, therefore, important to mix loose softbill food thoroughly with fruit, to which it will stick quite readily.

This problem has been largely overcome with the advent of pellet diets for this group of birds, which are available in a variety of sizes to suit all softbills. Some brands of pellets and loose softbill foods need to be soaked or mixed with water before use. This improves their palatability, especially to smaller softbills, such as tanagers, but you must select a suitable brand, as some pellets disintegrate into a nasty, turgid mass.

NECTAR DIETS

Some softbills, such as hummingbirds and sugarbirds, should be provided with a nectar solution on a regular basis. Proprietary foods, that are specially formulated for these birds, are available, either as a paste or a powder; both need to be mixed with a prescribed volume of water.

Nectar is a sugary fluid, which is rapidly absorbed into the body, making it a useful tonic for softbills, especially after a journey. Many tanagers also benefit from nectar, and some parrots are adapted to feed on nectar and pollen, which is primarily made up of protein.

Until recently, nectar-feeding parrots were fed a fluid solution rather like other nectivores. There is a trend now, however, to use dry nectar powder, as their artificial diet is excessively fluid. Pollen is a solid, and plant nectars also have a relatively firm consistency. Several brands of dry nectar food are now available for this colorful group of parrots, but you may need to sprinkle it over their fruit initially in order to persuade the birds to feed on it. Hanging parrots will also benefit from the regular inclusion of some nectar in their diet.

With all nectivorous species, do not be tempted to change their diet suddenly. Instead, make changes over a period of a few weeks in order to minimize the risk of intestinal upset. This is particularly important with newly acquired birds, because any significant dietary variation, coupled with the added stress of movement, could precipitate a fatal enterotoxemia – a condition in which toxins in the gut enter and infect the bloodstream.

·Feeding Equipment·

Most cages come equipped with two plastic pots, which are sometimes covered. Use one of these pots for grit rather than water. Water should be provided in a special drinker, which you can attach to the outside of the cage.

Winnowers, Containers, and Drinkers
Canaries tend to be wasteful when feeding, scattering their seed widely in search of a favored morsel, such as hemp. You can reclaim uneaten seed from the chaff by using a winnower, but this is not problem-free. With canaries in particular, the seed may be contaminated by droppings, which could cause disease if consumed by another bird. Seed must also be completely dry to ensure that it is free from mold.

Most winnowers do not work well with sunflower and the other heavier seeds that are usually offered to parrots; but parrots, generally, eat virtually all of their food without fuss. It is important, however, to provide parrots, especially the more destructive species, with sturdy food pots. Some individuals soon learn how to pull out food and water containers that hook over the mesh of their quarters unless you use pegs to clip them in place.

You can use plastic containers for smaller, less destructive species, such as the majority of Australian parakeets, but parrots with more powerful bills, such as African Grays, cockatoos, and macaws, need metal containers. Check that these have no sharp edges.

Special, relatively indestructible glass drinkers are available for parrots, although the larger macaws are capable of crushing a plastic spout, and so stainless steel is used instead. Bottles are usually colored green to discourage algal growth.

Food Containers

Containers that hook onto mesh or the front of a cage come in various sizes, making them suitable for a range of foods. Use smaller ones for soaked seed, and larger ones for diced fruit and livefood, such as mealworms and crickets.

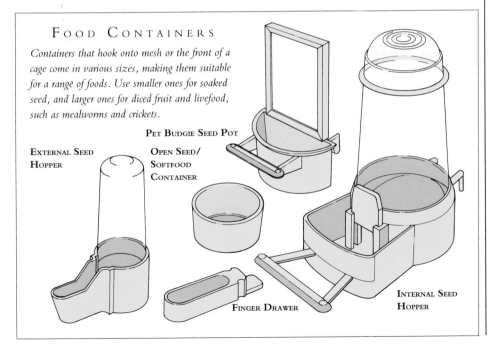

PET BUDGIE SEED POT

EXTERNAL SEED HOPPER

OPEN SEED/ SOFTFOOD CONTAINER

FINGER DRAWER

INTERNAL SEED HOPPER

FEEDING TECHNIQUES

The two covered plastic feeding pots that come with most bird cages (see page 155) can represent a problem for the young Budgerigar that is housed alone. Without a more experienced bird to show it the ropes, it may have trouble feeding and thus be reluctant to eat from such a container. To attract the bird's attention, sprinkle a little seed on the floor around the base of the pot, but not enough to satisfy its hunger, otherwise it will not try to eat from the pot.

Open containers can also be used for food, but not for water, however, which will rapidly become soiled with food, dust, and droppings. Place open food containers close to a perch so that the birds can alight close by, without scattering the contents.

A choice of feeding sites is always recommended so that birds are not kept short of food, and scared by one individual monopolizing a single food source. This is more likely when a number of birds are

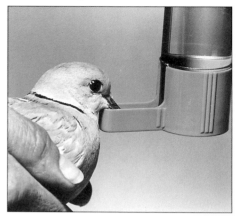

LEARNING TO DRINK To help a pigeon or dove locate water in an aviary, dip the tip of its bill in the water container for a few seconds.

housed together, but it can also happen in the case of a pair of parrots, where one bird is dominant for most of the year. In other birds, aggression of this type is more likely at the outset of the breeding period.

PROVIDING WATER

Never feed the birds in an outdoor aviary flight, where their food will become wet and moldy. Drinking water is safe in the flight, however. Normally, you should fill a drinker to the top, but in winter, leave a gap in case the water freezes and splits the bottle.

Check these drinkers after a cold night, because a plug of ice may form in the spout. Although the water in the bottle may not freeze, the birds will still be unable to drink. If you are in a hurry in the mornings, have a spare set of drinkers to replace any frozen ones. Check the water in the morning and again in the late afternoon, to ensure that the birds have an adequate supply, especially if you give them pellets in their diet.

MESSY EATERS
Position the food container for softbills so that it is easy to clear up food that these birds will scatter about.

Molt and Color Feeding

The coloration of certain birds can be influenced by their diet, such as the red plumage found in finches and softbills. Specific coloring agents are now available to ensure that plumage does not assume an undesirably pale shade of red over successive molts. Color feeding happened initially by chance toward the end of the last century, when a canary breeder gave some cayenne pepper to one of his birds, which was off color. He was surprised when the coloration of the plumage in its new feathers improved significantly.

Other foods, most noticeably carrots, can have a similar effect. Today, however, most breeders use synthetic coloring agents, available either as a soft food or as a liquid.

When To Color Feed

Start color feeding before the molting period begins so that there will be an even uptake of coloring agent into the new feathers. It is absorbed into the body and passes from the bloodstream to the site of feather development, and then into the plumage itself.

Canaries have a fairly defined molting period, and it is reasonably easy to assess when to begin color feeding, but it is more difficult with recently imported softbills, such as the Red-crested Cardinal.

Some breeders like to use the coloring agent once a week throughout the year, to ensure that any odd feathers that are shed are replaced by those of equivalent coloration. Do not use too much, however, because, over an extended period, it could create a deficiency of fat-soluble vitamins. In the case of softbills, sprinkle the coloring agent over their fruit, but with seed-eating species, you may have to resort to mixing it with their water. Mix the required amount of coloring agent with a little hot water, then dilute it with cold water. Even when prepared in this way, the coloring agent may precipitate. If you use tubular drinkers, invert them and gently shake the contents once or twice daily to ensure an even distribution.

Red color food containing the pigment called canthaxanthin is best known, and there are two other similar products also available. A yellow coloring agent, which occurs naturally in various citrus fruits and grasses, and is recognized as being a form of provitamin A, is now available for a variety of finches and softbills.

In the past, breeders of such canaries as Norwich and Yorkshire Fancies, and the Lizard, used a red coloring agent to induce the required shade of orange in their birds. In practice, this color was difficult to achieve and, frequently, an undesirable brownish tinge appeared. This can now be eliminated, following the introduction of a new coloring agent, which is designed to produce the correct shade of orange.

Coloring Agents

The easiest way to administer a coloring agent is in softfood form, and there is less risk of overdosing than with liquids. An excessive intake is not normally harmful to a bird's health, although the droppings will turn red, and the plumage is likely to become brownish. It should return to its normal coloration at the next molt. If you begin color feeding too late, the wing butts and probably some of the breast feathers may be paler than the rest of the plumage. Keep a note of the date of the molt, so that next year you can start earlier and begin color feeding at the right time. It is vital, if you intend to exhibit some foreign birds, to ensure that color food is used to maintain their natural coloration after the molt.

GENERAL CARE

Looking after birds successfully is not difficult, but it does involve daily care, both morning and evening. Always take the time to watch your birds for a few moments, so that you can become familiar with their normal behavior. You will then be more likely to notice if one is acting strangely, perhaps being excessively quiet, which may be an early indication of illness.

ACCLIMATIZATION

The term acclimatization is sometimes confused with quarantine in the case of imported birds. However, a bird that has recently been released from quarantine will not be able to withstand the rigors of a temperate winter immediately. The acclimatization process is much longer, and may take up to two years.

The ideal time to purchase birds that have just finished their quarantine is in the spring. You can then house them indoors for a month or so before releasing them into the aviary, where they will have the entire summer to settle down. You can then bring them indoors, or transfer them to sheltered and heated accommodation for the winter months.

Repeat this the following year, taking care not to release the birds until the risk of frost has passed. By this stage, they will have molted out, and should now be in good feather condition. You can allow parrots and larger softbills, such as mynahs, to remain outdoors for the following winter, provided that they have a snug shelter where you can shut them in at night. A nestbox for roosting should also be available within the shelter at this stage.

Clearly, if you live in a mild part of the world, this process need not be so elaborate. Even so, do not introduce newly acquired birds to an established group in the breeding period, because they are likely to be persecuted and bullied. Even when birds are a species that generally live in flocks, it is still very likely that they will resent a newcomer.

SIGNS OF DISTRESS

If you have only recently placed the birds outdoors, you will need to watch them carefully when it rains. This applies to softbills especially, whose plumage may be in poor condition. They can end up water-logged on the floor of the flight. This can happen if their tail feathers become muddy in a planted aviary with a grass floor. There is no effective way of preventing this, but encouraging the birds to bathe before you release them into the aviary should help. If possible, shut the birds in the shelter during heavy rain. If you find a waterlogged bird, bring it indoors in a cage and allow it to dry out before releasing it back into the aviary.

You can shut newly released birds in the shelter for a day or so before allowing them into the flight. The birds should then return readily to feed, whereas if you simply let them out they may be reluctant to enter the shelter. In any event, keep a close watch to check they are eating well.

Bear in mind that they will be nervous in their new quarters for the first few days, so try to avoid any disturbances in the general area of the aviary. Watch for cats, too, since they can cause a mad panic in

VACATION CARE

Vacations are always a slight problem unless you have an experienced friend who can look after your stock while you are away. The situation is more fraught during the breeding period, when there may be young chicks in the nest. One of the advantages of belonging to a local bird-keeping group is that you may be able to make a reciprocal arrangement over vacation times with a fellow fancier. Always leave clear and detailed instructions in writing, so that there is no confusion. If you have several pairs of birds in a birdroom or aviary, number them accordingly. It is also a worthwhile precaution to label foods, just in case there could be any doubt or confusion.

catch it and transfer it to indoor accommodation. This will enable you to keep a closer watch on its condition than would otherwise be possible. You can assess its food consumption, for example, and check its droppings for any obvious signs of a problem. Then, in due course, you can release it back into the aviary.

As a precaution, in case a bird does become ill, find out in advance the name and telephone number of a local veterinarian who is an avian specialist. You should use the same veterinarian on a regular basis so that he or she becomes familiar with your stock. It is also wise to have a hospital cage or other facilities for dealing with a sick bird – in an emergency, this could make the difference between saving or losing a bird.

It is not a good idea to purchase any new stock just before going away on vacation. Acclimatizing a bird to its new surroundings takes care and attention, and it would be an imposition to expect friends or neighbors to do this, even if they had the necessary knowledge.

the aviary until the birds have learned to feel secure in their quarters. Once cats realize they cannot reach the birds, they tend to lose interest in disturbing them.

You need not worry about acclimatizing birds that have already been established in an outdoor aviary. Nevertheless, if you purchase young birds, keep an eye on them, since they can be more delicate initially than adults of the same species. If you are unhappy about a bird, and think that it is looking off color, it is wise to

RED-BILLED FIREFINCHES
These attractive little waxbills may need particular care when first obtained. They can only winter outdoors with extra heating and lighting in mild areas. If in doubt, err on the side of caution, and keep them indoors over the winter.

SPRAYING AND BATHING

In order to keep a bird housed indoors well and healthy, regular bathing is absolutely essential. This will help to keep its plumage free of pests and parasites and in good condition. Without bathing, feathers tend to become dry and ruffled, a condition that may trigger feather plucking (see page 124), especially in parrots.

With the exception of lories and lorikeets, however, most parrots will not bathe themselves in a standing bowl of water, and so you will need to take a more active role by spraying them instead.

Start by removing any food pots in the bird's enclosure, so that the contents of the cage will not become damp and possibly turn moldy. The best time to bathe your bird is just before you would normally want to clean out its quarters, because at this time the floor covering will probably be wet anyway and in need of a change.

USING A PLANT SPRAYER

The best device to use is a plant sprayer filled with tepid water. Check to see that the jet is set to give a fine, mist-like spray.

At first, most birds will be nervous of the sprayer. To overcome this initial suspicion, direct its spray so that the water droplets fall on the bird from above, rather like rain would fall from the sky.

Never point the sprayer straight at the bird, squirting it directly with water. In time, most birds become excited with pleasure at the sight of the sprayer, and parrots call loudly. Mynahs also delight in bathing. Finches usually show less enthusiasm, so spray them less frequently when they are housed indoors, perhaps every two weeks or so, whereas parrots will readily bathe two or three times a week.

BUDGIE BATHS

You can purchase special baths for Budgerigars, which can be attached over the door of their quarters. Fill the shallow bath with water and then let your bird enter the chamber. It can then splash around in here as much as it wants, whilst the sides of the chamber help to keep

SPRAYING AN UMBRELLA COCKATOO
Note how the spray is being directed above the bird, so that the droplets fall like raindrops. Regular spraying will help to dampen down the feather dust of birds in the home, and should ensure that their plumage stays sleek.

your surrounding furniture dry. It is also possible to purchase special feather conditioners to add to the bathing water. These may help to give a final gloss to the bird's plumage, but they do little to ensure that its feathering is maintained in first-class condition. This aspect of its overall condition is for the most part a reflection of its diet and environment.

You will rarely need to wash a bird, unless some disaster has befallen it – for example, a lory that has fallen into an open jar of sticky honey solution. The plumage of softbills, especially the smaller species, may appear rather dirty when you first acquire them, but it is best to wait for a few weeks until the birds have settled down in their new home and regained their confidence, instead of rushing to wash them immediately. This would be very stressful for any bird that was not used to being handled. In any case, if you provide them with suitable surroundings, you may well find that they will clean themselves naturally and may even choose to bathe of their own accord.

PEDICARE

One situation where you will need to act immediately, however, is if the birds' feet are soiled with fecal deposits or food. This can happen on the journey home, after you have bought them, if they are transported with sticky food on the floor of the box (see page 127). If you pick up the birds yourself, you can minimize this problem by getting them home without delay. A few pieces of diced apple should be suitable for most softbills, and you can give the smaller nectivores a nectar solution in a special drinker suspended inside the container.

Dirt of this nature is extremely difficult to remove once it has dried hard. If this has occurred, however, then fill a suitable container, such as a clean, smooth-edged yogurt container, with tepid water and,

BATHING YOUR BIRD

- *Many birds are reluctant to bathe alone, but may roll in damp greenfood. This is not a sign of illness, although they may stumble about.*
- *Change the water in the bird bath once it has been used, and clean the bath thoroughly.*
- *A bird bath with enclosed sides will prevent surrounding furniture being splashed with water.*
- *Check that a bird bath on the side of a cage is properly attached, or the bird will escape.*

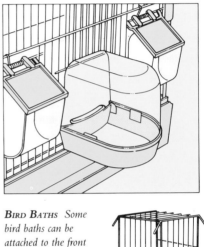

BIRD BATHS *Some bird baths can be attached to the front of the cage (above). Other designs may feature a hygienic removable base (left).*

one bird at a time, immerse their feet in the water for a minute or so. You can then carefully chip off the deposits once they have been softened by the water.

Under no circumstances should you rush this process. If you do, you may cause bleeding, and any damage to the skin will heighten the risk of infections setting in. Take particular care if the toes are en-circled with dirt, because this could cut off the blood supply resulting in the loss of the affected digit. Once you have cleaned their feet, as a final precaution you should rub them gently with a safe, germicidal ointment to cover any small nicks you may have accidentally inflicted.

Check the birds' feet again at frequent intervals to make sure that they are healing properly, and try to stop them from soiling their feet again. This is easier to do in an aviary than in a cage, because the droppings are not confined in such a small space. If they are in a cage, change the lining paper frequently, at least twice daily. In a flight of any kind, try not to feed the birds on the floor; they are more likely to encounter fecal matter there and, if you give them a large, shallow tray of food, they will hop over it in search of favored items. Various diseases can be spread from fecal contamination of the feet.

SHOWTIME

If you are intending to enter birds in a show (see pages 188 –193), you may need to wash them. This, again, is not a task you should hurry, and you should bathe a bird a couple of days before the show to allow time for its plumage to settle down again. Concentrate simply on washing the soiled areas of plumage in the morning, so that they can dry out naturally during the course of the day. You will need two

PREENING

Regular preening is a sign of good health – it serves to groom the feathers and remove the sheaths of new feathers as they emerge. The bird also spreads oil from its preen-gland, located above the base of the tail, and this helps to waterproof its plumage. Excessive washing with shampoo may remove this protective layer.

bowls, a soft brush, a bottle of children's mild shampoo, and some paper towels. Fill the bowls with tepid water and immerse the dirty area of feathering in one of the bowls. Add a small amount of shampoo, working it into the feathers to remove the dirt. Finally, blot the feathering with the paper towels, and move the bird to a cage, in a warm place on its own, so it can dry out.

Sometimes the bird's face may be stained with a trace of green food or carrot. For this reason, such foods are normally withheld just before a show. You should wash the face with particular care, since there is a risk you might get some shampoo in the eyes. Protect the bird's eyes with your hand while you apply the shampoo, and do not hold it on its back at any stage, since this may cause the soapy water to run back.

WASHING YOUR BIRD
Try to avoid washing a bird unless it is absolutely necessary. If there is a localized area of dirt on the plumage, this can be removed using a light cleaning instrument, such as a small brush or a cotton bud.

Dealing with Rodents

Both rats and mice are attracted to aviaries, and their presence will create problems. Rats, especially, are likely to harm birds and are quite capable of killing them. Mice can be just as destructive by disturbing sitting hens. Both are also a serious disease hazard to the bird-keeper as well as to the birds themselves.

It is not inevitable that you will be plagued with rodents, especially if you maintain good standards of hygiene in the birds' quarters. Spilled seed will attract rodents, so make sure you clear this away promptly, particularly in the flight. Otherwise you will find mice entering through any small gaps and, before long, some will have taken up residence in the aviary itself. Mice also frequently live behind the lining of an aviary. They are likely to breed and their urine will impregnate the surrounding lining, which you must then replace. As a precaution, feed the birds only in the shelter, and clean the floor twice weekly.

Traps

Alternatively, you can use traps. These come in various designs, but rats will soon learn to avoid them. A trap can be effective to eliminate a single rodent, but do not use one in an aviary where birds are present. It is best to catch all the birds, remove all the food, and then place the poison and traps in the aviary. This way, you will eliminate the rats before they become established.

In the birdroom, where there are no loose birds, breakback traps are a reliable option. Place these close to the area where the mice are known to be feeding. In an aviary shelter, traps are very dangerous. It may be possible to position a trap in a parrot cage, where it will be out of the bird's reach. But after dark, the noise of a trap going off can be disturbing, and may result in the birds flying around madly.

There is a trend to opt for live traps instead to deal with rodents. Some designs catch only one of these pests at a time, whereas others can hold a dozen or more. The latter ones are best, and simple to operate. After two or three nights, once you are certain where the mice are feeding, set the trap by placing the top unit in position, and bait the floor and the entry holes with seed. The mice enter and find themselves unable to escape. A trap of this type is safe for use in cages, aviaries, or birdrooms.

If you have a problem, seek the advice of a pest control expert, especially in the case of rats. Poisoning is still the preferred method for eliminating these pests, but it is sometimes possible to kill them effectively using sulfur fuses, sold by hardware stores and garden centers, if immediate professional assistance is not available.

It will be easier to detect the tunneling activities of rats if the lawn in your garden is kept closely cut. You should always take seriously any signs of excavation under the floor of the aviary, and try to identify the source of this problem immediately, by looking for the entry point outside.

New Technology
Rodenticides should not be applied in an environment where there are birds, but the recent innovation of an ultrasonic rodent scarer may be helpful. The ultrasonic sound waves are inaudible to our ears and those of birds, but they cause rodents great discomfort. To prevent rodents building up an immunity to the sound waves, such devices incorporate a variable frequency controller, which you can adjust at intervals. Obviously, you should never use equipment of this sort close to domestic rodent pets, such as hamsters.

CLEANING AND DISINFECTING

The risk of rodents greatly increases if you have other animals, especially poultry, near the aviary. Providing a clean environment is the best way to discourage rodents, and it will also alert you to their presence at an early stage.

Cleaning routines vary depending on the birds and how they are housed. In any event, you need a strong broom, a small shovel, and a dustpan and brush. You should also consider a protective facial mask, to prevent inhalation of dust while sweeping up.

The flight needs to be cleaned less often than the aviary. Most of the dirt accumulates under the perches, and during molting there are also plenty of feathers, which should be swept regularly. Try not to disturb the birds when they are breeding, and at other times enter the flight carefully so as not to upset them. Move slowly, never standing up for long, since this may cause the birds to panic. Once used to a routine, they will probably retreat to the shelter.

From time to time, scrub the floor of the flight to remove parasites, especially if you keep Australian parakeets or Cockatiels. After cleaning the flight, you may be able to hose it down from outside. Then, with a bucket of water and washing-up liquid, clean the floor using a long-handled broom. This is an important preliminary in the disinfection process, because organic matter reduces the effectiveness of disinfectant.

DIFFERENT DISINFECTANTS

There are different groups of disinfectants, and some are more appropriate for certain situations than others. Bleach (sodium hypochlorite) is used most often, and acts against many bacteria and viruses but a dirty environment will reduce its effectiveness.

Phenolic-type disinfectants are useful where it is not possible to clean the environment completely, and are sometimes recommended when washing out cages.

Try not to use quaternary ammonium compounds to clean dirty surfaces, such as the aviary floor. Like bleach, these tend to be rendered ineffective by dirt, and they are also incompatible with detergents. Quaternary ammonium compounds are best suited to such relatively clean places as a hand-rearing area, or food and water pots. It is vital to rinse everything thoroughly afterward or there is a risk, especially with finches, that they will fly down and drink from a puddle on the wet floor. Disinfectants of this type do not appear to be highly toxic, but it is clearly not a good idea to allow the birds to ingest these substances.

SAVING TIME

By lining the floor of the shelter with newspaper, spilt food and droppings can easily be removed. This is especially useful with softbills, because their food tends to go sour and moldy. The wings of larger

---

HINTS ON CLEANING

• *Clean the flight once a week.*

• *Clean the shelter twice a week.*

• *Clean the birdroom twice a week.*

• *Choose the right disinfectant for the job.*

• *Line the floors with newspaper, and tape it down if necessary to make cleaning easier.*

• *Invest in a small, portable, vacuum cleaner.*

• *Use a face mask to prevent breathing in dust when cleaning.*

• *Do not disturb birds when they are breeding.*

• *Move carefully to avoid causing panic.*

• *Rinse all containers thoroughly after they have been disinfected.*

• *Clean nestboxes and pans thoroughly after the breeding season commences to kill off any mites. You need to do this very carefully.*

it is both unpleasant and unhealthy. If you use an ionizer to combat this problem (see pages 142–143), wipe over surfaces where the dust settles every day to prevent it from wafting back into the air.

If the birdroom is a shed-type structure with a wooden floor, it is worthwhile lining the floor with hardboard and linoleum for a smooth, hard-wearing surface, which is also easy to clean and disinfect. Regular attention to cleaning will prevent a major buildup of dirt, but you should empty the birdroom at least once a year to scrub the interior thoroughly.

Cages and flights in the birdroom need to be stripped down as far as possible and washed at the same time. Redecorate, and repair them if necessary. However, you should avoid painting when the birds are in the aviary, as paint fumes will affect them adversely in such a confined space. Pay the nestboxes particular attention, to be certain that no mites are lurking, ready to infect the birds at the start of the next breeding season.

SPRING CLEANING *Use a preparation to kill mites just in case any have established themselves, especially in nestboxes, or any other dark areas.*

birds may disturb the newspaper, but if there is an adequate layer the floor will remain covered. You can also tape the newspaper down.

To reduce spillage of seed husks, in Budgerigar aviaries in particular, use a special hopper with a tray underneath to hold the husks. When this is full, simply empty it by tipping out the contents.

Hoppers for other birds do not usually have this facility. A small, portable vacuum cleaner is a useful investment to gather up seed husks and the other debris that inevitably accumulates in even the cleanest of enclosures.

Dust builds up surprisingly rapidly in a birdroom, and

LESS MESS *To reduce spillage of husks in Budgerigar aviaries, use a hopper with a removable tray. This catches the husks as the seeds are shelled by the birds. Empty it regularly to keep the aviary clean and fresh.*

BREEDING

With some bird species, distinguishing between the sexes is straightforward due to obvious differences in the plumage of the cock and hen birds, or by cere coloration – the soft, waxy swelling around the base of the upper bill – in the case of Budgerigar varieties. Yet, this is not possible in all cases, and two main methods exist to determine the gender of birds that cannot be sexed visually.

— SEXING METHODS —

Attempts to overcome the problem of sexing birds began toward the end of the nineteenth century with pelvic bone sexing. When a hen is about to lay, the gap between her pelvic bones enlarges to allow for the passage of the eggs. If you compare a hen in breeding condition with one that is not, you can see a difference. Unfortunately, this method is useful only when the birds are breeding. Outside this period, or with immature birds, you will be unable to distinguish cocks from hens.

Accurate sexing was a major stumbling block to breeding parrots, in particular, so scientific study in this field began in earnest during the 1970s. The first method devised, known as fecal steroid analysis, relied on difference in the ratios of the sex

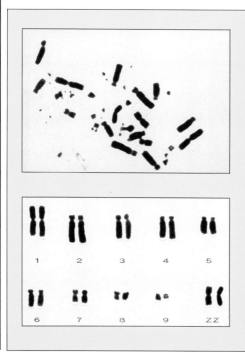

KARYOTYPING
Since the gender of the bird is determined by the time of hatching, fledglings can be sexed easily. All that is required is a growing feather. Chromosomal karyotyping is therefore a non-invasive method of sexing, which is becoming increasingly popular and, as a result, cheaper to carry out. A major advantage, especially for breeders of birds that take months to mature, is that birds can be sexed reliably when they leave the nest. This can save considerably on aviary space. You can determine almost immediately which chicks should be retained for the breeding program for certain color mutations.

CHROMOSOMAL DIFFERENCES *This karyotype of a male Scarlet Macaw shows nine chromosome pairs, plus the sex chromosome (ZZ). When the cell is not dividing (below left) the chromosomes are arranged in matching pairs. In males, the ZZ chromosome pairs are of equal length.*

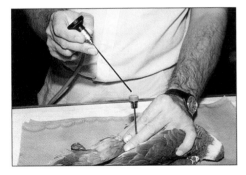

hormones between males and females of the same species. Unfortunately, however, there was no standard baseline, with the actual levels depending on the species, and a high degree of reliability proved allusive.

SURGICAL SEXING

During the 1980s, laparotomy sexing came to be widely used, and continues today. Better known simply as surgical sexing, this method is more satisfactory than others because the internal reproductive organs are viewed directly. The development of relatively safe avian anesthetics, along with the miniaturization of the endoscope, has ensured that all parrots and many softbills, for example, can be sexed in this fashion. There are some drawbacks to this method, however, especially with immature birds, which cannot be sexed with certainty.

KARYOTYPING

It seems likely that surgical sexing will be challenged by chromosomal karyotyping, which relies on the difference in the sexes encoded within the nucleus of each living cell. When the cell is not dividing, the chromosomes, on which the genes are located, are arranged in matching pairs. At this stage, when a chromosomal map, or karyotype, is prepared, it is possible to locate the pair of chromosomes responsible for determining gender.

The accuracy of chromosomal karyotyping is assured, since, unlike fecal steroid analysis, no ratios are involved. The bird experiences less stress than with surgical sexing, because no anesthetic is required, and the bird need not be moved. It is the safest method presently available.

SURGICAL SEXING OF AN AMAZON PARROT The advantage of using this method is that by looking directly at the bird's reproductive organs, a vet is able to recognize any abnormality here, or a generalized illness such as aspergillosis, and also observe whether the bird is likely to breed soon.

·THE REPRODUCTIVE SYSTEM·

The more prolific species, such as the Budgerigar, will nest at virtually any time of the year. Other birds, however, such as canaries, have a more closely defined breeding season, nesting only during the spring and early summer. Birds will not usually attempt to breed unless they are in good condition and well established in their quarters. You need, therefore, to ensure that pairs are set up before the onset of winter if you hope to breed them the following year. Placing a pair in a new aviary in the spring is likely to lead to disappointment, even if they have bred together before.

You also need to give recently imported birds plenty of time to settle down, and they will probably not breed until they have molted for the first time in their new home. The signs of breeding condition are unmistakable: cock birds become more attentive toward the hens, and more vocal, too. The song of canaries is attractive, but the raucous calls of parrots are certainly less appealing. This stage should pass quite rapidly, however.

Many aviculturists now specialize in particular groups of birds, and for serious breeding purposes you should aim to have at least two pairs of the same species. Then if they both breed, you will have unrelated youngsters to pair together to establish a second, F2, generation. The length of time taken to reach this stage depends largely on the species concerned. The small waxbills will breed by the time they are a year old, for example, but parrots may take four or five years to attain sexual maturity.

SEXUAL CHARACTERISTICS

When a bird is surgically sexed, the procedure is invariably carried out from the left side of the body, and the opening is made behind the last rib. The opening is usually just a tiny incision, the skin being pierced with a sharp trocar, and no

MALE ORGANS

Unlike the hen, the reproductive organs of the male bird are paired, so that there are two functional testes within the body. The spermatozoa travel along the tubules known as the vas deferens, before passing out of the body via the cloaca. When mating takes place, the sperm are transferred directly from here into the cloacal opening of the hen, and progress up her oviduct in order to fertilize the eggs here. A single mating will usually fertilize a whole clutch of eggs, with the sperm remaining active in the hen's reproductive tract during this period. Fertilization can only take place as each ovum is liberated from the ovary, every day or two during the laying period, depending on the bird concerned.

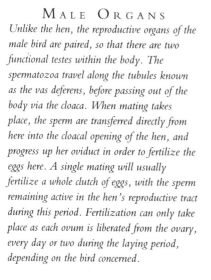
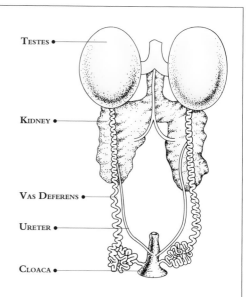

TESTES •

KIDNEY •

VAS DEFERENS •

URETER •

CLOACA •

FEMALE REPRODUCTIVE TRACT After being released from the ovary, the developing egg undergoes a series of changes as it passes down the oviduct, before it is finally laid. On rare occasions it may not pass down the oviduct, but into the body cavity, where it can lodge, and perhaps give rise to the condition peritonitis.

OVARY Ova develop here under hormonal control, and are released sequentially down into the infundibulum.

INFUNDIBULUM It is in this part of the tract that fertilization occurs, soon after the release of the ovum.

MAGNUM Here the egg white or albumen is added around the fertilized ovum.

ISTHMUS At this stage, the rubbery shell membranes are added and envelop the egg.

UTERUS The shell gland extracts calcium from the blood to form the eggshell. This consists of millions of tiny pores.

VAGINA The final part of the female tract, leading into the cloaca, from where the egg is laid.

REDUNDANT RIGHT OVARY Only the left ovary is functional.

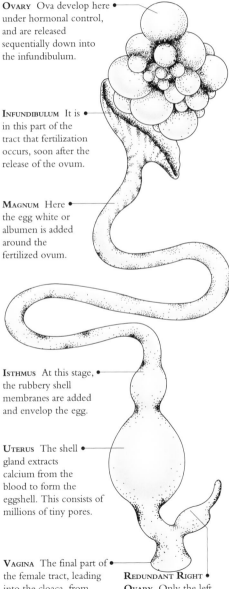

suturing is required. If gaseous anesthetic is used, the bird should be rapidly back on its perch showing no ill effects.

Cock birds have two testes, located near the kidneys, and hens have two ovaries, but only one, found on the left side of the body, is active. The ovary connects to an oviduct, through which the ovum travels down the reproductive tract until it reaches the cloaca, where the openings of the digestive, urinary, and reproductive tracts are found. From here, the egg will be voided by muscular contractions, and fall into the nest.

THE DEVELOPING EGG

The ovum undergoes a number of changes. Fertilization occurs shortly after its release from the ovary, in the vicinity of the infundibulum, the upper part of the oviduct. The white part of the egg, known as albumen, is added in the next section of the tract, the magnum, before being enveloped by the tough, leathery shell membranes in the isthmus.

The longest part of the process leading to the production of an egg takes place in the uterus. Here, calcium from the hen's bloodstream is extracted to form the shell. The color of the eggshell depends on the species of bird. Hole-nesting species, such as parrots, lay white eggs, while those that breed in open nests, such as canaries, have colored eggs, often marked with blotches and dots. This coloration comes from old blood cells, and helps to conceal the eggs from potential predators – white eggs would be very conspicuous in the open.

After spending just less than a day in this section of the hen's reproductive tract, the egg will be laid, normally in the morning rather than at night. The number of eggs in a clutch depends on the species, as does the frequency of laying. Pigeons and doves, for example, typically lay just one or two eggs, whereas finches may have clutches of six eggs or more.

→ PREPARING FOR THE BREEDING SEASON ←

Most birds can be bred in flights or aviaries, but exhibition birds are usually bred in specially designed cages so that breeders can be sure of the chicks' parentage. Plywood or hardwood cages are often used for this purpose. Alternatively, you may prefer a metal breeding cage. These are available in various sizes and tend to be more durable than wooden cages. Their enamel surfaces also facilitate cleaning and disinfecting. However, buying a metal cage can be a lot more expensive than making a wooden one.

When you are planning the position of the breeding cages in the birdroom, avoid placing the cages in a location directly in front of a sunny window, because it could result in birds succumbing to heatstroke. Most birds dislike breeding in an open environment. They prefer a darker location that is more secluded.

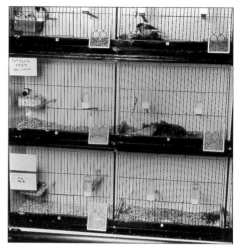

Breeding Cages in a Birdroom *Nesting activities can be more closely supervised here than in an aviary.*

PROVIDING FOOD

Use jam-jar hoppers to avoid disturbing birds with refilling seed dispensers daily. The hoppers fit easily through the door of a Budgerigar breeding cage. Fill a clean jam jar with seed of the appropriate size, and place a plastic base on top, which converts it to a seed reservoir, before inverting the whole unit. Hoppers are normally reliable, but check the seed flow twice daily because it may become blocked, either due to a slight tilt of the jam jar, or to a piece of debris, such as a stone.

Jam-Jar Hopper *This is ideal in small cages, for small seeds, but check that the jar does not tilt, restricting seed flow.*

Feed finches with a seed pot in the cage or a hopper outside, attached to the front. Check for blockage, an especially critical precaution with such small birds. Hoppers are unsuitable for birds that like to scatter their seed around, such as canaries. Instead, offer a limited quantity of food and encourage them to eat it, rather than have a week's supply spread over the cage floor.

Provide your birds with tubular drinkers attached to the outside of the breeding cage. Make sure that the base cannot slip down slightly from the tube itself, which is held in place by a clip. Otherwise, the water is likely to leak onto the cage floor.

Cuttlefish bone is absolutely essential during the breeding period. You can use a metal clip to secure the bone to the side of the cage. Do not provide large pieces, especially to Budgerigars, since the birds may perch on it, and their droppings will soil the cuttlefish bone. Also sprinkle grit on the floor of the cage, or put it in a small container, which you top up regularly.

BREEDING EQUIPMENT

The choice of breeding equipment will be influenced by the birds concerned. Parrots use nestboxes, which must be sufficiently robust to stand up to their bills, whereas in contrast, canaries breed in nestpans. Finches may use small wicker baskets, nestboxes, or nestpans, depending to some extent on the species. A good range of possible nest sites should be provided, in order to encourage breeding activity. Some birds, such as Pekin Robins, may nevertheless prefer to build their own nest, utilizing plants in a well-planted flight, such as shrubs or conifers. Here they will have privacy to conceal their nests. For parrots, hang the nestbox under cover, near the roof of the flight, so that there is no risk of the interior flooding when it rains. For finches, position nesting facilities in secluded parts of the flight, hidden close to the roof under a canopy of vegetation.

NESTING MATERIAL

Only lovebirds and hanging parrots generally use nesting material, in the case of parrots. Provide a good selection of branches at the onset of the mating season, as they will strip off bark for this purpose. Nestpan liners and nesting material for other birds are available from pet shops. You can also purchase dried moss, which is popular as a nestliner, from florists.

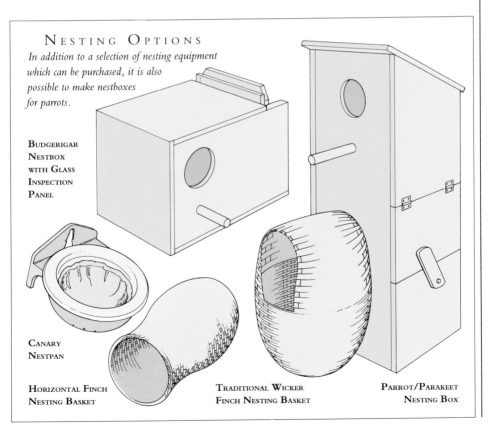

NESTING OPTIONS

In addition to a selection of nesting equipment which can be purchased, it is also possible to make nestboxes for parrots.

BUDGERIGAR NESTBOX WITH GLASS INSPECTION PANEL

CANARY NESTPAN

HORIZONTAL FINCH NESTING BASKET

TRADITIONAL WICKER FINCH NESTING BASKET

PARROT/PARAKEET NESTING BOX

SIGNS OF BREEDING ACTIVITY

When you see birds carrying nesting material – hay, pieces of cloth, hair, hemp or sisal fibers from rope, or whatever else you may have provided for them – breeding activity will probably follow shortly afterwards. Provide sufficient nesting material, although most parrots will not need this, as they do not build nests.

You may notice that one member of the pair starts to become absent for progressively longer periods of time each day. Do not worry if they both emerge when you approach the aviary; this is quite normal, and not an indication that they will abandon their clutch of eggs.

When chicks have hatched, provide additional food items, such as rearing food. This will distract the adult birds for a moment, and soon they will eagerly anticipate your visits, rather than being disturbed by your presence. This is certainly not the time to undertake any major maintenance or cleaning tasks in the aviary, however, since this degree of disturbance could well upset them and cause them to abandon their eggs.

EXTRA CALCIUM

As well as nest-building, one of the most likely signs of egg-laying activity is an increase in the amounts of cuttlefish bone a hen bird consumes. This material provides her with additional amounts of vital calcium for the production of strong, healthy eggshells. Most birds have no difficulty in chewing off pieces of cuttlefish bone for themselves, but some finches may need you to scrape off sections with a knife.

BODILY CHANGES

You may notice a slight swelling around the hen's vent area, especially in Budgerigars, immediately before she lays. This is quite normal. Her droppings are also likely

SNEAK PREVIEW It does no harm to have a quick glance into the unoccupied nest while you are in the aviary, but never drive a hen off her nest.

to alter noticeably both in consistency and size, becoming much larger and tending to be looser and stronger smelling than at other times of the year. Again, these changes are indications that egg-laying is imminent, and not a sign of ill-health. If you have covered the floor of the aviary with newspaper (see pages 164–165), you will be able to remove the droppings with the least amount of disruption to the birds.

It is important to bear in mind, especially if it is the first time that your birds have nested, that they are likely to be nervous. It is therefore advisable to try to restrain your curiosity. Do not delve into their nest in order to check on their progress, and under no circumstances should you be tempted to drive a sitting bird out of its box. Most birds, however, may leave the nest for a short period of time if you move into their immediate vicinity.

THE EGG-LAYING PERIOD

It is not unusual for the incubation period to start only after the second or third egg has been laid, so do not be concerned if the birds do not sit once the first egg has been laid. Bear in mind, when you are working out the incubation period, that the effective length of time that it takes for the first and subsequent eggs to hatch depends entirely on when incubation begins in earnest. In the case of a Budgerigar, whose eggs normally take 18 days to hatch, the first egg in a clutch will remain unhatched for 20 days until the chick emerges, assuming incubation did not begin until the next egg was laid. Make a note of when egg-laying commences, so that you can assess when hatching is most likely to occur.

Once the hen has started laying, everything normally progresses without problems, but you will need to watch for egg-binding. Although generally rare, it is a serious condition, and can prove rapidly

Sitting Tight Most birds will incubate without any problems, especially when they have nested in your collection before. However, it is important that you avoid disturbing them.

> ## NESTING BIRDS
> • *Provide adequate nesting material and rearing food for the birds.*
> • *Provide cuttlefish bone, which is a good source of the calcium essential for shell production in hens.*
> • *Watch for symptoms of egg-binding.*
> • *Give the birds as much privacy as possible.*
> • *If you remove eggs from the nest as they are laid, return them to the correct hen.*

fatal if not treated (see page 207). Affected hens usually emerge from the nestbox and appear decidedly ill, with their sense of balance affected. Unable to perch, they will be forced to stay on the floor of their quarters. This disorder is the result of an egg becoming trapped in the lower part of the reproductive tract and causing an obstruction there.

It is usual with canaries to replace their eggs with dummy eggs as each one is laid. The real eggs are then returned only after all the eggs – usually four to a clutch – have been laid. This ensures that the chicks will all hatch at the same time, and so all will have a better chance of survival. Otherwise, the eldest chicks tend to monopolize the food supply and the younger birds are likely to suffer as a result.

Some fanciers use egg-trays that fit into a special cabinet. Each compartment in the cabinet has a number corresponding to numbers on the breeding cages, so that in due course the eggs can be replaced under the correct hen. On the fourth morning, after laying is over, the eggs are put back under the hen, and the dummies removed. This system is often used when only one parent is responsible for rearing the chicks, as it makes feeding the chicks far easier.

HATCHING AND REARING

There is no need to disturb the birds during the incubation period, although some breeders do examine eggs for signs of fertility. This is straightforward in the case of parrots, because the white eggshells permit the penetration of light. If you do decide to "candle" the eggs, as this process is known, wash your hands first, and dry them on disposable paper towels.

Viewed with a good light behind them, fertile eggs after a week or so of incubation will have assumed an opacity, resulting from the development of the chick. Infertile eggs, or those that have failed to develop after laying, will look "clear," with the light showing through them.

This information is helpful for the more prolific species, such as the Budgerigar, because if once you know that none of the eggs are fertile, you can remove them without delay, shut the hen outside the nestbox, and then hope that mating will take place. In most cases, however,

INSIDE AN EGG Here all the components of the egg are shown. The yolk provides nourishment for the growing embryo, which also draws calcium from the shell into its body, and this ultimately gives the chick the strength to break out of the egg.

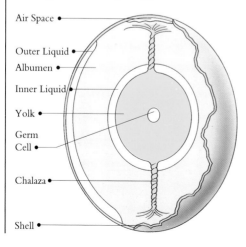

- Air Space
- Outer Liquid
- Albumen
- Inner Liquid
- Yolk
- Germ Cell
- Chalaza
- Shell

FEEDING CONTINUITY
Irrespective of whether or not you intend to keep the chicks, it is a good idea to house them in an indoor flight or cage when you first separate them from the adult birds. You can then monitor them and be certain that they are feeding properly. It is important to continue offering rearing food, and also to provide soaked seed, if this has been available to them previously.

especially when the birds are not yet fully domesticated, it is preferable simply to allow things to progress without disturbing either the birds or their eggs.

NUTRITIONAL REQUIREMENTS

Toward the end of the incubation period, start offering rearing foods in small quantities. Do not inspect the nest when you anticipate hatching. Some large parrots may become uncharacteristically aggressive at this stage. The vast majority of fertile eggs incubated naturally will hatch without any problems. This is in contrast to eggs that have been artificially incubated.

After hatching, the volume of food consumed will start to increase, and you must also cater for changes in dietary preferences. Many softbills and finches with chicks are almost entirely insectivorous, and if you do not provide adequate livefood, the chicks may be ejected from the nest. If you find a young bird on the ground close to the nest, do not despair, even if it appears to be dead. Pick it up gently and clasp it very carefully between your hands. After a minute or so it may start to wriggle slightly, having been revived by the warmth of your hands. If so, continue the process for a while longer before replacing the chick in the nest.

You rarely encounter this type of problem with parrots, because of their nesting habits. But if you have Budgerigar concaves – small wooden blocks in which eggs sit – that are too small for the box, there is a risk that a chick could slip down inside the gap.

Potential Problems

One unpleasant problem encountered with members of the crow family, such as jays, and other more omnivorous softbills, such as laughing thrushes, is their occasional tendency to eat their own offspring. This appears to result from the provision of too much food; the birds do not have to spend time foraging and treat their chicks as an extension of their food supply. With these birds, it is a good idea to scatter livefood on the floor of the aviary to encourage the adults to search for it, which should distract their attention from the nestbox.

If you are breeding exhibition birds, you will almost certainly want to ring them with closed bands while they are in the nest. You can use rings supplied by the society concerned. It is better to close-ring a bird at a relatively early stage, even if the ring is loose. Without the proper ring, you will not be able to enter the bird in a breeder's class. In contrast, split bands can be applied at any age. These are useful for identification, but offer no formal confirmation of breeding origins.

Nestling Budgerigars benefit from regular handling to ensure that they are steady when they leave the nest. This will also give you the chance to inspect the inner surfaces of the bill and the claws, which is especially important if concaves in nestboxes are wetter than usual. If the claws of the chicks become

soiled with fecal matter, this can lead to the loss of the claw, or it can cause the claw to grow at a deviated angle.

Young finches and softbills, and doves and pigeons, fledge at a relatively early age, often within a mere three weeks of hatching. At this stage, they are still rather frail, and thus very vulnerable to the elements. A summer storm, for example, can cause a fatal chilling, so it is vital to ensure there is good drainage of rainwater from the aviary. The birds will also tend to cling readily to the aviary mesh, not realizing that they will be a target for cats. There is little that you can do, although as a precaution you could fit some temporary panels around the sides of the aviary. Outside of the breeding season, these same panels will be useful for winter protection.

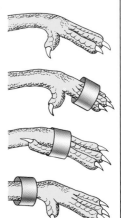

Ringing A closed band should only be fitted when chicks are young. The band must be slid over the bird's three longest toes. The fourth toe is then held parallel against the leg itself for a short period of time, while the ring is passed over it, and the toe is then freed.

Green-naped Lorikeet Chick Prior to a feed, the crop of the chick should slacken, as food from its last meal passes on down through its digestive tract.

⸻• ARTIFICIAL INCUBATION •⸻

During recent years there has been a trend toward the artificial incubation of parrot eggs. However, this process is costly, and, in inexperienced hands, results are not likely to be better than leaving the eggs with their parents.

Small incubators for hatching a few parrot eggs are available from avicultural suppliers. Talk to other breeders before purchasing one, though, to find out which models they have found most suitable. One with an automatic turning facility saves you having to open the incubator.

FACTORS INFLUENCING INCUBATION

The positioning of the incubator helps to determine how many eggs will eventually hatch. Site it on a level surface well away from direct sunlight, which can raise the internal temperature of the egg to a lethal degree for developing embryos. The ideal incubation temperature for parrot eggs is 37.2°C (99°F).

Relative humidity is the other significant factor. The egg loses water throughout incubation. When water loss is at a correct level, which depends on the humidity in the atmosphere, an air-space develops at the rounded end. Here, in a stage called internal "pipping," the chick first breathes air. However, inadequate water loss forces the chick to hatch prematurely, which is likely to make hand-feeding difficult. Alternatively, it may simply die, effectively drowning inside the shell. A rapid loss of fluid from the egg can be equally harmful, causing irreparable kidney damage. Such chicks are invariably smaller than normal.

AFTER INCUBATION

Young parrot chicks, like other birds, do not need to feed upon emerging from the egg. The yolk sac, which nourished them during the incubation period, continues

BROODERS

Chicks are usually placed in a brooder soon after hatching. At present brooders are not widely available, but they are not difficult to make from plywood. The heat source is built into the bottom of the unit in the form of a flexible pad or mat. Alternatively, light bulbs can be used, but these tend to fail regularly. For this reason, it is better to have two bulbs of lower wattage, in case one fails. Whether using a heat pad or light bulbs, a good quality thermostat is vital.

to sustain the chicks for a period after hatching. The first feed is usually mainly water, sometimes with probiotics added, designed to start establishing the gut flora. It is given about four hours after hatching, by which stage the chicks should have largely recovered from their exertions.

The feeding of young parrots formerly relied upon various recipes, often based on pediatric foods. Now, specially formulated rations are available in powder or crumb form. You should mix these with water and a probiotic compound, if required, following the instructions on the pack.

At first, the chicks are likely to need feeding every two hours or so. You can assess this by the state of the crop. This should have slackened off noticeably, but not emptied completely, since the last feed. If the food has not passed through the digestive tract, the chick may have a problem, such as a blockage in the crop, and you should seek advice immediately from an experienced avian veterinarian. Even in young chicks, it can be possible to operate and remove an obstruction safely. The coloration of the chick gives a clear indication of its state of health. It should be pinkish, with red usually indicating a disease. A whitish skin tone is typically a sign of chilling, or can be a symptom of fatty liver and kidney syndrome.

Monitoring Development
One of the best ways to monitor the progress of chicks reliably is to weigh and log them on a daily basis. For this, you will need scales capable of weighing in units of 0.1 gram. Consistently weigh them first thing in the morning, before a feed.

As the chicks grow, you can increase the intervals between feeds. Tiny chicks need feeding every two hours around the clock, but larger chicks can go for approximately four hours between 2 a.m. and 6 a.m. It takes from several weeks to three or more months of demanding attention to rear macaw chicks. Do not hurry to increase feeding intervals, as this leads to a weight loss that could stunt the chick's growth.

Weight loss is normal, however, as fledging approaches, and if you plot daily weight on a graph, you will see

that the growth curve dips downwards slightly. By this stage, the chicks are very active, and once they are able to climb out of their larger container you should plan to place them in a cage with low perches.

The youngsters will still beg to be fed by hand, but may now be reluctant to accept your offering. At this stage you should also be providing soaked seed and fruit on the floor of the cage. Make drinking water available, too, in a sealed vessel, so that there is no risk of the chicks becoming saturated with water. If, later, you think that any are not feeding properly on their own, then you must still feed them once or twice a day, keeping a close watch to ensure they do not lose condition. The young parrot's quarters must be kept scrupulously clean, so food here does not become soiled with droppings.

THERMOMETER
VIEWING PANEL
INCUBATOR
CONTROLS
PERFORATED TRAY WITH WATER BENEATH
LID
BASE

INCUBATORS
Compact, reliable incubators suitable for small numbers of eggs are now available. Cleanliness within the incubator is very important, so disinfect it thoroughly between batches of eggs to prevent harmful microorganisms from building up, which could be fatal to newly hatched chicks.

HAND-REARING

Newly hatched chicks are delicate and therefore need to stay warm, at about incubator temperature, for the first day or so. You can house them conveniently in clean margarine tubs, lined with tissue paper, in the brooder. You will need to change the tissue paper after each feed, however, so that the chicks do not become soiled with fecal matter. Do not use wood shavings, since these can be dangerous if swallowed by a chick.

If you have difficulty finding a suitable brooder, you can make one quite easily yourself (see right). The heat source can be either a flexible heating mat placed at

MAKING A BROODER

A basic box, with ventilation holes and a clear acrylic front to observe the chicks within, will work. It must be easy to clean. Melamine-faced chipboard, which you can wipe over with a moistened tissue, is ideal for this purpose. At the front of the unit, incorporate a secure sliding door. This will help to minimize the inevitable heat loss every time you open the front to remove the chicks to feed them, since it need only be opened a short distance. Keep heating elements out of reach of the chicks.

GROWTH RATE CHART This typical growth curve shows the slowing down in growth and weight loss prior to fledging. Drastic deviation from this pattern during hand-rearing is likely to indicate a problem.

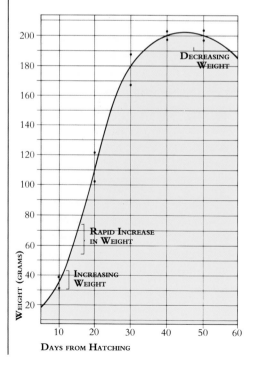

DAYS FROM HATCHING

the base of the unit, or a light bulb. Use two bulbs so that if one fails, the chicks are not totally deprived of heat and thus do not risk becoming perhaps fatally chilled. Be sure to have replacement bulbs available in case one fails in the middle of the night. And use bulbs of a more subdued color at night, such as blue.

Whatever method of heating you do finally decide on, make certain that you incorporate a reliable thermostat somewhere in the circuitry. You may also think it a wise precaution to install an alarm system, which will alert you if the temperature falls below the required level.

FEEDING

Chicks do not have to be fed as soon as they hatch. Their yolk sac, which nourished them through the incubation period, will continue to sustain them until about four hours after hatching. This is the time when the first feed can be given. A simple dropper can be used at this stage, but most bird-breeders prefer to use a teaspoon, with its edges bent inwards to act as a funnel. This helps to prevent spillage. Syringes (with the needle removed) are a useful device for feeding large chicks such as macaws, but they can jam and so there is a greater risk of choking a young chick as the food may be inadvertently squirted into its windpipe.

MONITORING PROGRESS

The best means of monitoring the chicks' progress is to weigh them each morning, before their first feed, using scales that are graduated in 0.1 gram units. By keeping a record of their weight increases, you will soon see if there is a problem with any of the chicks you need to deal with.

You should also take special notice of the crop, which should slacken noticeably, but not empty completely, between feeds. If this does not happen, the chick may be suffering from an infection, or it may have swallowed something, such as wood shavings, which is causing an obstruction. Alternatively, the crop may be reacting abnormally simply because the chick is cold. It is important, however, to identify the correct cause of the problem, and then to take appropriate action, seeking veterinary advice if necessary.

As the chicks grow and develop, you need to increase the interval between feeds. With the very tiniest of chicks, feeds every two hours around the clock will be needed. With larger individuals, however, you can cut feeding frequency down to about every four hours - from, say, 2 to 6 a.m. Do not be in too much of a hurry to extend intervals between feeds, because this could stunt the chick's subsequent growth. The amount of food remaining in the crop reliably indicates the best interval.

HAND-FEEDING CHICKS It is important not to rush this task. Mix the food fresh for each feed, ensuring that it is warm enough, around 38°C (100°F). Use different feeding utensils for each batch of chicks.

→• WEANING •←

It is quite normal for chicks to lose some body weight around the time that they would normally leave the nest. By this stage in their development, they should be very alert and active and entirely capable of climbing out of their containers, and so you should be thinking of placing them in a cage set up with a series of low perches.

The young birds still beg to be fed by hand, but they tend to toy with the food offered to them, rather than eat it greedily. This behavior is normal and should not cause concern provided that the chicks are healthy and lively in all other respects.

In order to encourage the chicks to start feeding independently, you should provide soaked seed (see page 147) and fruit, placed on the floor of the cage. Bear in mind, however, that these are perishable foodstuffs, which can turn moldy very quickly. To avoid waste, do not prepare more than the chicks will require for a single feed. Drinking water should also be provided in a suitable container to the young birds. Watch the youngsters closely during this process, and note those that feed well on their own. Less developed chicks may still require hand-feeding. It is always preferable to hand-rear and wean chicks in small groups, rather than keeping them on their own. Chicks hand-reared singly are more likely to become imprinted on their keepers, and can prove harder to wean and, ultimately, pair up for mating.

Periodically, the young birds may still attempt to solicit tid-bits from you. This is not unusual behavior by any means. In the case of macaws, for example, young, fully fledged birds remain with their parents in family groups and continue to beg for food long after they are capable of feeding independently.

BROODING At eight weeks old, these young Sun Conure chicks are nearly independent. They will already be starting to crack seeds by this stage.

SEPARATING YOUNG STOCK

It is important to transfer the youngsters to larger quarters where they can flap and build up their wing muscles and continue their development. Since chromosomal sexing has been developed, it is now possible to have chicks sexed without difficulty at this stage. You can then pair them up well before they start to breed. Young parrots housed together in this fashion will develop a much stronger pair-bond than two individuals placed together when they are mature. This enhances the likelihood of their breeding success and reduces the possibility of aggressive outbursts, which can occur, particularly with cockatoos, when the bird turns on its intended mate.

HAND-RAISED BIRDS
• *When settling in the young birds, confine them in the shelter for a few days to be sure they are eating and drinking properly.*
• *Place them in an outside aviary when the weather is mild and dry.*
• *Gradually reduce the temperature until they are receiving no artificial heat.*
• *Check that their plumage does not become saturated when it rains.*
• *Avoid introducing chicks alongside adult birds until they are well established outside.*

USING COMMERCIAL FOODS

Changing from a rearing food to an adult diet can be a difficult time, but certain commercial diets have been formulated to minimize the problems that may occur. Parrot pellets or crumbs, which must be soaked in water when first given to a very young bird, contain similar ingredients to the diet on which the chick would have been reared. As a result, this preparation is more likely to be taken readily by young birds, compared with the success rate of feeding them unfamiliar seeds. In emergenies,

foods of this type, which have been formulated specifically for parrots, can also be used for rearing other chicks, such as softbills. This is not usually undertaken on a regular basis, however, whereas chicks of larger parrots, such as the African Gray, are often hand-reared for sale as pets. The same guidelines apply, however, bearing in mind that such chicks usually fledge at a much earlier age than parrots. During weaning, when providing livefood, ensure that it is small and easily digestible. Whole mealworms are usually unsuitable due to their indigestible casing.

FEATHER-PLUCKING
Some parents feather-pluck their chicks. This young parrot will regrow its feathers, but until it does, it is at risk of becoming chilled if left with its parents. You should remove chicks from pairs known to feather-pluck before the chick's feathers develop.

COLOR BREEDING

Keeping records is an important part of bird-keeping, whether a note of bird behavior or simply the date that an egg was laid. However, in the field of color breeding, it is critical. Mutations have long been a source of fascination, and it appears that many birds possess a relatively high incidence of mutant genes coding their coloration. As domestication has proceeded, these genes have been widely transmitted through captive populations, and have begun to emerge, affecting the coloration of the individuals concerned.

SO MANY COLORS

In a captive population birds are likely to be more closely related than in the wild, and this increases the possibility of recessive color mutations emerging in their offspring. It is then a matter of identifying which birds may be carrying the mutant gene, through a study of the existing breeding records. These individuals can be then used most effectively in the program to establish a mutation.

THE SCIENCE OF INHERITANCE

Genetics was first studied in depth by the Austrian monk, Gregor Mendel, toward the end of the nineteenth century. Based on his work with pea plants, Mendel formulated a set of rules governing the inheritance of features, such as color, which are passed on from one generation to the next.

Each chick receives one set of genes from each of its parents, which combine as a result of the fertilization of the ovum. The genes occur on chromosomes, and usually there are two genes for each characteristic, although they may not be the same. In most cases, alterations to the genes, known as mutations, are said to be recessive to the normal form. These mutations are often harmful, either directly or indirectly.

A green Ring-necked Parakeet, for example, is relatively inconspicuous when feeding in a tree, but a bright yellow (lutino) bird stands out clearly to a potential predator, such as a hawk. As

GREGOR MENDEL (1822–1884)
Ignored in his lifetime, his work on inheritance was rediscovered in 1900.

a consequence, the lutino mutation is unlikely to survive well in the wild, but because it is colorful and attractive, it is popular in captivity, where it faces no pressure from predation. However, if this mutation were dominant, Ring-necked Parakeets would rapidly produce a relatively high proportion of lutino offspring, possibly endangering the survival of the group.

RECESSIVE MUTATIONS

In the case of recessive mutations, it is possible for a bird to carry the recessive gene while appearing perfectly normal in coloration itself. The recessive characteristic will become evident in offspring only when this individual mates with another individual possessing an equivalent mutant gene. Gregor Mendel's laws of inheritance are valuable tools for the breeder today, since they assist in formulating pairings that will maximize the production of mutant offspring, and also make it easier to establish new colors.

INTRODUCTION TO GENETICS

In this section on genetics, all of the basic pairings are given, including those of the sex-linked recessive mutations, where both the genetic makeup and the gender of the birds are significant. These tables will enable you to find the pairing that is most likely to yield the highest percentage of chicks of the desired color. The majority of color mutations in birds are recessive in their mode of inheritance.

You will need considerable aviary space, especially for establishing a new mutation, as you may be unsure which of the chicks may be split for a recessive character. This will enable you to work out which of the visually normal birds carry the desired mutant gene in their genetic makeup, by using test pairings with other birds of known genetic makeup. These birds can then be used to best effect in your breeding program. Not all color forms are considered equally desirable by bird-keepers. Generally, the most striking birds are most sought after. These include the blue forms of predominantly green parrots, such as the Ring-necked Parakeet, as well as the yellow variants.

DIAGRAM OF PAIRINGS

The complex diagrams on pages 184–185 show the starting point for pairings and the two genes from both of the adult birds, arranged at right angles to each other. It is possible to see the four basic combinations for these different genes, bearing in mind that every chick receives one set of genes from each parent. Shown in the divided inner boxes in these diagrams is the genetic makeup of the chicks in each case.

In the case of parrots, color mutations have currently been recorded in 21 out of 77 of the recognized different genera. Not all mutations have been successfully preserved, however. It is a slow process to establish color mutations successfully, and in the case of the larger parrots such as Amazons, this often takes many years. This is due to the length of time it takes for these birds to mature before they themselves can be used for breeding purposes.

ESTABLISHED MUTATIONS

In contrast, finches will nest when they are less than a year old. This has facilitated the breeding of mutations in such birds, since it is possible to increase the number of mutant individuals quite rapidly. In turn, this ensures that the mutation is less vulnerable.

Although some mutations have proved somewhat delicate at first, those that are now widely available are no more demanding in their care than normal-colored individuals of the same species. When new colors first become available, they are usually far more expensive than normal birds of the same species. In time, however, assuming that the color becomes well established, the price will fall as such birds are bred in much greater numbers.

TABLE OF PAIRINGS

Located along the bottom of the following pages there are tables, which show all the possible pairings for the various mutations, in combination with a normal individual. You need to read these horizontally, knowing the genetic makeup of the adult birds, so as to work out the likely coloration and genetic combinations of the chicks, expressed in percentage terms. If there are four chicks in a clutch, for example, and a 25% chance of a particular color combination, one of these chicks on average will be of this color.

AUTOSOMAL RECESSIVE MUTATIONS

These are the most common color mutations in birds, encompassing all blues as well as yellow and white varieties. The recessive pied mutation of the Budgerigar belongs to this group, as does the white-faced Cockatiel. In genetical shorthand, an individual known to carry different genes for a characteristic is said to be heterozygous, compared with homozygous for one known to carry identical genes.

"Split" is sometimes used by birdkeepers in place of heterozygous, and is indicated by an oblique line. Dominant genes or characteristics are written in upper case letters, with their recessive counterparts indicated by lower case. A green bird that is split for blue is "Gg," in contrast to a homozygous individual, "GG."

Bearing in mind that the genes from each parent combine at random, you can work out the potential offspring that would be produced from pairing two heterozygous birds of this type together, using the Punnett Square System. This is simply a matter of arranging the genes from both parents to show all possible combinations (see left). In percentage terms, you can see the results from this pairing in the table below.

In most cases, mutations are more expensive than normal birds, especially in the case of the blue form of Ring-necked Parakeets. If you cannot afford two blue individuals, the ideal pairing is number four in the table below. Not only will you have an excellent chance of breeding blues from just one blue parent, but you can be certain that all the green offspring will also be split for blue. Since it is impossible to distinguish between splits and normal (homozygous) individuals, this is a considerable advantage.

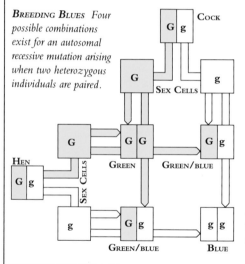

BREEDING BLUES Four possible combinations exist for an autosomal recessive mutation arising when two heterozygous individuals are paired.

AUTOSOMAL RECESSIVE MUTATION This shows the various possible combinations and likely percentages of offspring from pairing a blue with a normal green bird.

1 Green/blue	x	Green/blue	▶	50% Green/blue	25% Green	25% Blue
2 Green	x	Blue	▶	100% Green/blue		
3 Green	x	Green/blue	▶	50% Green	50% Green/blue	
4 Green/blue	x	Blue	▶	50% Green/blue	50% Blue	
5 Blue	x	Blue	▶	100% Blue		

SEX-LINKED RECESSIVE MUTATIONS

This particular group of color mutations is confined to the pair of sex chromosomes, as its name suggests. As a result, there is considerable difference in the mutation's mode of inheritance, due to the variation in the structure between the pair of chromosomes in male and female birds. Cock birds have two chromosomes of equal length, ZZ, so there are matching pairs of genes. In hens, the Y chromosome is significantly shorter than its partner, meaning that genes on the Z chromosome may be unpaired. This applies to the color mutations known to be sex-linked, including virtually all lutino mutations, cinnamons, pearl markings in the Cockatiel, and opaline markings in the Budgerigar.

With only one gene present in such cases, the hen must either be normal or show the sex-linked character. It is impossible for hens to be split for a mutation of this type; their appearance must always reflect their genetic makeup. In the chart (right), the absence of the gene is indicated by a dash.

With such a pairing you could expect just green chicks, although all the cocks will be split for the lutino characteristics.

Being pure green, hens have no significant role in establishing a strain of lutino birds. In fact, lutino cocks are considerably more valuable for this purpose than hens, as seen by comparing the results in numbers 1 and 2 in the table of potential pairings (below).

The second pairing is the most important if you plan to breed mutations of this type, because all the progeny can be used in the program, and lutino birds result in the first generation. In contrast to pairing 4, there is also no difficulty in sexing the offspring. In the case of lutino mutations, you can carry this out from hatching since these birds have red eyes.

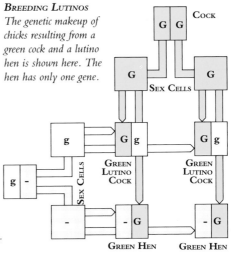

BREEDING LUTINOS *The genetic makeup of chicks resulting from a green cock and a lutino hen is shown here. The hen has only one gene.*

SEX-LINKED RECESSIVE MUTATION The various possible combinations and likely percentages of offspring from pairing a lutino with a normal green bird are shown.

1 Green cock	x	Lutino hen	▶	50% Green/lutino cocks	50% Green hens		
2 Lutino cock	x	Green hen	▶	50% Green/lutino cocks	50% Lutino hens		
3 Green/lutino cock	x	Green hen	▶	25% Green cocks	25% Green/lutino cocks	25% Green hens	25% Lutino hens
4 Green/lutino cock	x	Lutino hen	▶	25% Green/lutino cocks	25% Green hens	25% Lutino cocks	25% Lutino hens
5 Lutino cock	x	Lutino hen	▶	50% Lutino cocks + 50% Lutino hens			

DOMINANT TYPE MUTATIONS

These types of mutation are rare, but some pied mutations are of a dominant nature. This means that when a pied of this type is paired with a normal individual, a proportion of their offspring will also be pied. As a dominant genetic trait, a bird cannot, therefore, be split for this type of mutation.

Typical examples of this mutation are the dominant pied in the case of the Budgerigar and the Peach-faced Lovebird. The pied factor may affect the genes on one chromosome, in which case the bird is said to be a single factor pied (sf), whereas if both are modified, this will be a double factor pied (df). Apart from trial pairings, there is no way that you can distinguish these groups visually.

In the case of the dark factor, however, there is a visual difference between single and double factor birds, who are darker in coloration. In other respects, however, the pattern of inheritance is identical to that shown in the chart below. The dark factor, as its name suggests, is not a color itself, but modifies green or blue plumage.

A single factor green bird is known as dark green, while a double factor bird is olive. In the blue series, the equivalent forms are described as cobalt and mauve. The dark factor is at present well recognized in the Budgerigar, the Peach-

faced Lovebird, and the Ring-necked Parakeet and, to a lesser extent, in the Turquoisine Grass Parakeet. The ideal way to breed the entire spectrum of colors involved with the dark factor is to use pairing 5 shown in the chart, substituting dark green and olive as appropriate, for single and double factor dominant pieds. Similarly, when the dark factor combines with blue series birds, you have cobalt (one dark factor) and mauve (two dark factors), in place of dark green and olive.

DOMINANT MUTATION It is possible to predict the likely percentage of offspring, but with the dominant pied Budgerigar, one cannot predict marking patterns.

> **PERCENTAGES**
> *Remember that the percentages given in these various tables are actually averages. It is rather like flipping a coin, and calling heads or tails. Since the combination of chromosomes occurs entirely at random, there can be no guarantee that the chicks produced in a single nest will be as listed, but over a number of pairings, they are likely to approximate to the average. In any one nest, though, you may be lucky enough to end up entirely with youngsters of the desired color, or simply green offspring.*

1 Dominant pied (df) x Normal	100% Dominant pied (sf)		
2 Dominant pied (df) x Dominant pied (df)	100% Dominant pied (df)		
3 Dominant pied (df) x Dominant pied (sf)	50% Dominant pied (df)	50% Dominant pied (sf)	
4 Dominant pied (sf) x Normal	50% Dominant pied	50% Normal	
5 Dominant pied (sf) x Dominant pied (sf)	50% Dominant pied (sf)	25% Dom. pied (df)	25% Normal

CRESTED MUTATIONS

A number of species, including the Zebra Finch, Bengalese (Society) Finch, and Budgerigar, can be bred in crested forms, and crests have also been associated with a number of canary breeds. Closer study of their genetics has shown that, although this is a dominant mutation, a lethal factor is associated with it. Double factor crested birds fail to hatch or die soon afterwards. The number of potential pairings are restricted accordingly (see chart below).

As a result, crested birds of this type are always paired with a normal, and never with each other. If paired together, 25 percent of the potential offspring will fail to hatch. Lethal factors of this type are otherwise rarely encountered in breeding programs. The only other case of this type involves the blue mutation of the Splendid Grass Parakeet, of Australian origin. In contrast to crested mutations however, the blue is actually an autosomal recessive mutation. Pairing blue to blue was not recommended at first, because chicks bred in this way invariably failed to hatch or died soon after hatching.

Breeders resorted to breeding these blues by pairing a blue bird with a known split, in order to establish the mutation. This no longer seems to be a significant problem, but if you encounter difficulty of this type when breeding mutations, outcross back to normal individuals, rather than continuing to pair mutant birds together.

Some other mutations have also proved to be difficult to breed at first, such as the Elegant Grass Parakeet *(Neophema elegans).* Belgian breeders, working to establish this color, initially encountered poor fertility

> ### RECORD KEEPING
> *Maintaining accurate records based on the pairings of your stock is one of the vital requirements for color-breeding or establishing an exhibition stud. Traditionally, this has been carried out in written breeding registers, with each bird also having a stock card in a card index. This card gives details about their origins, breeding and show performances, using ring numbers for identification purposes. Now, however, records are being maintained increasingly on personal computers.*

and blindness. Although these difficulties have been largely overcome, stock of this mutation is still not readily available.

It has not been possible to maintain stocks of all the various documented mutations. Even with Budgerigars, some have been lost. In recessive mutations, the gene responsible for the color concerned may be preserved within the existing Budgie population and, when paired with a similar bird, the color can reemerge.

Not all mutations are actually considered desirable, such as long-flighted Budgerigars, distinguishable by long flight feathers that cross over at the backs of the wing. More recently, "feather dusters" have become a problem in some studs. With abnormally long feathering cascading over their bodies, and a short lifespan, this mutation affects the plumage, rather than its color.

BREEDING CRESTS *These pairings show the potential impact of the lethal factor, and how to avoid it.*

1 Crested	x	Normal	▶	50% Crested	50% Normal	
2 Crested	x	Crested	▶	50% Crested	25% Normal	25% Crested non-viable

BIRD SHOWS

S ome birds, such as canaries, Budgerigars, finches, and Bengalese Finches, are bred and reared largely for exhibition purposes. Specific standards have been established for the different varieties, laid down by the organizing bodies concerned. The standards, in essence, are really an attempt to encapsulate in words how the ideal bird of that particular variety should appear.

INTRODUCTION TO SHOWING

The standard for any particular breed is likely to vary somewhat from country to country, and judges in these different countries use the standard as a yardstick by which to assess the characteristics of the birds on display in front of them.

Good training will help a bird to present itself in the best possible manner, in the hope of attracting the judge's attention. Exhibiting birds successfully is an artform in itself, one which demands both time and patience on your part. One of the best ways to make a start is to visit as many

WINNING EXHIBIT There are various stages in most shows, and usually the winning exhibit in each section competes for the overall Best in Show Award.

shows as you possibly can, so that you can see how the birds are presented and displayed. Perhaps more importantly, you will also gain a clear impression of what the judges are looking for in their individual interpretation of the standard. But you should bear in mind that these standards are revised occasionally, reflecting the views of those concerned in judging at that time. Once you have a clear idea in your mind of what the judges prefer, you can then concentrate all your efforts on producing birds of a similar type and quality.

There is really no shortcut to exhibition success at the highest levels of competition. It is sometimes possible to purchase birds of outstanding quality, usually at inflated prices, but unless you have a stud of matching quality your success is likely to be of only a temporary nature.

DEVELOPING A WINNING STUD

If you are seriously interested in exhibiting, it is best to start with just a small number of the best-quality birds you can afford. The likelihood of these producing offspring of similar quality is much greater than if you have more breeding pairs of inferior birds. Purchasing older exhibition Budgerigars, which may be past their breeding peak, is one means of obtaining quality stock at a realistic price. But even for the experts, it is difficult to assess the

AT A SHOW Here the exhibits in the Border Fancy Canary section, benched in rows by class numbers, come under the scrutiny of enthusiasts after judging.

likely potential of young birds when they first leave the nest. However, to develop what potential is there, you should provide a good selection of foods. Budgerigars, for example, will often take soft food when young, and this helps them to grow into healthy adults. If you handle them as chicks and later when they are out of the nest, this will encourage them to become tame. With care like this, in time they will settle down happily within the confines of a show cage.

SHOW CAGES
The show cage you need depends to some extent on the bird concerned, but in all cases presentation is important. All birds should be benched in immaculate show cages – spotlessly clean and with no chipped paintwork, knocks, or grazes of any description. In order to accustom the birds to their show cage, so that they feel happy and not stressed when inside, you need to house them in the cage at frequent intervals for short periods of time. The birds may retreat to the floor at first, but they will soon be up on the perch and curious about their new surroundings.

Budgerigars and canaries are usually exhibited individually, but other birds, such as Zebra Finches, are shown as pairs. A pair of birds should be of opposite sexes, and both should be in top-class condition, otherwise the judge will mark down heavily the bird that is less than satisfactory. You may be able to enter one as an individual, but it will usually not fare as well when competing against a pair of birds of equivalent type.

PREPARING FOR A SHOW

Joining a local bird club will increase your knowledge of exhibiting and will give you the best preparation possible for the exhibition of your own birds. Judges come to some club meetings and speak informally about the merits of birds placed in front of them. Each club will also usually organize an annual show in which you can enter birds and learn the basics of competing. In most countries, there will be a national show, and in Europe there is a world show, which takes place each year in a different country.

Shows are usually advertized in bird-keeping periodicals. In order to enter, you will need to fill out an entry form. There is normally no charge for this, although you should enclose a stamped, self-addressed envelope. Study the schedule, which lists the classes, before completing the form. If you enter a bird in the wrong class, it will be automatically disqualified, and you will have wasted your time and any entry fee.

ROUTINE PREPARATION

Every exhibitor develops his or her own system when preparing for a show. There will inevitably be some upsets to your plans, such as a bird beginning to molt just before the event. Even a top-quality individual is most unlikely to win unless it is in peak condition, so rather than bench a bird that is less than this, it is preferable to leave it at home and forfeit the fee.

Some preparatory work is essential before the show. In the case of many Budgerigars, it is standard practice to trim the bird's mask – the area of black spots

TRIMMING THE MASK An important feature of exhibition Budgerigars is their mask. In many cases it may be necessary to trim the plumage as shown.

MANICURING THE MASK The spots forming the mask are randomly arranged, with more spots often being present than is deemed desirable, with the standard being based on the appearance of the wild Budgerigar. It is permissible, therefore, to trim the mask, using a pair of tweezers to pluck out unwanted feathers. This needs to be carried out with the utmost care.

extending round the chin. Use tweezers to create two sets of three perfect spots on each side of the face. In a few cases, however, as with the albino, this will not be necessary, since it does not have an obvious mask.

If you need to wash the bird, do this well in advance of the show. Indeed, you should complete all of your preparations at least a couple of days before the show starts so that the bird can settle down and preen itself after all the handling and fussing. Its plumage should then be in top condition once more by the day of the judging.

Most exhibitors drive their birds to the show, rather than using public transport. It is important to avoid any last-minute hitches, so leave home in plenty of time. Try to arrive as soon as the birds can be benched, rather than at the last minute before judging starts. The birds will then have the maximum possible time to settle down and compose themselves.

While the judging is taking place, exhibitors are not allowed to watch the proceedings. However, stewards help the judges in their task, so if you volunteer for

this job, you will probably gain some invaluable insights into the judging process and what particular characteristics in the birds are considered desirable, as well as learning some of the personal preferences of the judges involved.

It is always easy to criticize the judges, but remember that they can make their decisions based only on how the birds display themselves on the day. If a bird hides on the floor of its cage, the judge will not be able to assess its merits. This is why training is such an important aspect of preparing well in advance for a show. Familiarize your birds with being lifted up in a show cage and studied. In birds where "carriage" – movement from perch to perch – is important, encourage this activity, using a pencil in the same way that a judge will use a judging stick. Training of this type will inevitably help toward showing your bird to its best effect.

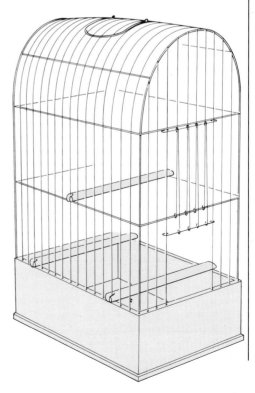

SHOW CAGE *Different show cages are produced for different birds. These can be purchased from specialist suppliers, and last many years if carefully maintained.*

Long-term Planning

Your results on the show bench are likely to mirror your breeding success, and once you have started to exhibit, you will then have to give particular thought to pairings. You must assess each bird for its individual strengths and weaknesses. If you have a bird that excels in one particular feature, try to find another bird that will complement it. By constantly reappraising your stock, you should notice a distinct improvement in the quality of the birds over a period of several years.

> ### HOW TO WIN ON A REGULAR BASIS
> • *Visit shows as often as possible, even if you are not exhibiting, to study the characteristics of winning birds.*
> • *Do not be in such a hurry to sell youngsters from your breeding program, or you may be discarding a potential winner prematurely.*
> • *Keep accurate records, considering each bird's strengths and weaknesses objectively.*
> • *Pay attention to detail. Show cages should be immaculate, as well as the birds in them.*

There is likely to come a time when you decide to pair closely related birds. By this stage, you will probably be specializing in, perhaps, a particular color, and you will be hoping to reinforce these traits. Line-breeding is the safest option, because it entails pairing related birds, such as cousins, but it also allows a degree of genetic diversity. Otherwise, if the pairings are too closely related, you risk compounding faults as well as emphasizing desirable features.

EXHIBITION STUDS

In the case of a top stud, the birds may be of sufficient quality, and with so few weaknesses, that judicious in-breeding may be advantageous. Pairings, such as father to daughter allow for little genetic variance, however, and you need to exercise great care. There is always a risk of weaknesses appearing and these can manifest themselves in various ways, the most significant being a decline in fertility and hatching rates.

Whenever you are purchasing birds to add to your stud, try to obtain those that excel in points where your stock is weak. Again, assess this by looking at birds on the

DIFFERENCE IN TYPE The exhibition Budgerigar (above) is larger than an ordinary pet Budgie, and has a bigger head. This is the result of selective breeding over the years.

show bench. You can then try asking the exhibitors concerned if they have surplus stock. They may be unwilling to part with a winning bird, but they may have a related individual, at a lower price, with the strengths you are looking for in your stud.

The current tendency is to increase the average size of exhibition studs, but there are plenty of successful exhibitors who keep as few as 12 pairs of birds. You do not have to make huge investments in stock in order to achieve good results. Attention to detail and an honest assessment of a bird's strengths and weaknesses are far more vital factors than sheer numbers.

NON-STANDARDIZED EXHIBITING

Prescribed standards do not exist for the vast majority of birds kept by enthusiasts, but it is still possible to exhibit them. In these cases, the judges are not relying on a standard, and so the actual condition of the birds is of paramount importance, rather than such features as the shape of the head.

The number of classes for non-standardized birds depends largely on the size of the show. Some specialist bird clubs stage their own shows, and here, as well as at national events, the competition is likely to be at its fiercest. The basic routine is the same as for exhibiting Budgerigars, for example, except that in many cases the cages are decorated with flowers, moss, and branches, depending on what is most appropriate for the species concerned.

If you are interested in exhibiting foreign birds, you will need to take particular care when you buy them. A missing or damaged claw will spoil your entry's chances of winning. The plumage will also need to be immaculate, so you may have to wait for a year or so until the bird has molted out. In cases such as the Scarlet-chested Sunbird *(Nectarinia senegalensis)*, it is vitally important to remember to color-

EXHIBITING FOREIGN BIRDS Birds are judged by their condition rather than to a standard. Long-tailed species are harder to stage than short-tailed species, so one in good condition stands a good chance of winning.

feed them (see page 157) before they start molting, so that they maintain their natural feather coloration.

There is growing encouragement for the exhibiting of captive-bred foreign birds, and such birds will obviously be easier to train. Many softbills reared in aviary surroundings, for example, will continue to feed from your hand throughout their lives, if you have accustomed them to this from an early stage in their development. If you are entering such birds in a show, you should check whether they need to be close-ringed. Without this proof of their age, you may not be able to enter them in such classes as current-year bred birds, although there is no reason why you cannot then show them alongside older individuals. Even if they do not win, the experience will stand them, and you, in good stead for the future.

UNDERSTANDING YOUR BIRD

B irds make excellent pets, being both intelligent and responsive. The long-standing trend for parrots as companion birds is not just because of their powers of mimicry, nor their coloration. Other birds can be taught to talk, and the popular African Gray Parrot has relatively dull plumage. It is because these birds interact so well with humans that their popularity has endured for centuries.

AVIAN INTELLIGENCE

D ocumented studies of the intelligence level of birds are limited, although experiments have been carried out to investigate their ability to count. The birds were shown a card that featured a number of spots, and had to relate this figure to a similarly marked food bowl. The numbers and patterns varied, so the birds did not simply identify with one set only. The outcome of this study showed that, in this fashion, the birds could master counting up to the number seven.

THE CASE OF ALEX

Investigations into a parrot's ability to reason and respond in words have been carried out by Irene Pepperberg at Purdue University in Lafeyette, Indiana. She chose a young African Gray Parrot christened Alex, from a pet store in Chicago. The bird was just over a year old at this stage, and did not speak at all. Pepperberg began her training of Alex using a method that had proved successful for a previous worker. She spoke to another staff member, using the words and phrases she wanted Alex to learn. In the wild, parrots mimic the calls of older birds, and some regional differences have been determined by fieldworkers in species that range over a wide area. Pepperberg did not offer food to Alex, but if he asked for a particular object to which she had referred, she gave it to him. After two years and two months of training, Alex had developed a reasonable vocabulary which he could actively apply to

AFRICAN GRAY PARROT
Although not very brightly colored, its intelligent and responsive nature ensures its popularity as a pet.

communicate with Pepperberg. He had mastered identification of nine objects, and could distinguish three colors, as well as count up to six. He was also able to distinguish between shapes.

Perhaps the most significant finding was that Alex learned to use the word "no" to refuse items he had not requested. If he wanted something, he would preface the object with the word "want," as in "want banana." It seems clear from this experiment that parrots are actively capable of communicating with people rather than simply repeating phrases with no understanding of them. Perhaps we sense this, seeing the pet parrot as somewhat akin to a young child. If intelligence can be equated with behavioral adaptability at its most basic, then clearly parrots must rank among the most talented members of the avian order.

Relatively little scientific research has been carried out into parrot behavior, but Irene Pepperberg's experiments offer a glimpse into a fascinating field. There are also a number of ways in which parrots use body language, both in their interactions with each other and with people. A bird that has been hand-reared on its own tends to have different responses to a bird that has been kept with others of its kind, either during hand-rearing or in the nest. A widely held view among breeders is that parrots which have been hand-raised subsequently prove more difficult to pair than parrots reared normally. This almost certainly relates not to the hand-rearing process itself, but to the manner in which they are reared. Socialization of young birds is clearly vital at an early stage, before the birds have intensive contact with humans. Otherwise, pairing up a pet parrot can prove rather more problematical, depending to some extent on the species.

PSITTACINE INTERACTIONS
Whereas Budgerigars and Cockatiels will usually accept another of their kind without too much reluctance, parrots can be far less enthusiastic about interacting with another bird of their own species. The reasons for this are presently not well understood.

One of the underlying problems may simply be that the parrot is out of condition. Many pet birds are too fat, and this can compromise any interest in breeding with a new partner. The best means of introducing a long-established pet to a potential mate is to allow the tame bird to spend a summer becoming acclimatized and fit in a long outdoor aviary. Encourage it to fly as much as possible by spacing the perches widely apart. Problems almost inevitably result if you simply place a pet parrot outside in the company of a fit individual.

Carefully introduce the birds on neutral territory, later in the year, by which stage they are more likely to be receptive to one another without showing aggression. During the following spring, they will, one hopes, have become accustomed to each other and be showing signs of breeding activity.

A BALANCED DIET
There is evidence to suggest that food preferences are formed at an early stage in a bird's life. Parrots in the process of being weaned should therefore be offered a wide range of foodstuffs, so that in later life they are willing to take these nutritious foods when they themselves are nesting. The reluctance of adult cockatoos, for example, to try new foodstuffs, can also be overcome in this way. A sound early diet may also influence the onset of sexual maturity. In the case of the larger parrots particularly, captive-bred offspring tend to breed earlier than equivalent birds in the wild. This is almost certainly related, at least in part, to nutritional factors.

INTERACTION WITH OTHER BIRDS

In the wild, many bird species live in large flocks, which have a distinct hierarchy. For this reason, introducing a new individual to an established pet can be fraught with difficulty, and jealousy can arise. Cockatiels and Budgerigars are reasonably tolerant, but parrots may attack newcomers. For this reason, it is much better to start with two birds, rather than to start with one and then acquire a second one later on. To emphasize the existing order of dominance, ensure that the established pet receives plenty of attention, and offer it tid-bits first. Do not encourage the newcomer to challenge the position of the established bird, but instead allow your original pet to be fed first, and give it treats so as to reassure it.

DISPUTES BETWEEN PARROTS

In time, the birds should grow used to each other, but at first there is a real risk of fighting if they are allowed out together. Each should be allowed to keep its own territory, and it is a mistake to force them together, even in larger surroundings. This will help to eliminate the risk of jealousy, but never be tempted to allow just your established pet out into the room, while the newcomer remains confined to its quarters.

There is a risk that the established parrot will be attracted to the newcomer's cage, and, if it settles, its feet are likely to prove an irresistible target for the caged bird. The resulting bite could lead to a serious injury. There is also the risk that the newcomer's feet could be attacked from outside its cage if it climbs onto the bars.

If parrots are of the opposite sex, this will not always assure a smooth transition. You will need to be in the room in order to supervise the introductory process, when the birds are let out simultaneously. Depending on how tame your new arrival is, you may need to remove this bird from the room while your established pet is allowed a daily period of exercise. When they are sharing the same room, both birds must either be allowed out together, or kept confined in separate quarters, so that there is no risk of a conflict between them.

In order to prevent possible territorial disputes it is advisable to remove their cages while the parrots are out in the room. Otherwise, if one attempts to enter the

GIANT BARBET The stout beak and aggressive nature of these birds make it essential that they are housed separately. Watch carefully for any signs of aggression, especially during the breeding season.

AGGRESSION BETWEEN BIRDS

If you plan to keep more than one bird, you must consider how the birds will interact, as some species can be very aggressive and jealous toward others of their own kind as well as other species. There is less risk of conflict in pairing up a pet bird that has never been especially tame, but, again, this needs to be carried out on neutral territory. Other birds are far more tolerant than the larger parrots, and it is usually quite safe to put one finch in with another. They will almost certainly start to roost together immediately, even if they are of the same sex. Softbills tend to be more unpredictable, and toucans are often highly aggressive toward any newcomer in their territory. The same applies to barbets, the great barbet *(Megalaima virens)* having a reputation for hostility toward other birds. Also, with certain softbills, such as barbets, compatibility can be difficult.

EYE FLARING

This behavior is most obvious in larger parrots, such as Amazons, often as a prelude to mating, and is a sign of good health. The bird constricts the pupil, and the eye momentarily assumes a more colorful appearance. This transient change is often related to raising of the feathers on the head, and vocalization. Similar behavior is also noticeable in Budgies, for example, when they play with a favorite toy.

NORMAL IRIS

FLARED IRIS

SHOWING FEAR If frightened by an unexpected noise, parrots draw their feathers tightly together and raise their heads rapidly.

other's cage, fighting between the birds is likely to result. Alternatively, you can simply close the cage doors.

You should never try to force the pace of the introduction. The birds should ultimately come to accept each other of their own accord, although this process may take several months.

INTERACTION WITH PEOPLE

Establishing a bond with a new parrot will take time, but if you start with a hand-reared parrot, this preliminary stage should pass quite quickly. Even so, do not expect the bird to respond to you in the same way as it did to its previous owner. There is no doubt that these birds can distinguish between individuals, and so you will also need to win the bird's trust.

Talk quietly to the bird, and move slowly and deliberately when in the vicinity of its quarters. Try to avoid having to catch and handle the parrot during these early days, as this will probably be unsettling for it. Offer the bird every opportunity to come toward you. A hand-raised parrot should soon feed from your hand, and identify with people as a source of food. You can then build on this bond, waiting until the bird is ready to allow you to touch its

Bonding Establishing a bond with a parrot requires both time and patience on the owner's part. Choosing a young bird in the first place also helps in this process.

plumage. At first, it may shy away but then, once it knows you well, it will approach you to be petted, rubbing its body on the sides of the cage. It will also hold its neck slightly on one side, ruffling the plumage as an indication for you to stroke this area.

On occasion, if your parrot feels that it is being ignored, it may call out loudly to attract your attention, and this can serve as a greeting. Different species also have other ways of greeting a person – a tame cockatoo will raise its crest. Calling out can also be a sign of excitment, for example, when the bird is being sprayed.

ADAPTABILITY

To some extent, the behavior of tame parrots with people mimics their natural responses. However, tame parrots also display behavioral traits not observed in the wild. The most notable of these is the way a tame bird will lie on its back, with its feet in the air, often in the palm of its owner's hand. This leaves the bird in an extremely vulnerable position, on its back and unable to fly away from danger. Further evidence of parrots' adaptability is the way in which they can be taught to pedal small bicycles and other vehicles. In the wild, if a bird lands on an unstable perch, equivalent to a pedal, it will fly off almost instantly.

THE IMPACT OF PAIR BONDING

The significance of pair bonding in tame parrots has only recently been appreciated. But it has long been recognized that some species are far more confiding companions in domestic surroundings than others.

In some parrots, such as the psittaculid species, hens are naturally dominant to cocks for most of the year, outside the breeding season. Cock birds also tend to be shy, while hens may prove to be somewhat aggressive, resenting any close contact. These parakeets are less satisfactory as pets than other species, such as *Pyrrhura* conures, which will accept human companionship more readily then any of the psittaculids. There is usually close contact between these birds, and they are naturally affectionate with each other. Even when two birds of the same sex are housed together, they will sit close together, and preen one another.

The personality of a large parrot, notably Amazons and cockatoos, may change once it has matured. It may also alter its response to you for periods of time corresponding to the normal breeding cycle. Such birds can then become temperamental and may bite with little provocation. They are also more raucous and destructive than usual.

PSITTACINE BODY LANGUAGE
Parrots are generally not aggressive birds, and only very rarely attempt to bite without provocation, usually giving a series of signals before acting this way. It is no coincidence, however, that species such as the Ring-necked Parakeet have red bills, and that these birds do not readily allow you to get close to them. This coloration is important for communication in parrots. A dominant bird, for example, will advance along the perch with its bill clearly displayed. The subordinate individual will then normally turn its head away, hiding its bill, and move to another perch. A more forceful challenge is indicated if the parrot keeps its bill low, and slightly open, as it moves toward a rival. Under these circumstances, it may well resort to biting if the opportunity arises, usually in defense of a mate.

Although parrots are social birds, they sometimes do not want attention from other birds or their owners. Red serves in some species to highlight this reluctance, as with the Severe Macaw. The bird's coloration is mainly green, but along the leading edge of each wing, there is red plumage, extending under the wings, where it is usually hidden.

If you approach a tame bird when it is disinterested or unsure of its surroundings, it will raise its wings, holding one or both slightly away from its body, to reveal its red plumage. If this is not an adequate deterrent, it will flap its wing, usually on the side of your approach, and may inflict a blow. It may also lunge with its bill, but this is little more than a gesture of annoyance. If your attention persists, the parrot is then likely to fly off a short distance.

SIGNS OF AGE
Hand-reared chicks tend to be very playful and inquisitive, rather like puppies, but, as they mature, they become more settled. Most parrots show few signs of aging, the most likely sign of this being evident in the bird's molting pattern. This period tends to be more prolonged in older birds, and so a parrot will display less readiness to preen itself. Consequently, the long tail feathers of macaws may emerge and grow to their full length while still in their sheaths. The molting pattern will also become less predictable. Toward the end of an old parrot's life, the plumage will typically regrow in a sparser fashion than normal.

LIFESPAN
Parrots rank among the longest living of all birds. Only condors, cranes, and owls may have a similar lifespan. But there are considerable variations between individual species, with Budgerigars, for example, having relatively short lifespans. Although we know that parrots can live for perhaps a century in captivity, their life expectancy in the wild is usually very much shorter. Faced with many dangers, even cockatoos may not live more than 25 years. Similarly, the life expectancy of many smaller birds, such as the African finches, is typically less than a year.

COMMON BEHAVIORAL PROBLEMS

Apart from repeated screeching, you are unlikely to encounter any problems with a parrot until it approaches sexual maturity. This is likely to be around the age of four years old for larger species, and as little as one year old in the case of Budgerigars. A likely symptom of behavioral problems in a cock Budgerigar is that it may resort to feeding toys in its cage, and it may even try to mate with them, or with your finger when it is out of its cage. A hen bird at this age will start to become broody, laying eggs on the floor of its quarters. If you leave them alone, she will soon lose interest in them. Do not be tempted to remove the eggs until she reaches this point, otherwise she is likely to lay again. This phase, however, should soon pass in both sexes.

CURING PROBLEMS

• *Start with a genuine youngster, which will settle readily into the home.*

• *If you are likely to be out for long periods each day, start with two birds, so that they can keep each other company.*

• *Choose a large flight cage, and offer your birds branches to gnaw, as well as providing them with a selection of safe toys.*

• *Be sure to give your bird a regular spray, two or three times a week.*

• *Always provide a balanced diet, with plenty of fresh fruit and vegetables.*

AGGRESSION

In the case of the larger parrots, aggression is frequently an indication of a desire to breed. Cockatoos will display frequently, raising their crests and calling loudly, and they may also bite unexpectedly and uncharacteristically. They will also be more destructive, but this behavior should only last for a few weeks and it is not normally a major problem, provided that you are aware of its likely cause. If you have a choice of a cock or hen bird at the outset when you are choosing your pet, and breeding is not a consideration, it may be better to opt for a hen, since in general, females tend to be less aggressive.

FEATHER-PLUCKING

Feather-plucking is far and away the major behavioral problem owners encounter with their parrots. And, sadly, it is one of the most difficult to deal with, partly because there is no clear-cut, single cause for its occurrence. Feather-plucking varies in severity, with some birds virtually denuding themselves; whereas other individuals concentrate on the feathers in just one particular area – for example, those on the breast.

This behavior pattern can rapidly become habitual, and you must take immediate action to prevent any further feather loss. The first step is to try to understand why your bird is behaving in this fashion in the first place. Boredom is generally cited as being one of the most significant causes, and, almost certainly, moving the parrot elsewhere in your home may be of some help in curtailing this distressing behavioral pattern.

Pet birds kept indoors pluck themselves far more frequently than their aviary counterparts. This may also be related to the fact that indoor birds do not bathe as frequently, so regular spraying is essential.

DIETARY FACTORS

You should also make a point of reviewing the parrot's diet, so that you can decide if you can introduce more variety there. The use of an additional nutritional supplement may help, as may providing more toys inside and outside the bird's quarters. In the case of sensitive birds, notably African Gray Parrots, macaws, and cockatoos, which are most prone to the feather-plucking vice, a change in their routine may have triggered the initial episode, which then became an established behavior pattern. The risk remains that, as new feathers emerge through the skin, so they too will be pulled out. In severe cases, special "Elizabethan" collars have been fixed round the bird's neck to keep the parrot from being able to reach its newly emerging plumage. Even if you manage to resolve the problem, relapses are unfortunately not uncommon. If all else fails, transferring the parrot to an outside aviary and providing it with a mate can sometimes prove to be the answer. Be careful that it does not become chilled in the aviary, however, until its plumage has fully regrown.

DISTINGUISHING BEHAVIOR PATTERNS

Tame parrots may develop behavioral traits that are not observed in the wild. The most striking of these is the way in which a tame bird will often lie on its back to have its stomach tickled.

Parrots will also often utilize their normal body language when communicating with their owners. It is important to be aware of these signs, especially when you are introducing your pet to other people. If in an aggressive mood, parrots will often stalk along a perch with their head held low in a manner that is quite deliberate, and this is intended to displace rivals. In less charged situations, a parrot may simply lift a foot, which is then used to fend off an advance.

Parrots are sensitive birds, and will avoid the attention of an onlooker, especially one they do not know well. Even tame birds may turn away from you if you are close to their cage, until you have won their confidence. A frightened bird will rear up, looking taller than normal. Parrots can greet you excitedly, often by calling loudly. It is then generally possible to tell when you have their attention, because of the way in which they cock their heads to one side and stare at you. Parrots normally sleep with only one foot on the perch, with this grip being alternated. Only if a bird shows reluctance to use its other foot may there be cause for concern. Parrots tend instinctively to be most active in the morning and evening, rather than in the daytime.

POOR FEATHERING Plumage *problems are quite common in parrots, which are kept indoors as pets. Rapid action will be needed in the case of feather-plucking so as to prevent this disorder from developing into a habit.*

HEALTH CARE

Although there have been significant advances in the health care of birds during the last few years, and bacterial diseases can now largely be controlled and cured with the help of antibiotics, it is becoming increasingly clear that viral infections may have been underestimated. These are a serious problem, especially where birds are kept together, as they are in commercial breeding units.

HOW DISEASES SPREAD

Birds used not to leave a collection unless they were sold, but, in the case of parrots, eggs and young birds are now routinely moved to hand-rearing specialists, thus mixing with birds from varying backgrounds. One of the most serious diseases facing parrot-breeders, psittacine beak and feather disease (PBFD), has undoubtedly been spread by this route.

Obviously, moving stock to a show also entails the risk of contracting disease, but there are significant differences. The birds are away for a much shorter period of time, and those that were sickly would not be taken anyway. They are also not handled, or allowed to mix directly with other birds. Nevertheless, it is still a wise precaution to isolate birds returning from a show for at least a few days.

Diseases can be introduced in a number of ways. Such problems as parasites may have been left by a former occupant of the flight or cage, so if you are tempted to purchase second-hand cages, scrub and disinfect them thoroughly to ensure the removal of mites and any viruses.

Other creatures in the vicinity of the aviary can also be a problem. Vermin represent an obvious hazard, and the droppings of wild birds perching on the aviary can cause disease. An accumulation of dirt in the aviary is also potentially dangerous: soiled perches are likely to lead to infections of the feet, especially in softbills such as the Fairy Bluebird.

It is important to bear in mind that visitors can introduce diseases on footwear and clothing. At least one case of PBFD has been confirmed as being caused in this fashion. The infection was thought to have been brought into a closed breeding unit by someone who had visited a pet store. If you have susceptible birds, take all necessary precautions – perhaps going as far as excluding visitors who regularly come into contact with parrots elsewhere, at least from young stock. You, yourself, may want to change your shoes and clothes if you have recently visited any other birds.

INSURANCE POLICIES

As avian medicine has advanced, so the tests and treatment options available have become wider and, consequently, more expensive. It is now possible to insure against veterinary fees, and even against the loss of a bird for various reasons. As with all insurances, check that the policy is suitable for your needs. With several companies now attracted to this field, premiums are not exorbitant, and you may decide to cover the life of a valuable imported bird for the first couple of years, until it is settled in your collection.

DIAGNOSING AILMENTS

Although a bird may appear perfectly healthy at the time of purchase, it may be carrying a burden of intestinal parasites. These can vary widely, from parasitic worms to unicellular protozoa. As a preliminary measure with any new bird you acquire, it is well worth while having its droppings screened for parasites, and then, if a problem is detected, administering the appropriate treatment as necessary. This is usually an inexpensive procedure, and it is something about which your veterinarian should be able to advise you.

Accurate diagnosis of avian ailments by visual observation alone is exceedingly difficult in many cases, simply because the symptoms are not sufficiently specific. The bird often just appears to be off color, and huddles up. You may already have noted that it seems slightly duller and less active than normal. Irrespective of the cause, it is vital to transfer the sick bird to a warm place, where you can maintain the temperature at about 30°C (86°F). With their high metabolic rates, birds normally lose heat rapidly if they are not eating properly, and the resulting hypothermia

can lead to death. It is possible to purchase specially designed hospital cages, and these are suitable for finches and other small birds, up to the size of a Budgerigar.

ADDITIONAL WARMTH

For larger individuals, you will need a different arrangement. An infrared lamp, of the dull-emitter type, which gives off heat rather than light, is ideal as a heat source. You can suspend it over the bird's cage, if it has a mesh top, or angle it at the side. The bulb should have a reflector to concentrate the rays of warmth, and you can control its output by a thermostat in the bird's quarters. A unit of this type, located over the flight, is also useful as an extra source of heat for delicate softbills. In contrast to the relatively sealed surroundings of the hospital cage, the bird can move to a position within its quarters where it feels most comfortable. Having warmed up, and feeling stronger, it may move away from the direct influence of the heat source.

One of the main advantages of using a heat lamp rather than a hospital cage, is that the bird can move to a temperature where it feels comfortable, rather than being kept at a constant temperature. As the bird's condition improves, you can gradually lower the temperature by adjusting the heat output from the lamp. If possible, choose a model that has controls for this purpose. Never be in too much of a hurry to reacclimatize the bird, however, as this is likely to be counterproductive.

Provide additional lighting to encourage the bird to feed, so that it makes up the inevitable weight loss, which accompanies most avian illnesses. Do not transfer a bird that has recovered from illnesses straight back to an outside aviary. You may need to keep the bird indoors right through the winter until the weather warms up.

CONSULTING A VET

Most sick birds tend to lose their appetites, so, in order to rekindle or maintain their interest, place their food in suitable containers beside their perches. This also applies in the case of water. The condition of a sick bird usually deteriorates rapidly, so you should seek advice from your vet without delay. Describe the symptoms as clearly as possible, and have a brief summary of the bird's history in hand. This should include details of how long you have kept the bird, whether you bred it, if it has had any illness before, and its usual diet.

·TREATMENTS·

Because of the need to begin treatment rapidly, veterinarians usually prescribe broad-spectrum antibiotics. They may take samples beforehand, which can be studied in the laboratory while the treatment is in progress. Then, in the light of these findings, changes to the treatment regimen can be made. Sick birds, especially if they have enteritis, tend to dehydrate, so giving special fluids can help save their lives.

ADMINISTERING MEDICATION

The size of the bird will influence the likelihood of its recovery; small finches are relatively difficult to treat compared with large parrots. An antibiotic powder added to the drinking water can be successful for small birds, but it must be mixed strictly in accordance with the veterinarian's instructions to avoid a potential fatality.

Recovery in the warm will, one hopes, be rapid if the bird is drinking properly, but do not be tempted to stop treatment too soon. It is important to continue for the period specified. After the course of antibiotics has been completed, a probiotic preparation should be added to the bird's diet to help stabilize the bacteria in the gut.

For larger birds, medication via drinking water is unsatisfactory; they need to drink an unrealistically large volume to receive a therapeutic dose. Birds that usually have a relatively fluid diet, such as lories and lorikeets, also dislike the bitter taste of the solution and avoid it. Your veterinarian may therefore advise, at least initially, an injection of antibiotics. Although this can be more stressful than simply leaving the bird to drink on its own, it is also likely to be more potent and give quicker results.

With a softbill, you may subsequently be given a powder to sprinkle over its food, or even tablets. These can be given to most larger softbills, such as touracos, and

> ### BIRD AUTOPSY
> *If all fails and a bird dies, refer back to your veterinarian, who will arrange for an autopsy if you wish. If the bird died of an infection that could have been treated with antibiotics, a sensitivity result will be available. This alone can be crucial in saving the lives of other affected individuals in your stock, since it will indicate any resistance which that particular strain of bacteria has to specific antibiotics, as well as revealing those to which it is most sensitive. Other findings, such as the presence of gut parasites, may also be of practical significance in diagnosis and treatment.*

to many pigeons and doves, without difficulty. Simply restrain the bird, not stressing it more than necessary, and open its beak. Place the tablet as far back in the mouth as possible, avoiding the opening to the respiratory tract. Quickly close the bill, and hold it shut for a couple of moments to encourage the bird to swallow.

A bird that has recovered from illness will still need careful management for a while, so do not place it straight back into the aviary. In a communal flight, it may well be bullied, and could succumb again. Lower the temperature of the bird's environment gradually, so that it reacclimatizes properly. If you bring a sick bird indoors in the winter, you will probably have to keep it there until the following spring. Even in the warmer months, check that the bird is fully fit and active. Weight loss usually occurs during a period of illness, causing the breastbone to become more prominent than usual. Wait until this weight has been put back on, and the bird is alert and lively, before releasing it into unheated quarters again.

⸻•Respiratory Tract Ailments•⸻

The tail movements of a bird at rest are one of the most obvious indicators of health. These should be barely discernible. If pronounced and labored, they may indicate a problem with its respiratory system. Look, too, for discharge from the nostrils, or even a blockage.

If the bird is having particular difficulty in breathing because it has blocked nostrils, it may be possible to relieve the congestion with a suitable medication treatment. Hold the bird on its back, and place a drop of the treatment in each of its nostrils. If there are pronounced deposits here, bathe the area with warm water to remove the worst of the external blockage before you start applying the decongestant.

Where the sinuses are involved, long-standing cases can be difficult to resolve, even when they are treated with the aid of antibiotics. The bird's condition may seem to improve for a time, but relapses again if you attempt to move it, or it becomes stressed in any way.

ASPERGILLOSIS The cause of this dreaded fungal disease is seen here magnified under the microscope.

BLOCKED NOSTRIL *Nasal plugs of this type are not uncommon in the larger parrots, and can indicate a minor infection of the upper respiratory tract.*

An infection that is less evident in the early stages, but that will ultimately prove fatal, is the fungal disease known as aspergillosis. This is most likely to be encountered in pionus parrots and the Philippine Red-vented Cockatoo *(Cacatua haematuropygia)*, as well as in numerous softbill species. If it occurs in overwhelming concentrations, and the bird is stressed, the clinical signs start to become apparent. Its breathing will be labored and it will have difficulty in flying. The bird's condition will noticeably deteriorate, and weight loss will be evident.

Diagnosis of the condition at an early stage can be achieved with endoscopy, the same process used for surgical sexing. X-rays can also be of assistance, especially if the bird's breathing is affected for any reason. Sadly, at present there is no truly effective treatment for this condition, although some drugs used in human medicine have provided some relief.

AILMENTS OF THE DIGESTIVE TRACT

Bird-keepers refer to an upset of the digestive system that results in loose, typically green droppings as enteritis. It is not a specific condition, but a description of an inflammation of the gut, which can be infectious or non-infectious in origin. If birds are not accustomed to receiving green food regularly, a large quantity can trigger enteritis. However, recovery is usually rapid. Colored seed treats can also affect the color of the birds' droppings but, again, they will return to normal once the colored food is discontinued.

SERIOUS CONDITIONS

If a bird also appears sick and huddles up, often on the floor of its quarters, the situation is far more serious. You should seek veterinary advice immediately, since there are certain conditions, such as salmonellosis, that can spread to humans. It is necessary to observe strict hygienic precautions whenever dealing with a sick bird, and always wash your hands in disinfectant after attending to its needs. The veterinarian can test for the likely cause of the disease, and may give the sick bird fluids and antibiotics.

DIGESTIVE TRACT PROBLEMS Birds may be at risk from contracting infections, or from swallowing objects which lodge in the digestive tract, and cause irritation.

Dirty, unsanitary surroundings encourage enteric diseases. The presence of rodents, or rodent-contaminated foodstuffs, is especially dangerous. After the bird has recovered, it may continue to excrete the bacterial organisms for a period, making it a hazard to others. Antibiotics and testing the droppings help to overcome this state.

THE IMPORTANCE OF HYGIENE

If the bacterium *Escherichia coli* is identified, it may signify a failure of hygiene on your part. Although widely present in the gut of mammals, this microorganism is not usually found in parrots and many other birds. Inadequate hygiene when preparing food is a likely cause. Even after washing your hands, the organism can return if you dry your hands on a contaminated towel.

Proventricular dilatation syndrome, first known as macaw wasting disease, currently causes concern among breeders of larger parrots. Affected birds become depressed and start to pass whole seeds undigested. The cause is unknown, but it seems to be a viral disease that attacks the proventriculus, which normally grinds up the seed with its muscular action. No treatment is available, and the outcome is usually fatal. It could be spread by contact with the bird's droppings, or by regurgitated crop contents. Keep affected birds separate.

FOOD SOILED BY WILD BIRDS As a precaution, always wash fresh foods.

VERMIN-INFECTED FOOD Buy food from reputable sources, and store in bins.

RUSTY CAGE BARS Rust particles can be injested, especially by parrots.

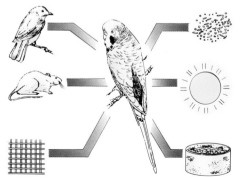

UNCLEAN FOOD Birds' food must be fresh and hygienically prepared.

FOOD SOURED BY SUN Soaked seed and milk food may sour in the sun.

DIRTY FOOD BOWL AND DROPPINGS These can easily spread disease.

REPRODUCTIVE TRACT AILMENTS

Egg-binding is the most significant ailment in this group and can strike hens at any time. The signs of egg-binding are reasonably specific, especially in a bird that has previously been fit and healthy. Characteristics are unsteadiness on the feet and inability to perch due to pressure build-up caused by the egg, which affects the surrounding nervous system. Once you have caught the hen, handle her with great care, since there is a risk of rupturing the egg, which could trigger peritonitis. You should be able to feel the egg as a slight swelling between her legs, but if trapped at a higher point in the reproductive tract, an X-ray may be necessary.

Several factors predispose hens to egg-binding. Young hens laying for the first time, and old birds at the end of their reproductive lives, are the most vulnerable. The major factor is probably a shortage of dietary calcium or an abnormality in the hen's calcium metabolism, leading to a soft, rubbery shell, and affecting the muscles that force eggs through the reproductive tract.

Rapid treatment is required to overcome the obstruction. The best response is usually an injection by a veterinarian of a

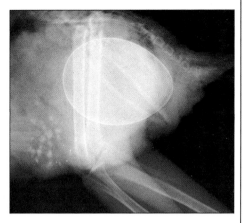

CONFIRMATORY DIAGNOSIS OF EGG-BINDING This radiograph clearly shows the shape of the egg as a large white solid, lodged in the reproductive tract.

calcium compound. As a last resort, surgery may be necessary. If no veterinarian is available, lubricating the vent may enable you to manipulate the egg free.

Other disorders affecting the reproductive tract are generally uncommon, although veterinarians are concerned about the disease known as cloacal papillomatosis. This contagious condition is best documented in macaws, but it also affects other species, notably Amazon parrots.

The growths (papillomas) in the cloaca form a physical barrier to mating, and can cause constipation. They can also protrude through the vent, and may initially be confused with a prolapse, except that they bleed readily. Various treatments, including a vaccine, have been tried. One of the more reliable remedies seems to be the application of silver nitrate to the growths – which should bring improvement within a week or so. Provided that there is no recurrence for a year, the affected bird can be safely reintroduced to a breeding group without fear of spreading the disease.

CLOACAL PROLAPSE

A complication stemming from a protracted period of egg-binding, resulting in a pink ball of tissue protruding from the vent, is known as a cloacal prolapse. This tissue must be washed off, if dirty, and pushed back inside. This is most easily done with two fingers, on either side of the prolapse. A lubricant may be of help in a stubborn case. Should it prove impossible for the bird to retain the tissue in place, a veterinarian will need to insert a temporary suture.

AILMENTS OF THE BILL AND EYES

Deviations in the normal arrangement of the upper and lower bill have already been mentioned (see page 122). There is nothing you can do to correct such problems, except to cut the bill back regularly so that the bird can continue to eat without difficulty. Cock Budgerigars kept as pets are especially susceptible to overgrown bills. It is a good idea to provide plenty of fresh branches for them to gnaw on in the hope that they will keep their own bills in trim, particularly if they ignore cuttlefish bone. Trimming the lower bill is simply a matter of nipping off any overgrowth at the front, caused by a deviation of the upper part of the bill, so that it curls behind rather than over it.

EYE PROBLEMS

The first signs are swelling of the eyelids and a discharge, followed by the eye being kept closed. Softbills develop similar symptoms if their feet become dirty, as scratching the skin around the eyes can set up an infection. To treat, use a sterile preparation. Hold the bird for a few moments after applying the treatment, so that it dissolves in the eye, and is not wiped off. Repeat this three or four times a day, as tear fluids wash the medication out of the eye. There is usually a rapid response, but continue treatment as directed by your vet.

EYE AILMENTS

An eye ailment may be a symptom of a more generalized infection, such as the disease variously known as psittacosis or, more recently, chlamydiosis. This is potentially a serious infection, because it is a zoonosis – a disease that can spread from birds to people. It usually produces symptoms resembling pneumonia, and should respond to antibiotic treatment. A wide range of animals – not just birds – can be infected with this disease, which is why it is more accurately known as chlamydiosis, after the causal microorganism, *Chlamydia psittaci*. Parrots are the birds considered to be most significant in terms of human health, although it is generally agreed that the incidence of infection from birds is low. Studies suggest that there are about ten cases a year in the United States, with both captive-bred and imported birds being implicated. Contrary to some statements, this is not just a disease of imported stock. Again, your veterinarian will be able to advise you if you are concerned about this disease. Testing and treatment are both possible, and birds entering the United States are routinely medicated with tetracycline antibiotics against chlamydiosis. There is, of course, nothing to stop them contracting the disease subsequently, however, since it is endemic in wild birds everywhere.

Red-eyed Budgerigars are perhaps more susceptible to eye infections than other varieties. Treatment of a simple localized infection is very straightforward, using a special ophthalmic ointment. You can also use drops, but these are less satisfactory, as the bird tends to blink them away before they have had a chance to be effective. However, it can be helpful to use drops with an exhibition bird, since ointment tends to mat feathers, but drops leave hardly any trace. Once you have completed a course of treatment, discard any unused medication. You should also replace or disinfect the perches, as the bird may have wiped the discharge here and it could be a hazard to others. The infection is more likely to be local than general, if one eye is affected. Once recovered, relapses are rare, and the bird suffers no long-term ill effects.

NUTRITIONAL DISORDERS

One of the most significant members of this group of disorders is candidiasis, which is a particular problem in young birds. It is most noticeable in those that are being hand-reared, but it can also be a major cause of mortality in Cockatiel chicks. The microorganism responsible can be present in the mouth of adult birds without causing obvious signs of disease, and chicks can become infected as a result of being fed by their parents. The infection can then be spread within a group of hand-fed birds by the feeding implements.

A chick that feeds actively is most at risk, since it may rub the roof of its mouth on the sides of the spoon and abrade the tissue there, thus allowing the infection to develop. It appears as a white, rather slimy area and, if it spreads unnoticed, may cause the bird to stop eating. In severe cases, candidiasis will affect the crop and lower parts of the digestive tract. Antibiotic medication from your veterinarian should normally overcome the disease, provided it is identified in the early stages. Adult parrots that have recently been imported may well be susceptible to this disease. It

CANDIDIASIS A problem most likely to be encountered in birds deficient in vitamin A, and often associated with Cockatiels, lories, lorikeets, and Eclectus Parrots.

can be triggered by low levels of vitamin A in their diet, which depletes stores of this vitamin held in their liver. Using a suitable vitamin A supplement is recommended, as is also food containing natural sources of vitamin A, such as carrots.

Pet Budgerigars can be susceptible to the problem of small fatty lumps known as lipomas. These normally affect the underside of the body, in the vicinity of the lower chest, but they may occur elsewhere, such as close to the vent, preventing effective mating. Lipomas usually develop over several months, and you should consult your veterinarian as soon as possible, so that the bird can be operated on with minimum risk to its safety. Try to encourage the bird to take more exercise afterwards – perhaps placing it in a larger enclosure where it will need to fly. The development of lipomas may be linked to an underlying thyroid problem, and recurrences are not unknown. Although a bird may live for some time with lipomas, they are likely to interfere with its ability to fly, and it will resort to climbing around its quarters.

LIPOMAS Common in pet Budgies living indoors, a lack of exercise may be partially responsible for such growths, perhaps linked with a thyroid gland disorder.

→PARASITIC PROBLEMS←

Avian parasites can be broadly divided into two categories: those that live on the bird and those found inside the body. Most mites and lice come into the former group, with the exception of air-sac mites, which live in the bird's respiratory system. You are likely to notice the signs of these parasites at dusk. Affected individuals will wheeze, and may later show respiratory distress after mild exercise. Ivermectin, a drug that is absorbed through the skin, is now used to treat this and other ailments.

In their effects, the most noticeable mites are scaly-face mites *(Knemidocoptes)* – a scourge of Budgerigars in particular. Starting as snail-like tracts across the upper bill, the infection proceeds to form coral-like encrustations, which may spread right around the beak and eyes. You should remove affected birds immediately from the aviary. Proprietary remedies are readily available from pet stores.

Some mites are not host-specific, and red mite *(Dermanyssus gallinae)* represents a potential hazard to all bird-keepers. Under favorable conditions, numbers build up rapidly and, in a heavy infestation, chicks will become anemic. There is also the risk that red mites will transmit microscopic blood parasites when they feed, weakening birds still further. Treat all new arrivals with a special avian spray.

Intestinal roundworms *(Ascaridia)* are a problem particularly associated with Australian parakeets and Cockatiels. This can be related to their feeding habits, since they tend to seek their food on the ground where it may have become contaminated. Make every effort to eliminate these parasites before you release the birds into your aviary. You can give suitable medication either in soft food or water, although the bitter taste of the drug may deter the birds from drinking.

SCALY FACE IN ITS EARLY STAGES Here showing as tiny tracks across the upper bill of this Budgerigar, scaly face results from mite infestation, spread by contact.

ADVANCED SCALY FACE This condition can be treated easily, and should not cause long-term distortion in the bill, for example, if it is identified early.

Protozoa are tiny, unicellular organisms. They occur in the intestines of birds and can cause chronic, sometimes fatal, diarrhea. Protozoal infection can also lead to trichomoniasis. This is most often found in doves and pigeons, and also in Budgerigars, where it is passed from adult birds to chicks in the nest. The parasites attack the esophagus lining and crop, and deposits form here that cause a blockage. The drug dimetridazole is the usual treatment of this problem.

PARASITIC WORM LIFECYCLES Here the distinction between the typical lifecycles of tapeworm and roundworm can be seen. Roundworms are spread directly from bird to bird, via eggs passed in droppings, and therefore pose a more serious threat to birds' health.

TAPEWORM

Bird eats invertebrate
• containing immature worm.

Invertebrates eat worm eggs; egg
• develops into worm.

Proglottids then passed •
out of gut.

Proglottids rupture and •
spread eggs.

ROUNDWORM

Birds eat parasitic worm eggs •
absorbed by earthworm casts.

Birds feeding on ground; highest
• concentration of eggs here.

Eggs not infectious just •
after passing out of bird.

Soiled food pot; bird •
ingests worm eggs here.

Always suspect intestinal roundworms when chicks emerge from the nest healthy, but then lose weight or appear suddenly ill. Immediate treatment should produce the characteristic short, white worms in their droppings. However, there is no point in simply treating affected birds, as they will only acquire the parasites' eggs from the aviary floor again. After treating any birds, you should strip and thoroughly disinfect the aviary. This should help to ensure that the condition does not reoccur.

Tapeworms are less of a problem, since the infection must pass through an intermediate host, usually an invertebrate, such as a beetle. Treatment in tablet form is usually prescribed for infections.

·PLUMAGE PROBLEMS·

Parrots as a group are most susceptible to feather complaints, and French molt has been a serious problem for Budgerigar breeders for over a century. It typically affects young birds as they leave the nest. The flight and tail feathers are more fragile than normal, and break off, impairing the bird's ability to fly. Not all chicks in a nest will be affected, but the disease sometimes reaches epidemic proportions.

VIRAL DISEASES

It is now clear that French molt is caused by a virus, but its effects may be influenced by other factors, such as nutrition. The virus is present in the nest, presumably being excreted in the droppings or from the feathers, so you

> ### PLUMAGE DISEASES
> ◆ *French molt differs from PBFD in that only chicks are affected, the condition is not usually fatal, and recovery may occur in mild cases. Birds may continue to shed the virus, however, which can make the disease a hazard to any birds that are breeding.*
> ◆ *Loss of flight and tail feathers in recently fledged Budgerigars is indicative of French molt. Traces of dried blood in the feather shafts suggest past infection in older birds.*
> ◆ *PBFD results in the bird's plumage becoming thinner and sparser, and causes abnormal growth in the beak and claws. This disease is progressive, and usually proves to be fatal.*

FRENCH MOLT This feather disease, caused by a virus, affects Budgerigars and other species, and results in stunted plumage, as here.

should take particular care when cleaning an affected nestbox. Use a separate brush, and avoid mixing these chicks with healthy ones in a temporary container. Such birds are best sold as pets, rather than being kept to form part of a breeding program.

Routine disinfection in the birdroom will help to overcome this disease, as will an ioniser. There have been reports of a similar problem being encountered in other species, notably in Peach-faced Lovebirds and Ring-necked Parakeets, but it does not seem widespread at present.

Psittacine beak and feather disease is undoubtedly the most serious viral disease identified in recent years. From its origins in cockatoos, it has been confirmed in at least 36 different species. Efforts are being made to market a means of testing affected birds, and ultimately to produce a vaccine. At present, however, affected birds pose a serious risk to others. The virus is present in their droppings, feather dust, and crop, which suggests that chicks can acquire the infection before leaving the nest.

FRACTURES

Fractures in aviary birds are relatively uncommon, but do occur on occasions. Young grass parakeets and pigeons are most at risk from skull fractures when they first leave the nest. At this stage, they will be unaccustomed to the confines of the aviary, and may fly about wildly if alarmed. In most cases, injuries of this type are fatal.

FRACTURES OF THE LIMBS

In contrast, limb fractures can often be dealt with satisfactorily, giving the bird a good chance of recovery. Fractures are most often treated with external splints of various types. If you suspect that a bird has fractured its limb, take it to a veterinarian, who will be able to confirm the problem and assess its severity. If a fracture is

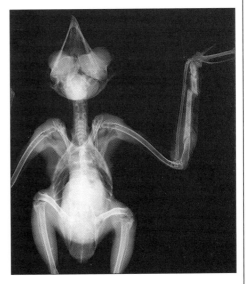

FRACTURED LIMBS *The use of an X-ray will help the veterinarian to ascertain the severity of a fracture, and then to decide on the best course of action.*

confirmed, the veterinarian may decide to anesthetize the bird, in order to fix the splint. You will then need to keep the injured bird in a cage by itself for perhaps eight weeks or so until the fracture is likely to have healed completely.

This is not the end of the story, however. After this period of enforced inactivity, it takes a further period of time, especially following a wing fracture, before the muscles are fully functional again. The likelihood of a complete recovery depends partly on the site of the fracture. A break in the middle of the shaft of the humerus, for example, is reasonably straightforward to remedy, but a fracture at the far end of this bone, close to the joint, will be much harder to treat. This is because of the difficulty in immobilizing the ends of bone satisfactorily at this point, which is essential if they are to heal properly.

LEG FRACTURES

External splinting of fractures can be carried out using items from paper clips to coathangers. The choice will obviously be influenced both by the size of the bird, and the severity and position of the fracture. It is also important to ensure that the bird cannot remove or dislodge the splint. Parrots, in particular, may have to wear a special neck collar for this purpose.

SUPPORTING THE LEG	KEEPING THE SUPPORT SECURE

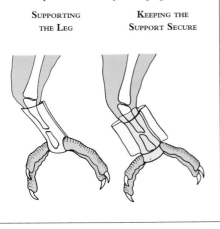

→Veterinary Care and Treatment←

Because symptoms are usually not specific, it is exceedingly difficult to diagnose accurately most avian ailments by visual observation. A sick bird often just huddles up, with its feathers fluffed, and generally appears off-color. Irrespective of the cause of the illness, however, you must transfer the sick bird to a warm environment, with a constant temperature of about 30°C (86°F). Birds, with their high metabolic rates, will lose body heat rapidly if they are not eating properly, and the resulting hypothermia can lead directly to their death. To encourage them to eat, position food and water in suitable containers next to their perches.

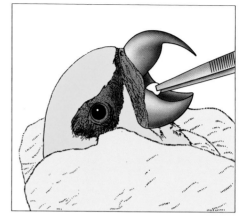

Dosing a Parrot *Parrots can often be given tablets more easily using forceps, as shown here.*

Consulting a Veterinarian

Since the condition of a sick bird will deteriorate rapidly in most cases, seek veterinary advice without delay. Describe the symptoms as clearly as possible, and have a brief summary of the bird's history to hand. This should include how long you have kept the bird, whether you bred

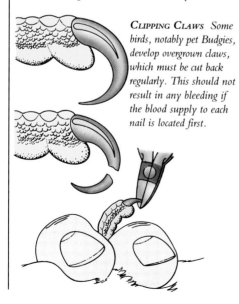

Clipping Claws *Some birds, notably pet Budgies, develop overgrown claws, which must be cut back regularly. This should not result in any bleeding if the blood supply to each nail is located first.*

it, if it has been ill before, its diet, and whether any other birds in your collection have been affected with similar symptoms.

Since treatment must commence without delay, it is usual for veterinarians to prescribe a course of broad-spectrum antibiotics, which should be effective against a range of bacteria. They may take samples beforehand, however, which can be studied in the laboratory while treatment progresses. This allows any change to be made, in the light of these findings, after several days when the results are determined. In addition, sick birds, especially those suffering from enteritis, tend to dehydrate rapidly, so administering fluids can be as important as medication in ensuring the bird's recovery.

Administering Medication

The size of the bird may also affect the likelihood of its survival, since small finches, for example, are more difficult to treat than larger birds such as parrots. Nevertheless, an antibiotic powder added to the drinking water may be successful if used in accordance with a veterinarian's instructions. Never use more than directed, as an overdose can be fatal, affecting both the liver and the kidneys.

You will need to mix a fresh antibiotic solution two or three times each day, because its potency declines rapidly. Use only plastic or ceramic drinkers, as they will not react with the drug.

Recovery should be rapid, provided that the bird is kept warm and is drinking properly. It is important to continue the course of treatment for the period specified, to prevent a relapse. Finally, the use of a probiotic should help to stabilize the effects of the bacterial population in the gut, after the effects of a course of antibiotics.

PROBLEMS WITH LARGER BIRDS

To be effective, the drug must be absorbed from the gut and build up to a therapeutic level in the body. However, for larger birds, medication in the water can be an unsatisfactory method since the birds often need to drink an unrealistically large volume in order to receive a therapeutic dose. In addition, the taste of the antibiotic solution is usually rather bitter, and a bird may be reluctant to drink it. Your veterinarian, therefore, may advise an initial injection of antibiotics. This can

CONVALESCENCE

*   *Bring a sick bird into warmth without delay, to prevent any unnecessary deterioration of its condition.*
*   *Seek veterinary advice as soon as possible, and begin treatment at the earliest opportunity, taking care to follow the dosage instructions.*
*   *Put food and water within easy reach, but withhold greenstuff if medication requires water, as this lessens the bird's desire to drink.*
*   *Reacclimatize the bird slowly and carefully.*

actually be more stressful for the bird, but it does ensure that the drug can start to work almost immediately.

You may be given tablets to treat larger softbills, such as touracos or pigeons. Restrain the bird as usual (see page 134), and then open its bill. Place the tablet as far back in the mouth as possible, taking care to avoid the entrance to the respiratory tract, which is usually evident as an opening at the front of the throat. Then quickly close the bill, and hold it shut, to encourage the bird to swallow the tablet. Stroking the base of the throat in the direction of the chest can also help to encourage the swallowing reflex.

HOSPITAL CAGE You can purchase various designs, usually incorporating an internal heat source, a thermostat, and a thermometer. Check ease of cleanliness as the cage will need to be cleaned and disinfected after use. It must also be possible to adjust heat output easily. Cages of this type can be used to provide extra warmth for young birds that have fallen out of the nest, or that may have been abandoned.

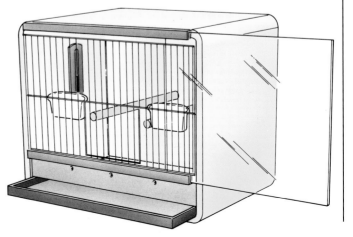

——ACCIDENTS AND EMERGENCIES ——

In certain circumstances you may have to undertake emergency action to help a bird in distress. It may have become caught up on a sharp piece of wire in its quarters, for example, perhaps trapped by its leg ring. This situation is not that unusual, so you need to check the condition of the wire regularly. If you catch yourself on a strand of mesh in the aviary, so too could one of your birds. When you find a bird caught by its leg ring, try not to alarm it further. Restrain it carefully with your left hand, and inspect its situation closely. You may be able simply to manipulate the ring off the wire, or you may have to cut the strand of wire in order to free the bird. This problem is most likely with Budgerigars, but finches and canaries may become caught up in the aviary by their claws.

RISKS IN THE HOME

The pet bird in the home is at risk if it attempts to fly through a pane of glass, so always screen windows. There is a greater possibility of it being caught by a cat, however. If you succeed in rescuing a bird from the clutches of a cat, bear in mind that it will be in an exceedingly stressed state, so avoid holding it for any longer than is necessary. Contact your veterinarian, if the skin is broken anywhere on the bird's body, as a generalized infection could develop from this site. Otherwise, simply leave the bird to recover quietly in its cage.

YOUNG BIRDS

You should watch young birds carefully when they first leave the nest, especially Australian parakeets. These birds can be nervous, and fly about wildly if alarmed. They may not appreciate the presence of mesh, and attempt to fly through it at speed.

Unless you are in the aviary when an accident occurs, you may discover it later. Young parakeets are prone to night fright, perhaps disturbed by cats, and will start to fly around wildly as a group, and in the morning, you may find a bird on the floor that is disorientated. Examine it closely, paying attention to the inner surfaces of the wing. If it has flapped against the aviary mesh, it may have cut itself here, and also on the head if it has collided with the mesh.

Move the bird carefully into a box or cage lined with tissue paper, so that it can rest comfortably, and put it in a quiet place. You can offer some water, but never give fluid in an open container to a bird in this state, as they could drown. In a few hours, it should show signs of improvement and be more lively. By this stage, it will have passed the danger period, and will regain its strength rapidly. For a few days, the bird may be somewhat uncertain when perching and flying, but one hopes there will be no permanent damage.

It is possible that the bird may have fractured a limb (see page 213), which would account for any on-going disability. In the case of some fractures of the leg, the

---

PARROT FIRST AID

For a parrot with a bleeding tongue, mix up a solution of powdered alum and cold water, and apply it by dipping the bird's mouth in the solution. In other, more accessible places, you can use cotton balls or a piece of tissue dipped in the solution. Press this to the affected area for a couple of minutes or so; the pressure of your fingers will also help to stop the flow of blood. If the flow does not stop promptly, or it is profuse, you will need to contact your veterinarian immediately for professional assistance. Keep pressure on the wound to prevent further loss of blood.

limb becomes slightly shortened, although this rarely causes serious disability. Fractures of the wing are more of a problem, and can seriously impair the bird's future flying ability. Even so, most individuals adapt well, and are soon climbing about their quarters.

A Soggy Start

On occasions, you may find a young bird, which has left the nest prematurely, and ended up saturated on the aviary floor in a shower of rain. You should take it indoors and dry it off as much as possible, using a paper towel. Then, assuming that the adult birds are still returning to the nest and feeding the chicks, it will probably be best to place it back with its nestmates. Alternatively, if the youngster is virtually

> **AVIAN FIRST AID KIT**
> • *Alum powder or a styptic pencil to stop minor bleeding.*
> • *Germicidal ointment to treat small cuts.*
> • *Powdered aloes to stop feather-plucking.*
> • *Proper nail clippers, to trim claws as necessary.*
> • *Paper toweling and a clean yogurt or margarine container to use as a disposable container for cleaning dirty feet.*
> • *Ophthalamic ointment for the treatment of minor eye infections.*

independent, you may need to keep it indoors in a cage. Otherwise, it might end up becoming fatally chilled in the aviary, should it flutter back onto the floor. This applies especially to young Diamond Doves *(Geopelia cuneata)*, and related species, which frequently leave the nestpan before they are able to fly properly. Waxbill chicks and other finches are also very vulnerable, particularly if the adult birds have built their nest in an exposed part of the aviary.

BLOOD LOSS

There is no truth to the story that it is fatal for birds to lose more than a couple of drops of blood. However, uncontrolled blood loss is very dangerous. In the aviary, this may occur in certain circumstances, most likely in the case of parrots. If pairs are housed in adjoining flights, which are not separated by a double-wired intervening panel, they may attack each other through the mesh. This is most probable during the breeding season, and lovebirds and conures are among the worst offenders. Fighting in this fashion can result in serious injury if a parrot's toe or tongue is bitten. The tongue is especially vascular, and bleeds profusely. You can stem the flow of blood from a torn nail using a styptic pencil, but professional attention may be required if the tongue is affected.

> **BUMBLEFOOT**
> *A relatively minor injury to the skin, usually coupled with dirty perches, can lead to this chronic condition, and potentially cripple the bird. A toe or possibly a joint higher up the limb swells up as a result of the bacterial infection. On the underside of the foot, this area can develop into an open sore, making it painful for the bird to use the affected limb. Effective treatment may entail surgery. Certain species, especially some softbills, are more prone to this condition than others. Keeping perches clean will help to prevent bumblefoot occurring.*

⟶ GLOSSARY ⟵

Words in *italic* within an entry have their own entry in the glossary.

Albino Pure white bird with red eyes, lacking any trace of color pigment
Autosomal recessive mutation A *mutation* affecting the autosomes; those chromosomes not associated with determining the bird's gender.
Aviary A combination of an outside flight and shelter used for housing birds.
Aviculture The keeping and breeding of non-domesticated species in controlled surroundings, such as an aviary.
Aviculturist A person who practices aviculture.

Backcross The pairing of a chick back to one of its parents (see *inbreeding*).
Bobhole Entry point for birds, connecting shelter to flight.
Birdroom Area equipped with flights and/or cages, used to house birds under cover, sometimes indoors.
Buff Description of a coarse feather (see *yellow*).

Cap Area on the top of the head, especially significant in Lizard Canaries.
Cere Area above the beak, usually unfeathered in parrots. Differences in coloration here enable budgies to be sexed.
Chick A young bird which is not yet independent of its parents.
Chromosomes Microscopic structures present in the nucleus of all lining cells in the body, occurring normally in pairs.
Chromosomal sexing A laboratory means of determining the sex of birds, which is carried out especially in the case of *monomorphic* birds. Birds sexed in this way are sometimes advertised as "C.S." (see also surgical sexing).
Clear egg An egg which was not fertilized, or where the embryo died at a very early stage.
Cloaca The point where the urinary, digestive, and reproductive tracts meet, prior to the *vent*.
Closed ring (band) A ring which can only be applied to a chick soon after hatching, and generally accepted therefore as a reliable indicator of its age and origins.

Clutch The number of eggs laid in one nest.
Cobby Chunky appearance, often used in descriptions of some breeds of canary such as Norwich Fancy birds.
Cock A male bird.
Color-feeding An artificial means of improving the coloration of certain birds, by providing a coloring agent in either the drinking water or food.
Crop Storage area for food, which is located at the base of the neck.

Dead-in-the-shell Chicks which fail to hatch.
Dilute Paler form.
Dominant Genetic trait which tends to cause this color to predominate.
Double-buffing Mating of two buff birds together, which may result in an apparent improvement of size of the offspring, because of their coarser feather type. Also increases the risk of *feather lumps*.
Down Fluffy feathering, providing insulation.

Egg-binding Failure of hen to expel egg from her body, resulting in a blockage.

Fancy Selective breeding of birds for particular features, such as their type.
Fancier Breeder of domesticated stock, often for exhibition purposes.
Feather lumps A condition typically associated with canaries caused by the inability of a developing feather to emerge normally. Results in localized swellings, often over the back.
Flecking Unwanted darker markings on the head, typically associated with Budgerigars.
Fledgling A chick which has left the nest, but is not yet feeding independently.
Flight A mesh structure, usually made with a wooden frame, where birds are kept.
Frugivore A softbill that feeds on fruit.

Genes The structure located on chromosomes which directly influence the appearance of the individual, and can give rise to mutations.
Gizzard Seeds and other foodstuffs are ground up by its thick muscular walls, and by grit.

Going light Weight loss, noticeable over the breastbone. More typically associated with some groups of birds, e.g. Gouldian Finches, than others, and often of infectious origin.

Hand-raising (rearing) Artificial feeding of chicks not able to feed themselves. Such chicks may then be advertised with the initials "H.R."

Hen A female bird.

Hybrid Chick resulting from the pairing of two closely related species, and usually infertile.

Inbreeding Mating together of closely related birds, such as mother and son, usually carried out to emphasize desirable traits.

Insectivore Bird which feeds predominantly on invertebrates.

Iris (*pl.* irides) Often brightly colored area surrounding the pupil at the center of each eye. Useful for recognizing young parrots.

Line-breeding The practice of pairing related birds together, but not birds showing a direct relationship, e.g. hen-son, which is *inbreeding*.

Melanistic Showing abnormal areas of black feathering in the plumage. Often a sign of poor condition, but may be associated with natural variations in some populations, such as Stella's Lorikeets, where both normal and melanistic birds occur together.

Molt Shedding of plumage, with matching growth of replacement feathers. This occurs annually in most cases.

Monomorphic Opposite sexes have identical external appearance.

Mule *Hybrid* offspring produced from mating of a canary with a British finch.

Mutation Unexpected alteration in coloration or appearance from one generation to the next.

Nectivore A bird which feeds on nectar as a major part of its diet.

Pied A bird showing abnormal areas of light plumage, mixed with normal dark coloration.

Pin feather Small feathers, typically around the head, which are still covered in a sheath.

Plainhead Describes a bird without a crest, in cases where crests normally occur.

Preening Grooming of the feathers with the bill. Usually a sign of good health.

Psittacine Collective term used to describe any or all members of the parrot order.

Quill The feather shaft, especially in the case of longer feathers, such as those of the tail.

Saddle Plumage that is located in the middle of the bird's back.

Seedeater Collective, but inaccurate term used to describe finches.

Self Not variegated in any way.

Sex-linked genetic Characteristic linked to the sex chromosomes.

Sexual dimorphism A means of distinguishing the sexes of birds on their external apearance.

Shelter Enclosed part of the aviary, providing cover from the elements.

Softbill A bird which does not feed predominantly on seed. Encompasses *frugivores, insectivores and nectivores*.

Split Carries a hidden genetic characteristic, which differs from its actual appearance. This is abbreviated to an oblique line, to green/blue, for example, with the recessive feature written last.

Split rings Usually celluloid, and can be applied at any age to assist identification, e.g. cock Bengalese finches whose song during the breeding season distinguishes them from hens.

Standard Lists the desirable features of exhibition birds, with points for each feature.

Surgical sexing A means of sexing the larger *monomorphic* species. Such birds are indicated by the letters "S.S." in advertisements.

Type Physical appearance of a bird (as distinct from its coloration). Important in exhibition stock, being specified in the *standard*.

Unflighted A bird, typically a young canary, which has yet to molt its flight and tail feathers.

Vent External opening from the cloaca.

Yellow As well as being a color, can also refer separately to plumage type, being relatively soft and the opposite of *buff*.

INDEX

ACKNOWLEDGMENTS

Author's Acknowledgments:
I would like to thank the many enthusiasts whom I have met on my travels in both Britain and overseas, and those with whom I have corresponded about bird-keeping matters. I am also exceedingly grateful to Mrs. Rita Hemsley for processing my manuscript on to disc, and the editorial and design team at Dorling Kindersley for their help and enthusiasm. My wife Jacqueline and daughters Isabel and Lucinda deserve special thanks for their patience and understanding during my endeavors.

Illustrators:
Color artwork (page 25) provided by Sean Milne; genetics charts provided by Anthony Duke; all other artworks by Hardlines, Oxford.

Credits:
Ghalib Al-Nasser and Janice Foxton, George Anderdon, Bill Austin, Paul and June Bailey, Ron and Keith Baker, Eric Barlow, Fred Barnicoat, Christine Baxter, Tony and Jean Beard, Bob Beeson, Blean Bird Park, Trevor Bonneywell, Tony and Brigitte Bourne, Alan Brooker, Kevin Browning, Trevor and Maura Buckell, Jack Chitty, Frank Clark, Dulcie and Freddie Cooke, Databird Worldwide, Bill Dobbs and Jean Kozicka, Danny and Robert Dymond, Nick Elliston, Keith Garrett, Roger and James Green, Fred Hill and Dinah Hawker, Phil Holland, Bernard and Jean Howlett, Alan Jones and Sue Willis, Colin Jackson, Alec James, Ron James, Tim Kemp, Shirley and George Lawton, Maureen Loughlin, Gary McCarthy, Stanley Maughan, Albert and Monica Newsham, Mick and Jean O'Connell, Mike and Denise O'Neill, Joanne O'Neill, Peter Olney, Ron Oxley, Bill Painter, Andy and Audrey Perkins, Mick and Beryl Plose, Peter Rackley, Janet Ralph, Walter and Jenny Savoury, Bernard Sayers, Raymond Sawyer, Ken Shelton, Charlie and Jane Smith, Nigel Taboney, Patrick Taplin, Peter and Ann Thumwood, Joyce Venner, Keith Ward.

Dorling Kindersley would like to thank:
Southern Aviaries, The Mealworm Company, Zoology Museum at Cambridge University, and South Beech Veterinary Surgery. Judy Walker for copy editing, Jonathan Hilton for invaluable editorial assistance, Andrea Fair for support with the manuscript, Michael Allaby for compiling the index, Heather Dewhurst and Irene Lyford for proofreading the text, and Kevin Ryan for additional design assistance.

Picture Credits:
Ardea: Peter Steyn: 9 (top); Dennis Avon: 60 (bottom), 76 (top), 95 (top), 120; Cage and Aviary Birds Magazine: 189; J.E. Cooper: 213 (top); Simon Joshua, University of London: 166; Mary Evans Picture Library: 15 (bottom); Hulton Picture Co.; 10 (bottom); A.D. Malley, South Beech Veterinary Surgery: 207; Mansell Collection: 130 (top), 182; Photograph Collection Maurithius, The Hague, inv. no 605: 13 (top); Oxford Scientific Films: London Scientific Films: 165 (top); Bild-Archiv Okapia: 17 (bottom); Science Photo Library: David Scharf: 205 (bottom), CNRI: 209 (top); Schubot Exotic Bird Health Center, Texas A&M: David L. Graham: 211 (top): Mrs Mattie Williams: 130 (bottom).